DUCATI

Belt-Drive Two-Valve Twins

Restoration Guide

Ian Falloon

REVISED EDITION

OCTANE PRESS

Originally published by MBI Publishing Company as ISBN 0-7603-0697-4
Octane Press, Edition 2.0, October 2012
Reprint Edition 2.1, October 2013

ISBN 1937747115
ISBN-13 978-1-937747-11-4

Design by Tom Heffron
Edited by Charles Everitt

About the Author

Ian Falloon has a life-long passion for Italian motorcycles and Ducati in particular. In the 1980s, Ian moved to Australia and began writing for motorcycle magazines as a freelance journalist and photographer, an occupation he continues to this day. Falloon›s first book, The success of his first book, *The Ducati Story,* has led to the publication of fifteen additional books on Ducati, and more on motorcycle marques including BMW, Moto Guzzi, Laverda, Honda, and Kawasaki. An avid collector and restorer of older Italian motorcycles, Ian Falloon is considered one of the world authorities on Ducati motorcycles. He resides in Melbourne, Australia with his wife and two sons.

OCTANE PRESS
octanepress.com

Printed in Canada

CONTENTS

INTRODUCTION

Although responsible for many magnificent engine designs during his 40-year involvement with Ducati, Ing. Fabio Taglioni's most enduring has been the two-valve belt-drive V-twin. Starting production life in 1979 as the Pantah, this engine continues in production with minimal updates more than 30 years later. Over that time it has comfortably grown from 498cc to 1078cc, and also spawned the Desmoquattro and later Testastretta. No other single Ducati engine has had such a strong influence on the direction of the company. So superior was the Pantah engine in terms of reliability and cost effectiveness that within six years it was the only engine being produced by the company. Single-handedly the Pantah has also managed to change the public perception of Ducatis and their reliability. Once only for enthusiasts prepared to time consumingly maintain their machinery, the Pantah brought the Ducati legend to a far wider audience.

While the Pantah engine remained largely unchanged up to 750cc until 2002, production levels have increased dramatically in more recent times. Thus in documenting these motorcycles I have emphasized the aspects relating to authenticity of earlier Pantahs, particularly the SL and 750 F1 series. These machines are now relatively rare and deserve to be preserved. This is true also for the 750 and 906 Paso and *nuovo* 750 Sport. While much maligned I am sure their time will also come when they assume collectability status, purely because they are rare and unusual. Already these models have gained a dedicated and loyal following and they have been covered in depth. The same also applies to the Cagiva Ducatis such as the Alazzurra, Indiana, Elefant and Gran Canyon. Although not exactly sought after, I am sure that their time will come sometime in the future. As they are now getting older, the restoration of an early Monster or post-'91 900 Supersport may also be considered down the track.

Every motorcycle featured in this book has desmodromic valve gear. This feature alone characterizes Ducati, and the Pantah was the first Ducati engine designed and produced only with desmodromic valves. While using the desmodromic system, the engine doesn't have dauntingly complicated valve gear. Much of the appeal of the Ducati two-valve belt twin is due to its simplicity, and until 1998 all two-valve belt-twins still used carburetors. These are engines that don't overwhelm with their technology.

As this is essentially a reprint of the earlier book published by MBI, *Ducati Belt-Drive Two-Valve Twins Authentic Restoration Guide,* 2002 remains the cut-off year for most of the models covered. Updates have incorporated 750 and 900 models until their replacement by the 800 and 1000. The original book has long been out of print and the reprint is totally due to Octane Press publisher Lee Klancher. The earlier edition also dealt with modification but this one less so. This book is now more a guide to authenticity. If you are more interested in modifying these bikes I suggest L.T. Snyder's excellent *Ducati Desmodue Maintenance & Modification Guide.* Although the two-valve belt twins will always be locked in time everything else changes. Apart from Livio Lodi, the curator of *Museo Ducati,* and chief tester Andrea Forni, all the individuals who helped me at the Ducati factory 13 years ago are no longer working for Ducati. The same goes for the various motorcycle magazine editors who contributed photographs. Some are unfortunately no longer with us, and others have moved on from motorcycle journalism. Only Brian Catterson remains to be thanked individually, although he has also moved from *Cycle World* to *Motorcyclist* in the intervening years. I will always be grateful to my family for supporting these projects, and thanks as always to my wife Miriam, and sons Benjamin and Timothy for their patience while preparing this manuscript for the reprint.

Ian Falloon
May 2012

CHAPTER ONE

Historical Background and Racing History

Originating from two racing engines, the belt-drive Ducati twin followed a tradition first set by Ducati in 1957 with the first overhead-camshaft 175cc single. This was the production of a street motorcycle based on a racing design. In that case the 175 grew from the Marianna, or Gran Sport. The belt-drive 90-degree V-twin emanated from a synthesis of the 500cc bevel-drive Grand Prix motorcycle of 1970, and the belt-drive double overhead camshaft four-valve Armaroli racer of 1973. Ducati designer Ing. Fabio Taglioni managed a clever synthesis of these two designs to create the Pantah. Not only did the Pantah provide considerably improved reliability over any earlier designs, it was also the first Ducati to be produced only with desmodromic valve gear.

Following a Ducati board meeting in October 1970, the directors of Ducati, Arnaldo Milvio and Fredmano Spairani, gave Taglioni the go-ahead to design and produce a 500cc Grand Prix racer. The 750cc V-twin was already being developed and while the 500 grew out of that design it differed in many details. The plan was to initially build ten 500cc V-twin bikes to race in Italian Championship events and some 1971 Grands Prix, but only five bikes ended up being built. With Agostini totally dominating Grand Prix racing at that time on the three-cylinder MV, the purpose of the Ducati 500 was not so much as to win races, but to prove that the idea of the V-twin was sound. It would also promote sales of the 750 that was struggling in the marketplace. Working tirelessly through the winter, Fabio Taglioni managed to design and build the complete bike from scratch to race debut in under six months.

With a bore and stroke of 74mm x 58mm, and a 10.5:1 compression ratio, the 90-degree V-twin bevel-

The 1971 version of the 500cc Grand Prix V-twin featured a Seeley frame. While raced in selected Grands Prix it was also entered in the Italian championship. This is Gilberto Parlotti at Ospidaletti where he came third.

drive 500 initially produced 61.2 HP at 11,000 rpm. All the 500 GP bikes built used two-valve engines with desmodromic valve gear and an 80-degree included valve angle. Carburetion was by remote float bowl Dell'Orto 40mm SS carburetors, and they differed to the 750 by featuring a six-speed gearbox with a dry multi-plate clutch. Ignition was electronic, provided by nearby Ducati Elettrotecnica, but this was generally unreliable in early races. When first raced, the 500 used a Ducati-designed chassis with a single Lockheed disc brake on the front and a twin-leading-shoe Fontana at the rear. Dry weight was 297 pounds (135kg) and 18-inch wheels were fitted front and rear with 3.00- and 3.25-inch Dunlop racing tires. Wheelbase was a moderate 56.3 inches (1430mm). A noted Anglophile, Spairani wanted a frame developed by Colin Seeley, and a set of 500cc prototype engine cases was dispatched to him late in 1970. His brief was to develop a racing frame along the lines of his successful G50 Matchless. The Seeley frame was displayed in February 1971, but not tested by Phil Read until June. The better handling Seeley frame was then adopted on Bruno Spaggiari's bike, then raced with limited success as a 500 Grand Prix bike by Spaggiari, Ermanno Giuliano and Read during the 1971 and 1972 seasons. In March 1972 direct injection was tested on the 500, but soon outlawed by the FIM, ruling it as a form of supercharging. Development throughout 1972 also saw twin front disc brakes and 40mm PHM Dell'Orto carburetors.

Besides the two-valve head, Taglioni also produced a four-valve version, still with the single overhead camshaft driven by a vertical shaft and bevel gears. These heads ultimately didn't produce as much power as the two-valve versions. Thus they contributed to Taglioni's suspicion of four-valve cylinder heads that would last through until the mid-1980s. Initial power from the four-valve heads was 65 HP at 12,000 rpm, but by the end of 1972 this had only risen to 69 HP at 12,500 rpm. Over the same period the power from the two-valve engine increased to 71 HP, so the four-valve version was never raced.

1972 saw the 500 similar to the Imola 750 racing machine. This is Spaggiari's 500 at the factory at Borgo Panigale before the Italian Grand Prix at Imola. Spaggiari still used a single front disc brake while Smart's 500 sported twin front discs.

Ducati's first experimentation with belt-driven overhead camshafts was the Armaroli-designed double-overhead-camshaft 500 twin of 1973. The basic engine and running gear was inherited from the bevel-drive 500 and the four-valve engine featured a reversed rear cylinder head. Only one of these machines was built.

Race results during 1971 were disappointing due to a spate of gearbox and ignition problems. The best result was Phil Read's second to Agostini in the San Remo Grand Prix, and a fourth also by Read at Monza in the Grand Prix delle Nazione, although Spaggiari looked like taking second before breaking a valve. In May 1972, Bruno Spaggiari finished third at Imola, beating Paul Smart into fourth. They had finished the other way round one month earlier in the Formula 750 race, possibly the most important race win ever for Ducati. According to Paul Smart the 500 was a fabulous motorcycle by 1972, lighter and with more nimble handling than the long 750. Lap times at Imola were only fractionally slower than on the 750, Spaggiari finishing third at 153.24 km/h (95.2 mph). Smart had won the Imola 200 at an average speed of 157.35 km/h (97.8 mph).

The final Grand Prix 500 appeared in 1973, with belt-driven double overhead desmodromic camshafts. Not actually built by Ducati, this engine was constructed by another Bolognese company, Armaroli, but still used the 500cc bevel-gear crankcases. It had the gearshift on the right side, and primary drive and dry multiplate clutch on the left. The exposed toothed belts were driven from the crankshaft inside the primary gears, so the camshaft drive moved from the right side of the engine to the left. Ignition was by a set of contact breakers mounted on an external reduction gear. In a move pre-empting the Paso 13 years later, the rear cylinder head was reversed so that both Dell'Orto carburetors faced forward between the cylinders, with a rear exiting exhaust pipe. Unlike the bevel-drive 500 racing engine, the front cylinder had radial finning. Power was 74 HP at 12,000 rpm, not significantly increased over the two-valve bevel-gear engines. Mounted in one of the Seeley frames with triple Lockheed discs and leading-axle Marzocchi forks, it was raced occasionally by Spaggiari in some Italian events during 1973 without success. This was to be the final 500cc Grand Prix twin.

To design a motorcycle engine with toothed rubber-belt camshaft drive in 1973 was unusual, and was instigated by Fabio Taglioni. The only other motorcycles with toothed-belt camshaft drive at that time were Morini's 3½ (also from Bologna), and the Honda Gold Wing, both of which were still in their development stages. Coming from Italy's technological center, Emilia Romagna, Taglioni always had close connections to the automotive industry and followed the development of toothed rubber camshaft belts with interest. Although he preferred two-valve cylinder heads, Taglioni was always involved with the Armaroli four-valve project. It was only because the new management was less sympathetic to racing that the belt-drive 500 contract was outsourced. During 1973 there were no longer the resources available to develop another competition engine alongside the short-stroke Imola 750 and Montjuich 24 Hour 860. Although the Armaroli 500 wasn't successful, it still provided Taglioni with much inspiration when he came to design the Pantah a short time afterwards.

The years 1973 and 1974 were difficult ones for Ducati. The new manager Ing. De Eccher was determined to make the company more profitable, and this affected not only the racing program, but also the production lineup. Thus the square-case 860 and the ill-fated parallel-twin replaced the expensive round-case 750 twins and bevel-drive overhead-camshaft singles. Even as the venerable bevel-drive 750cc 90-degree engine was being developed and enlarged it was obvious that its days were numbered. Not only was the engine extremely expensive to manufacture and assemble, it was also difficult to silence adequately and still suffered reliability problems. With these two problems foremost in his mind Ing. Fabio Taglioni set about designing a new engine in 1975. Where this differed from the bevel twins was it started life as a 500 and was intended as a complementary smaller-capacity engine to the larger twins. At that stage Taglioni envisaged the big-twin replacement would be a four-cylinder, created by doubling two 350 or 500cc Pantahs side by side. Little did he realize that within ten years his new design would become the sole engine produced by Ducati and continue to form the basis of the range over 30 years on!

In the meantime Taglioni's idea for a small-capacity 90-degree V-twin was overruled in favor of the parallel -twin. Taglioni subsequently refused to be involved in the parallel-twin project and it was left to Ing. Tumidei to finalize it. Unfortunately it was a flawed design that did little to enhance the reputation of the company. So disastrous were both the 860 and parallel-twin for Ducati that in 1976 Taglioni was asked to resurrect his design for a belt-drive V-twin. While it was virtually ready for construction and development, this also coincided with another particularly turbulent time at Ducati. The EFIM Group that controlled the company was unable to make any commitment to further investment so the development of Taglioni's Pantah was severely slowed. When the company became part of the IRI Group in July 1978 work toward a production version was further delayed. IRI at that time also controlled Alfa Romeo and Alitalia, but was only interim management before Ducati became part of Finmeccanica in the VM Group during 1980. This was the beginning of a very poor period for the company. Under the management of Dott. Cosimo Calganile, Ducati was only able to produce between 3,000-5,000 motorcycles a year. VM was more interested in manufacturing diesels and considered motorcycle production secondary. Thus these managerial problems severely affected the birth and early development of the Pantah.

Assisted by Gianluigi Mengoli and Ing. Giuseppe Bocchi, fresh from the MV Agusta and the Ferrari Formula One racing teams, Taglioni proceeded with the Pantah's development. The first prototype appeared during 1977 with bodywork from the 500 Sport Desmo parallel-twin. The engine still featured the built-up

By the end of 1978 the prototype was in this form.

The 1977 prototype Pantah had a Campagnolo conical front brake.

crankshaft, with the roller big-end bearings, of the bevel-drive Grand Prix 500 and shared the same bore and stroke of 74mm x 58mm. By the end of the year, though, at the Milan Show, the Pantah appeared with a one-piece crankshaft and full-flow oil filter, features of the parallel-twin so despised by Taglioni. The move to plain big-end bearings was a big step for him as he still relied heavily on 1950s motorcycle racing practice and he still didn't go as far as incorporating the parallel-twin's plain main bearings. Other features carried over from the parallel-twin were the two-valve desmodromic cylinder heads with a 60-degree included valve angle. The desmodromic heads on the 500 Sport Desmo parallel-twin had been the only aspect of that engine that had received any Taglioni input. Introduced from experience gained with the 1973 Imola 750 racers, the narrower valve angle would be a feature of all two-valve belt-drive twins. The late 1977 prototype also had Campagnolo Hydroconical brakes and a full fairing. Also a first for a Ducati was the absence of a kickstart. During 1978 development continued. The engine still featured finned-aluminum belt covers, but twin Brembo disc brakes were used along with the rear Campagnolo. The front 18-inch wheel was also Campagnolo, and this prototype had an oil cooler mounted underneath the headlight in the full racing-style fairing. Carburetors were Dell'Orto PHF 32A and claimed power at this early stage, with air filters and silencers, was 48.5 HP at 8,500 rpm. Later in 1978 the final form appeared, but with Speedline wheels and a two-tone blue-and-white paint scheme.

While obviously drawing heavily on the bevel-drive 500 for inspiration the Pantah design differed in a number of important details. Still using the 90-degree twin-cylinder layout with vertically split crankcases, the swingarm pivoted on bearings within the gearbox casing. This was to bring the pivot as close as possible to the countershaft sprocket, reducing chain snatch. To facilitate a properly incorporated left-side gearshift the Pantah was almost a mirror image of the bevel version. The crankshaft was still supported by axial-thrust ball main bearings, with the helical primary-drive gears on the right side and the alternator on the left. Whereas the cylinders were offset, with the horizontal cylinder to the left on the bevel-drive twins, in the interests of keeping the exhaust pipes more compact, this was also reversed on the Pantah. Also, unlike the big twin, the flywheel with ignition trigger sat inside the 200-watt alternator. The Bosch BTZ ignition system was new, and was adapted from the same system used on the Darmah SD900. The starter motor was neatly fitted under the front cylinder and drove through reduction gearing to a sprag clutch attached to the back of the flywheel. The toothed belts and valve gear were driven off a jackshaft running between the cylinders and geared from the crankshaft on the left side. This enabled the engine to be kept much narrower (14.8 inches, 776mm) than the bevel-drive engines that needed to fit the geared camshaft drive inside the alternator rotor.

A usual helical-geared primary drive drove a standard Ducati-style wet multi-plate clutch. The Pantah clutch was also the reverse of the larger twins, in that the six springs clamped the driving and driven plates from the inside outward of the alloy clutch drum and hub. The forged one-piece crankshaft necessitated the change to two-piece connecting rods with plain bearing big-ends, and a corresponding increase in oil pressure. Whereas the old engines, with all their ball and roller bearings, could run with only 15 psi from its geared pump, the Pantah flow rate was regulated to 70 psi. The geared oil pump resided in the same location as the earlier engines, but was now driven by the primary drive gear.

Unlike the larger twin, maintaining a short wheelbase wasn't such a problem, so the gearbox was now the indirect type, with separate input and output shafts. Consequently the engine rotated forward, not backward as the bevel-drive twins did. The cylinder barrels were also Gilnisil (an Italian Nikasil), a plating incorporating silicon and carbon particles that was much harder than iron, lighter, harder wearing, and offered better heat transfer. The only disadvantage was that the cylinders couldn't be rebored.

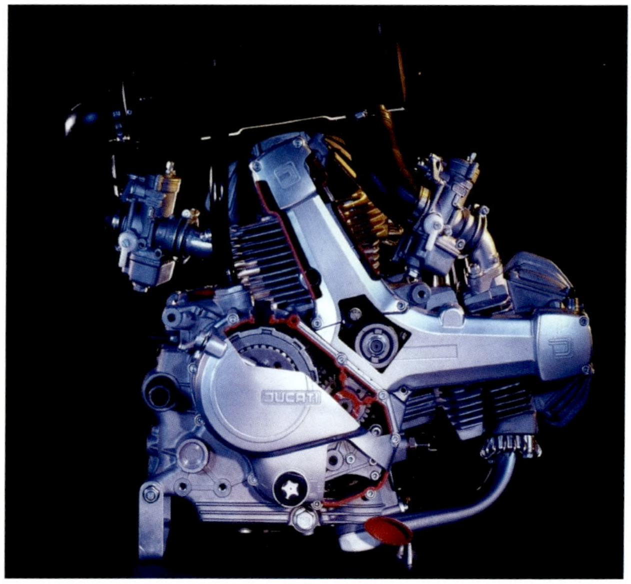

A cutaway of Ing. Fabio Taglioni's 500cc Pantah engine from the right side. The air cleaner above the engine was particularly restrictive.

Supporting this engine was a trellis frame, also designed by Taglioni. Two pairs of parallel tubes running from the rear cylinder to the steering head met another

In every respect the Pantah was more compact than the bevel-drive V-twin. The narrower 60-degree included valve angle came from the 1973 Imola 750 racers.

pair of tubes running up from the rear of the crankcases. This was braced, especially around the steering head, for extra rigidity. The engine hung below the trellis and was bolted to it at six points. It wasn't the most compact frame, as the wheelbase was still 57 inches (1450mm), but it was considerably shorter than the larger bevel -drive twins.

Although it was clearly close to being ready for production, there was little development to the Pantah during 1978. By the end of the year another prototype was ready, first for the Cologne Show, and later for Milan. These were blue and white and closer to the eventual production form. The Cologne version featured Speedline cast magnesium wheels, while there were aluminum FPS wheels on the Milan Show Pantah. Brakes were normal 260mm Brembo discs by this stage. The first production series of two hundred 500 SL Pantahs was red and silver and produced in September 1979 and sent to distributors around the world to test the market. These were considered production bikes and detailed in Chapter Two. They also featured Marzocchi suspension and Taglioni's own design for a trellis frame.

As soon as the Pantah was in production the factory developed it for Formula Two racing in Italy. It was immediately obvious that the new engine could provide levels of reliability the earlier bevel-drive twin could only dream about. As the racing success of the 900 NCR waned, the Pantah took over, and during 1980 chief racing mechanic Franco Farnè prepared two 600cc race-kitted Pantahs. These were campaigned successfully in the Italian national junior championship (TT2) by Vanes Francini, Paolo Menchini and Guido Del Piano, and with five victories were unbeaten. They were based on the standard SL frame, but with Marzocchi racing suspension. The red-and-yellow bodywork was similar in style to that of the 900 NCR, and power from the 583cc engines up to 70 HP at 9,800 rpm. Also during 1980 Pantahs won the Spanish TT2 Endurance championship and the German and Canadian championships for 500cc production motorcycles. In Australia Lee Roebuck won the Adelaide 100-kilometer production race outright, beating a field of 750 and 900cc machines. Then, for the 1981 season Fabio Taglioni released his tour de force, the TT2.

Angel Nieto (14 times 50cc and 125cc World Champion) and successful Ducati endurance racer Salvador Canellas tested the prototype TT2 in Spain over the winter. So good was its design that, at its debut race meeting on March 29, 1981, the TT2 in the hands of Sauro Pazzaglia won the opening round of the Italian TTF2 series at Misano. Yet even as the TT2 was making its presence felt on Italian circuits, Sports Motorcycles' Steve Wynne and Pat Slinn had prepared a modified 500 SL Pantah for Tony Rutter to race in the Isle of Man Formula 2 race in June 1981. Originally promised two factory bikes, these didn't eventuate, so finding an insurance write-off, they installed a factory race kit, sent the frame off to Ron Williams of Maxton for some extra bracing, and signed up Isle of Man veteran Tony Rutter. Rutter won at an average of 101.91 mph (164 km/h), with a fastest lap of 103.51 mph (167 km/h). Ducati were pleased enough with this victory to offer Rutter a TT2 factory bike for the next round at Ulster on August 22. In atrocious conditions, Rutter finished second to secure the 1981 Formula Two World Championship.

The TT2 marked the return of the factory to international competition after an official absence since 1975. Though the NCR racers were factory bikes they were entered under the NCR banner to avoid conflict with the management. By using an 81mm bore, capacity was increased to 597cc, almost the class limit, and a completely new frame was designed by Taglioni, and made by Verlicchi. Weighing only 7kg (16 pounds), rear suspension was by a cantilevered single Paioli shock absorber. This frame was exceedingly compact and strong, being heavily triangulated around the steering head, and comprising essentially straight tubes. It bolted to the engine in four places, still using the engine as a stressed member, with butt-fitted bosses rather than flat tabs as

Vanes Franchini took two victories in the Italian Junior TT2 championship on a factory modified Pantah during 1980.

on the SL. This frame encased the 18-liter fiberglass petrol tank. A significant advancement over the earlier Pantah frame was a reduction in fork rake from 30 degrees to 24 degrees. Fitted with 35mm Marzocchi racing forks with magnesium sliders and 280mm Brembo front discs, the racer weighed in at a mere 270 pounds (122kg). It was also extremely compact, with only a 55-inch (1395mm) wheelbase.

In the engine department, the TT2 was pure factory racer. The 81mm Borgo pistons only had moderate compression of 10:1, but valves were larger at 41mm inlet and 35mm exhaust. Desmodromic camshafts giving 12mm of intake lift and 10mm of exhaust operated these valves. Italian regulations permitted the use of 40mm Dell'Orto carburetors, but for the TT World Championship, standard 36mm carburetors needed to be retained. Claimed power was 76 HP at 10,750 rpm. There was much evidence of weight saving. Exposed camshaft drive belts, a magnesium primary drive cover, and hydraulically operated dry clutch. A lightweight

The 500 SL was also successful in the German 500cc Series Production championship of 1980.

two-into-one exhaust system was also used. Internally most gears were drilled for lightness, and ignition was still by electronic Bosch BTZ, with the small battery

Future Grand Prix star Kevin Magee rode a Bob Brown-tuned Pantah in Australian Superbike racing in 1982 and 1983, often defeating much faster machinery.

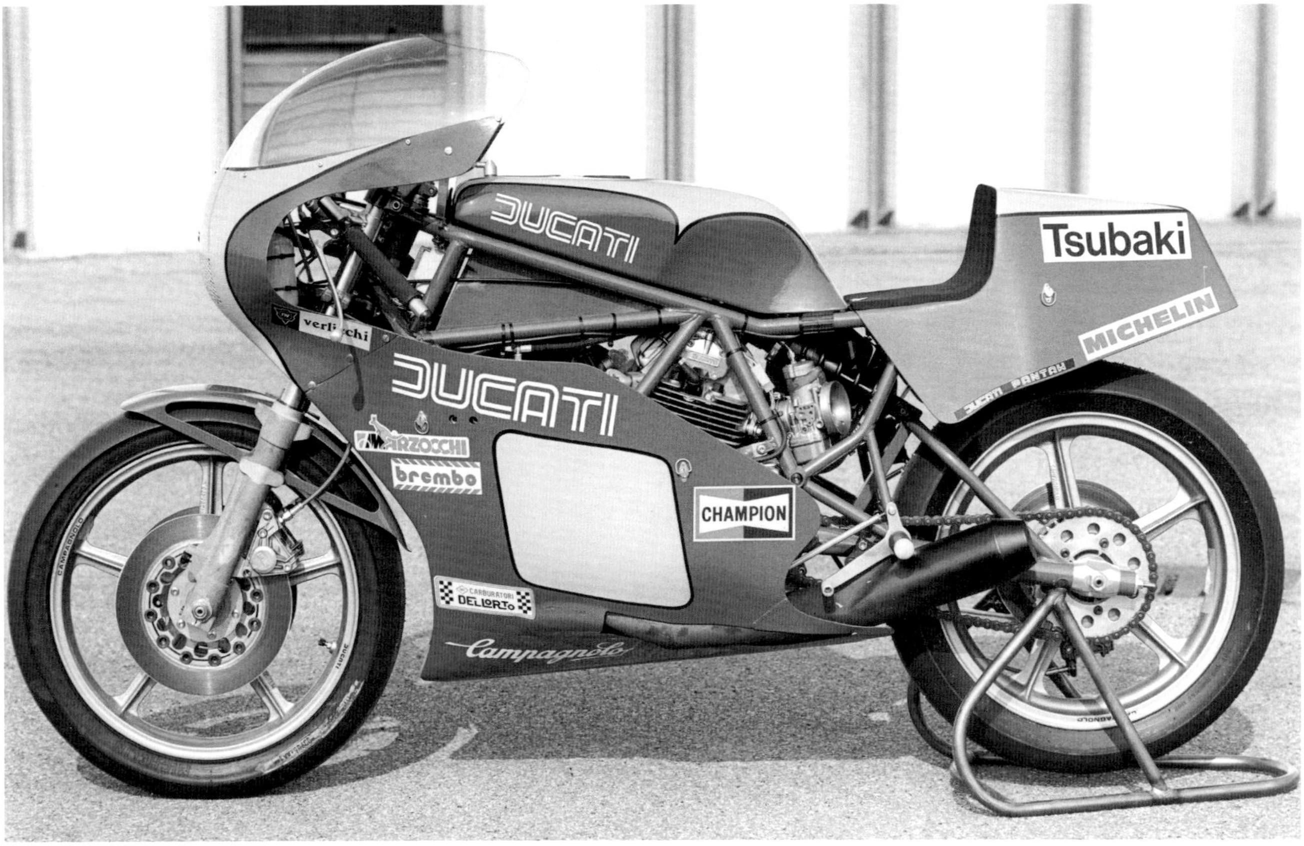

The factory TT2 of 1981, one of the classic racing Ducatis.

mounted in the rear tailpiece. Because Italian regulations required an electric starter, both this and the 200-watt alternator were retained.

The TT2 was a very effective racing machine, in the best Taglioni tradition of achieving maximum results through a balance of power and weight. It was light, athletic, slim, had a wide powerband, and Taglioni was especially proud of the specific fuel consumption figures of 187 gr./HP/hr. Just how effective it was as a racer was displayed by Massimo Broccoli in October 1981 at the final round of the Italian 500 series at Mugello. On a TT2 sleeved down to 500cc, he finished 7th in a field of 500GP Suzukis and Yamahas. Broccoli had already secured the Italian Formula 2 championship ahead of the Kawasaki-powered Bimota KB2s. In its first full year the TT2 had won the two championship

The 1981 factory TT2 with an engine that still looked similar to the production Pantah, at least on the left side.

On the right side was a magnesium dry clutch assembly and the closeness of the frame to the engine didn't allow for timing belt covers.

series they had contested. At the Milan Show at the end of 1981 the 500 Pantah Speedway was also unveiled. This was intended for Ice Trophy racing during 1982 but failed to meet expectations. A joint Ducati/Alfa Romeo project, ten ice racers were built. Based on a 500 SL, the 500 Pantah Speedway was without brakes and was fitted with spiked tyres. There were 190 spikes on the front and 235 on the rear, and the Austrian rider Hans Maier raced it unsuccessfully during 1982.

The TT2, though, was even more successful in 1982. In the Italian Formula 2 championship Walter Cussigh won every round on his factory TT2, and the now 40-year-old Tony Rutter again won the TT2 World Championship. For the Italian events power was up to 78 HP at 10,500 rpm using 41mm Malossi Dell'Orto carburetors, and Cussigh favored a 16-inch Campagnolo front wheel while Rutter still used the 18-inch wheels, preferring them to the 16-inch on the bumpier street circuits. At the Isle of Man he was considerably faster than the previous year, winning the Formula 2 race on the factory bike at an average speed of 108.50 mph (175 km/h), with a fastest lap of 109.27 mph (176 km/h). He was timed at 144 mph (232 km/h) at a speed trap at the Highlander. With the World Championship now extended to three rounds, Rutter scored perfect points on his factory bike. He won at Vila Real in Portugal, following this with a victory at Ulster.

During 1982 ten 500 Pantah Speedway were constructed for "Ice Trophy" racing. These had spiked tires and no brakes or rear suspension.

Tony Rutter won four consecutive world TT Formula 2 championships on the TT2. Here he is on his way to victory at the Isle of Man in 1982.

During 1982, a limited number of production TT2 replicas were built for privateers. These bikes were very close to the factory bikes, but lacked items such as the magnesium primary drive cover and hydraulically operated dry clutch (details are covered in Chapter Three). Racing results for the TT2 in 1983 weren't quite as spectacular as the previous year. Tony Rutter again won the TT2 World Championship, but not quite as convincingly. At the Isle of Man he headed a Ducati one-two with Graeme McGregor, at an average speed of 108.20 mph (174 km/h), with a fastest lap of 109.44 mph (176 km/h). At the other two rounds at Ulster and Assen, he could only manage second, but it was enough to win the championship again. Another batch of TT2 replicas was built for 1983, quite similar to those of the previous year except for a 16-inch front wheel.

With the possibility of the World Championship TT2 class disappearing completely, Ducati hastened development of a 750cc TT1 version of the Pantah for 1984. Both TT1 and World Endurance were becoming limited to 750cc, so a longer, 61.5mm stroked crankshaft was homologated with the 650 SL Pantah. Even as far back as March 1982, Jimmy Adamo raced a 750cc version of the TT2 for Reno Leoni at the Daytona 200, finishing 13th overall. This bike had produced nearly 95 HP at 10,250 rpm, with a top speed of almost 155 mph (250 km/h). Two months later, on May 15 and 16 at Imola for the inaugural 24 hour *Bol d'Or Italia*, Taglioni prepared another 750 from a TT2. Weighing 135kg (297 pounds) with full lighting equipment, this prototype produced 92 HP. It was also fitted with a 16-inch front wheel and four-piston Brembo front brakes. The following year at Daytona, this time in the Battle of the Twins race, Tony Rutter took the 750 TT1 to third place. Then in July 1983, at one of the most successful venues for Ducati, Montjuich Park, a TT1 won the now non-championship 24-hour race with Benjamin Grau, Enrique de Juan and Luis Reyes. Prepared by Franco Farnè, the 135kg (297 pound) racer produced 86 HP at 9,000 rpm.

While Tony Rutter still raced the 600TT2 in 1984, and won the Formula 2 World Championship for the fourth successive year, he also campaigned a 750cc version of the same bike in Formula 1. He failed

A factory TT1 engine on display in the Museo Ducati in Bologna. Former factory mechanic Primo Forassasi painstakingly restored this example.

to win the Isle of Man F2 race, coming second, but won at Vila Real (at 90.81 mph). Trevor Nation, also on a 600TT2, came second in the championship. In Formula 1, Rutter managed third overall on the new Ducati TT1 during the 1984 season, and the 750 had limited success in endurance racing. At the non-championship Le Mans 24-Hour race in April, a 750 TT1 ridden by Marc Granie, Philippe Guichon and Didier Vuillemin finished fourth. They followed this up with a fourth at the Österreichring 1000km race, third in the Liege 24 Hours at Spa, and fourth at the Mugello 6 Hours, eventually finishing fifth in the championship. The works bike of Walter Villa and Walter Cussigh came fourth at the ADAC 8-Hour race at the Nürburgring, but was plagued with problems throughout the season.

The catalog TT1 differed only slightly from the TT2 (see Chapter Three), but the factory racer used by Walter Villa was significantly more developed than any customer bikes. The steering head angle was reduced to 24 degrees, and a rising-rate suspension system, similar to the Suzuki full-floater type, was used, along with a box-section swingarm. The bikes immediately suffered suspension problems, with retirement at Le Mans. During 1984, 41.7mm Kayaba front forks with hydraulic anti-dive from a Suzuki RG500 were tried, before settling on new 42mm aluminum-slider Marzocchis. Brakes were the new type of quickly detachable four-piston Brembos with larger, 300mm discs, and a small, 230mm disc at the rear. Marvic three-spoke 16-inch front wheels were used, along with 16-, 17- or 18-inch rears. Rim widths ranged from 3.5 inches on the front to 5.5 inches on the rear. By the end of the season, a 16-inch front and 17-inch rear wheel were fitted, along with the new series of Michelin radial. The claimed dry weight was 287 pounds (130kg).

The factory TT1 prototype endurance racer at Le Mans in April 1984. This was the first factory racer to feature a rising-rate rear suspension and was ridden by Walter Villa, Dominique Jaubert and Carlo Perugini. Early in the season Kayaba Suzuki RG500 forks were used.

The factory TT1 engine was considerably developed over the TT2. Camshafts with intake lift of 11.45mm and exhaust lift 10.35mm operated the larger valves (44mm and 38mm). Stronger, American-made Carrillo con rods were used on a standard, polished crankshaft. The 10.3:1 pistons were the cause of one failure during the season, as were problems with valve seats, but the engine still produced 94 HP at 10,000 rpm with the 41mm Dell'Orto-Malossi carburetors, reduced slightly to 90 HP for 24-hour events. The Bosch ignition rotor and alternator were now fitted in the magnesium left-side case, away from engine oil, and a mechanically operated dry clutch replaced the previous hydraulic one. The factory TT1 was by now very well developed, and ready for another assault on the World Endurance Championship, and Italian F1, in 1985.

The factory TT1 for 1985 featured a new 12-plate dry clutch and magnesium engine cover. The crankcases were also one-off castings.

1985 was also the final year for the official TT2. Tony Rutter, riding a factory TT1 with the rising-rate rear suspension, but fitted with a 600cc engine, again won the Formula 2 race at the Isle of Man, but at the slower speed of 107.79 mph (173 km/h). He followed this with a second at Vila Real, and a third at Montjuich Park. Unfortunately, a serious accident in the F1 race at Montjuich on a Suzuki GSX-R750 tragically ended Rutter's career, and he was lucky to survive, initially being pronounced dead. Despite not completing the season, Rutter still managed to finish second in the TT F2 World Championship that year. His record of four

In the foreground is the 1985 factory TT1, with a customer model in the background. On the factory machine there was a new frame with a rising-rate-linkage suspension. There was also a new magnesium left-side engine cover with externally mounted Bosch ignition.

Walter Cussigh on the 1985 factory TT1. While he had mixed fortune in the Endurance series that year, the machine was very competitive in the Italian Formula 1 championship.

consecutive World Championships rates as amongst the most significant racing results ever achieved by Ducati.

Despite all the development on the TT1 by Taglioni, Franco Farnè and Walter Villa, the 1985 Endurance season was even less successful than the previous year. The only notable results were a fifth and sixth at the opening 6-hour round at Monza with Walter Cussigh/Oscar La Ferla and Virginio Ferrari/Marco Lucchinelli. In the Formula 1 World Championship, Dieter Rechtenbach managed sixth overall, by virtue of finishing second at Montjuich, always Ducati's most successful venue. Another significant result for the TT1 was Marco Lucchinelli's sixth place in the Daytona Formula 1 race in March. It was a different story in the Italian Formula 1 Championship. Here TT1 Ducatis filled the first seven places, with Virginio Ferrari taking the title from Marco Lucchinelli.

The 1986 season started well with Marco Lucchinelli winning the Battle of the Twins race at Daytona in March on an experimental 851cc (92mm x 64mm) 750 F1 based racer at just over 104 mph (167 km/h). Lucchinelli raced in both the Formula 1 and Battle of

The winner of the 1985 Italian Formula 1 championship was former Grand Prix star Virginio Ferrari.

the Twins, and later went on to win the Battle of the Twins race at Laguna Seca. He also won the opening round of the TT Formula 1 World Championship at the Autodromo Santamonica at Misano on April 6, at an average speed of 90.14 mph (145 km/h). Unfortunately he couldn't repeat this performance in other rounds. Graeme McGregor eventually came sixth overall in the championship on a non-factory TT1. There was no factory involvement in the Endurance World Championship until the debut of the new water-cooled four-valve 748 at the Bol d'Or in September, but that was the beginning of a new Desmoquattro generation, and is outside the realm of this book. However, at the Jerez 8-Hour race on September 28, Juan Garriga and Marco Lucchinelli were teamed together on a two-valve 750 TT1. They had pole position and initially led the race, eventually finishing second. Later, at the Barcelona 24-Hour race on October 26 1986 (a non-championship event), Juan Garriga, Carlos Cardus and the steadfast Benjamin Grau won using the 851cc version of the TT1, proving the reliability of the larger engine. An 818cc (92mm x 61.5mm) version of the engine was also tried during 1986, notably by Jimmy Adamo at the Battle of the Twins race at Daytona.

The final outing for the factory air-cooled two-valve racer was at the Laguna Seca Pro Twins race at Laguna Seca in 1987. Marco Lucchinelli again rode,

Marco Lucchinelli with mechanic Giuliano Pedretti after winning the 1986 Daytona Battle of the Twins race. The TT1-based machine displaced 851cc and produced around 97 HP.

Lucchinelli also rode a modified 750 F1 in the Daytona 200 of 1986, the TT1 ineligible. This machine had the stock Forcelle Italia forks and cantilever swingarm, but he retired during the race.

The final factory TT1 of 1987 with its upside-down single-damper White Power fork.

and this 851cc bike featured revised inlet ports and ducting, and metal shrouding around the rear cylinder to keep it cool. The standard TT1 chassis was fitted with a new type of 43mm upside-down GCB (Gazzaniga-Ceriani-Bianchi) fork with a single, centrally located spring damper unit. At the rear, a lightweight GCB shock absorber was used. Wheels were Marvic 17-inch front and rear, and Lucchinelli repeated his victory of the previous year.

Besides the factory bikes, which were undoubtedly the most spectacular, TT1 replicas were widely raced with some success throughout the world. In Spain, Antonio Cobas built a frame for the F1, and Kenny Roberts tested this bike at Misano in August 1985. Juan Garriga had raced it at the Montjuich round of the Formula 1 World Championship (the same race where Tony Rutter was injured), and had actually led at one stage before crashing. In Battle of the Twins classes around the world, replicas of the TT1 took over where the bigger twins left off, but as a competitor to the Japanese head-on, it was now outdated. The two-valve Pantah heads had reached the limit of their development, and a new cylinder head design was needed.

CHAPTER TWO

The Pantah

350/500/600/650 SL, 350/600 TL, 350 XL

As with some other models of Ducati, only a small number of the first series of Pantah was produced. While these didn't include any special parts as the first 750 GT had done back in 1971, they were built primarily to test the quality of the design and market acceptance before regular production commenced. It must be remembered that when the first Pantah was created it was one of the most expensive machines available in its capacity class, and in October 1979 distributors around the world received small quantities of pre-production 500 SL Pantahs. This immediately set new standards for performance in the 500cc category, even in the standard trim that included restrictive air filters, mufflers, and extremely high gearing. The design characteristics of the Pantah were such that while much was shared with Taglioni's earlier bevel-drive twin, in most respects this was a new-generation engine.

500 SL
1979

Released at the same time as the 900 Mike Hailwood Replica, as with the initial series of that model, only a small number (163) of the first series of 500 Pantah were produced following the August summer break of 1979. While they differed in several details to later production bikes, essentially the design was to remain unchanged. Apart from the red-and-silver paintwork, along with red front and rear fenders and a single/dual seat arrangement similar to the early 900 MHR, this model formed the basis of the 500 and 600 Pantah until 1984.

Engine and Drivetrain

Engine numbers for the 500 SL started at DM 500L.1 600001, stamped on the rear left half of the crankcase. As with limited series of earlier 750 and 900 Super Sports the first Pantahs carried the .1 designation, presumably indicating they were an initial series. Many of the engine design features were carried over from earlier Ducatis, notably the vertically split crankcases and finning that differed between the front and rear cylinders. But inside, the Pantah engine was virtually all-new. Compared with the bevel-drive twin it was considerably more compact, lighter, and much more

The final 500 SL prototype before the model went into limited production in late 1979. The seat, screen, taillight, filler cap and positioning of the rear brake caliper differed to the eventual production model.

In production form the 500 SL still featured a rather crude solo seat and red and silver decals.

oil-tight. It was also amazingly reliable from the outset, with only minor modifications over the first few years.

The first 500s featured three-ring 74mm 9.5:1 Borgo pistons with matching Gilnisil cylinder liners. In an effort to reduce engine noise, 61 rubber plugs were positioned between the cylinder fins, along with a further 20 in the rear cylinder head and 23 in the front head. Just as with the larger twins there was no cylinder head gasket, the head and barrel being located by bushes and sealed by O rings. On the early engines the front cylinder used one 8mm -diameter bush and one 12mm -diameter bush, the rear featuring three 12mm -diameter bushes.

It was interesting that when the engine was initially designed in 1975 it was intended for a maximum displacement of 500cc, along with a smaller 350. Consequently the general construction reflected that of a small engine. The cylinder heads, while incorporating the 60-degree valve angle of the larger racing Ducatis, provided for quite small valves, 37.5mm inlet and 33.5mm exhaust. It was only several years later, with the 500cc engine already in production and the advent of Formula 2 racing, that a larger displacement was considered. These valves had 8mm stems and were located in the usual short valve guides favored by Ducati with their desmodromic engines; 38mm long for the inlet and 37mm for the exhaust. The inlet and exhaust ports were also on the small side, 32mm for the inlet and 34mm for the exhaust.

A pre-production Pantah on display at the London Show of 1979. The general specification was as for the production version although the colors were red and green.

The desmodromic valve layout for the Pantah mirrored that of the bevel-drive Super Sport. The same basic system features on all motorcycles in this book and continues today.

The desmodromic valve layout was almost identical to that of the earlier 500 Sport Desmo parallel-twin, and followed that of the 750 and 900 Super Sports. Each valve was opened by a normal rocker and closed by a lower forked rocker. Small springs seated the valves to ensure sufficient compression for starting. Adjustment was by a set of opening and closing caps identical to those of the larger twins. Sizes ranged from 2mm-5mm for opening clearances (in 0.05mm increments), and 5mm-9.6mm for closing clearances (in 0.2mm increments). The 10mm hard-chromed grooved rocker pins too were shared with the 750/900 Super Sport. Valve guide sealing though was new, no longer with an internal O ring, but with a more usual rubber seal on top of the guide. The valve lift was 10mm for the inlet and 9mm for the exhaust.

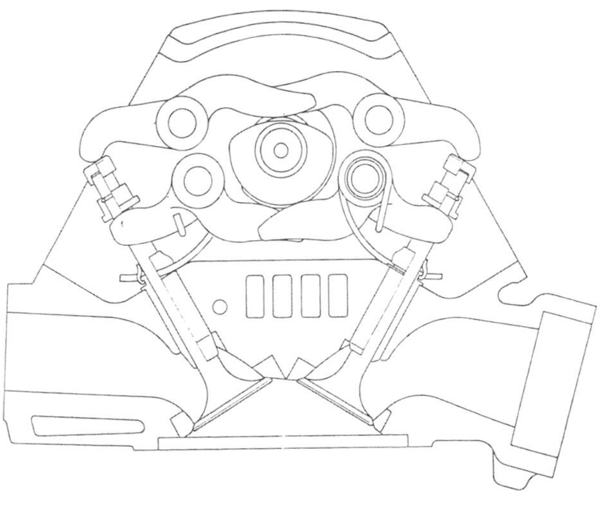

While the general valve operating system was as with the larger twins, the narrower included valve angle was more modern. This design also carried through for more than 30 years.

Unlike the bevel-drive desmos that used four identical camshaft support bearings, the single overhead camshaft in the Pantah was supported by two ball bearings in the cylinder head, one 20mm x 42mm x 12mm and one 17mm x 35mm x 10mm, along with a 15mm x 35mm x 11mm bearing in the external support housing. The shorter camshafts of the Pantah didn't warrant additional bearing support. The camshaft drive was by two 68-tooth rubber belts, driving aluminum pulleys on early engines. Each belt had its individual tensioning system.

Forged two-piece con rods with an 18mm wrist pin and 40mm crankpin also represented a departure from the one-piece con rod and pressed-up crank assembly of the bevel-drive twins of that period. Con rod

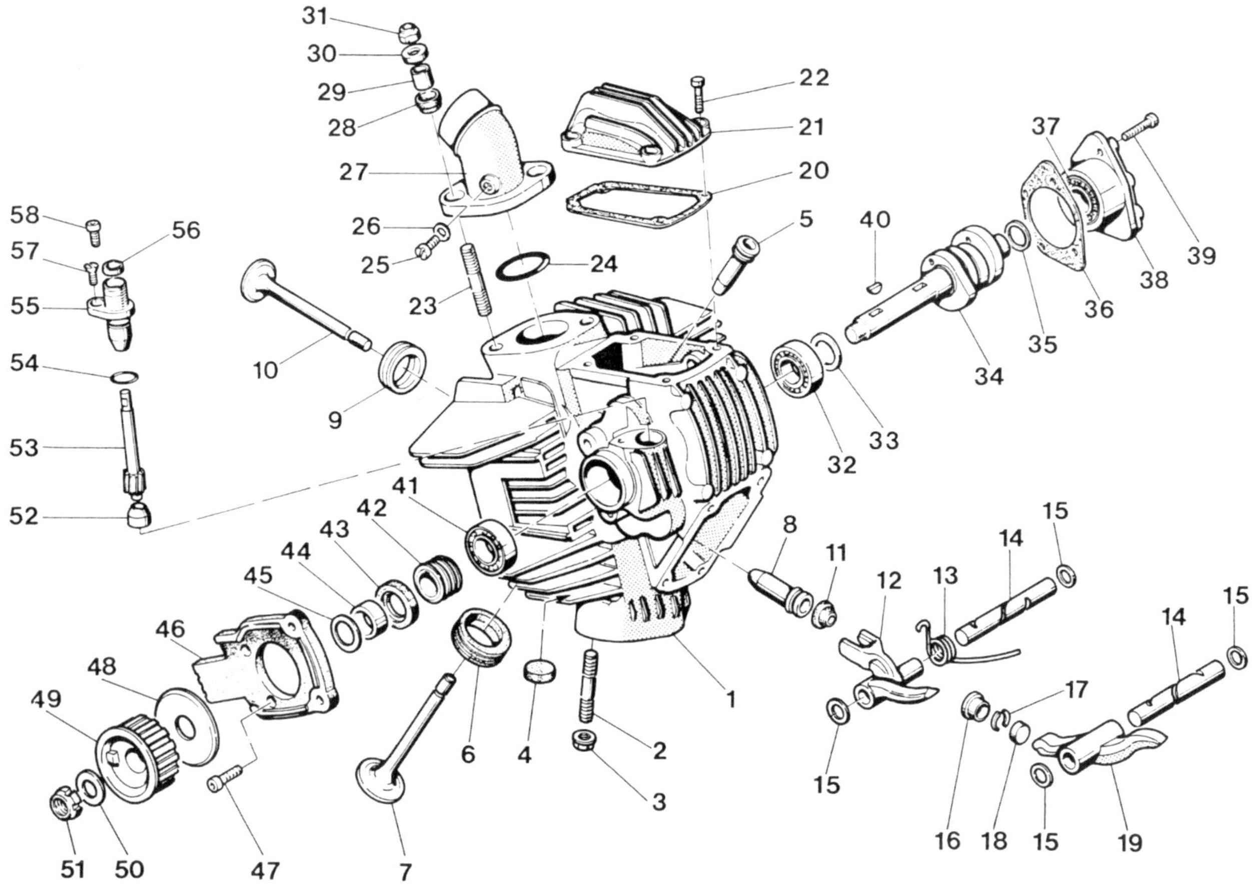

The design of the Pantah cylinder head showed a strong family resemblance to the bevel-drive twin. Even the rocker covers were shared with earlier models.

eye-to-eye length was 124mm, giving a con rod length-to-stroke ratio of 2.14:1. These rather long rods would eventually prove useful when the engine stroke was increased for the 650. Width of the big-end eye was 22mm. If there was single factor that contributed to the improved reliability of the Pantah engine it was the plain big-end bearings. While requiring more specialized repair facilities, big-end failure was now virtually a thing of the past. The crankshaft was forged one-piece and was constructed in UNI38 NiCrMo4, nitrided at −50 degrees Celsius. Although the crankshaft was similar to that of the ill-fated parallel-twin, the use of axial-thrust ball main bearings was more reminiscent of the bevel-drive twin. These included different sized main bearings, a 35mm x 80mm x 21mm on the drive side and a smaller 35mm x 72mm x 17mm on the ignition/alternator/jackshaft side. As with the larger twins these main bearings ran in steel bushes that were an interference fit in the crankcases. Early Pantahs also sometimes suffered main bearing failure, generally the smaller bearing collapsing. Twelve screws—six M8mm x 80mm, five M6mm x 35mm, and one M6mm x 50mm— retained the crankcase halves. These were obviously adequate because a very similar setup featured on 600 and 750 engines until the end of the 1990s.

1979 engines also used different nuts to secure the primary drive and alternator. The primary drive was secured by an M22mm x 1mm x 8mm hex nut, while the alternator used an M20mm x 1mm x 7mm hex nut. Drive to the clutch was now on the right, still through helical gears, with a ratio of 31/69 (2.226:1). The clutch drum was alloy and attached to the primary gear by eight rivets along with rubber bushes to absorb shock. These were supported by two 25mm x 47mm x 12mm bearings separated by a spacer and circlip. It was essential that the circlip was thicker than this spacer by 0.15mm to maintain the correct axial preload to the bearings. If the preload was too high this could cause

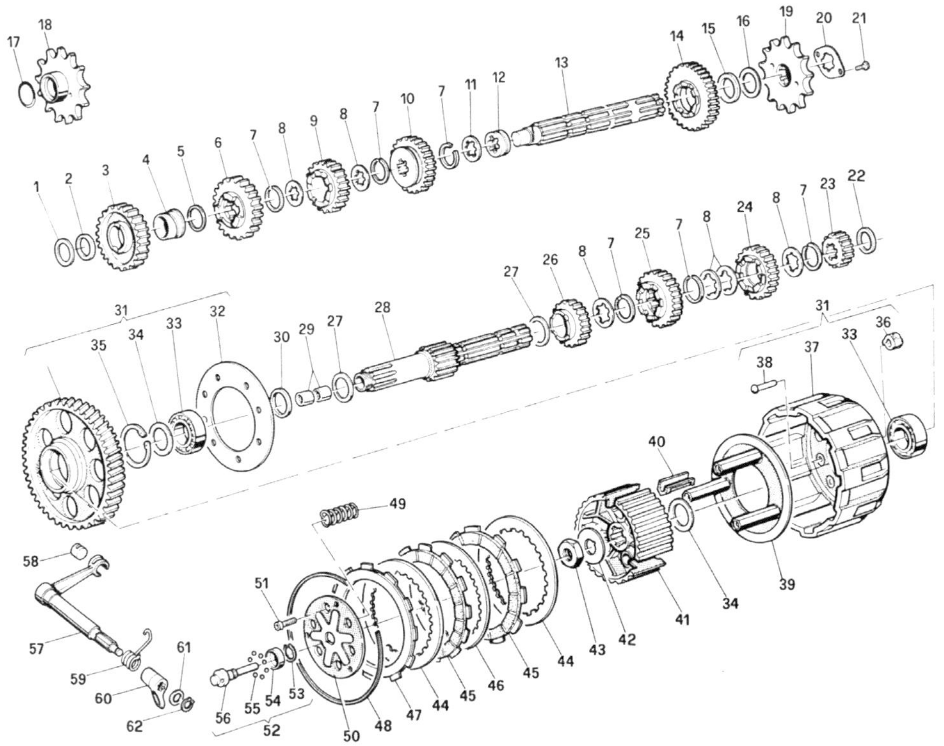

The clutch and gearbox of the 500 SL. Early gearboxes featured six-dog gears and an alloy clutch drum.

premature bearing failure. A spacer too thick in relation to the circlip could cause clutch problems. To rectify any problem with assembly by the time the Pantah entered regular production the circlip and spacer were offered as one spare part (0660.88.630). Another spacer (0660.16.225) fitted between the outer drum and alloy inner clutch drum. The combination of clutch plates was quite a lot more sophisticated than on the bevel-drive twins. Seven fiber driving discs, seven steel driven discs, with a thinner driven disc either end and a special steel driving disc on the outside for a total of 17 plates. These were retained by a large outer circlip, and like all Ducati clutches of this period were Surflex (S7). While the clutch seemed more advanced than that of the bevel-drive twins, this would still be the major area of weakness in the new design with numerous clutch modifications occurring over time, especially as the engine grew in capacity. The cable operation also required a Herculean hand to operate.

A more normal indirect five-speed gearbox, with separate input and output shafts, featured gears with six dogs. Directly behind the 25mm x 52mm 15mm and 17mm x 40mm x 12mm output shaft bearings were the bronze bushes that supported the swingarm pivot. As it was lubricated by engine oil mist it wasn't anticipated that wear would be a problem so on early models only one size of pivot pin was specified. A spur gear drove the geared oil pump, this integral with the helical primary drive. For the first time on a Ducati there was an automotive-style full-flow spin-on oil filter, along with an oil level sight glass in the right-side engine cover. Surprisingly the screw-in mesh sump filter was also retained, this no longer needing to be removed to drain the oil as there was now a magnetic oil drain plug. The early series Pantah featured a countershaft sprocket (either 14- or 15-tooth) with an internal O ring, but this part was superseded in 1980, along with the early layshaft. Sprocket retention was also improved over the bevel-drive twins with the sprocket located by a plate and two M6mm x 10mm screws.

For a 500cc twin, very large Dell'Orto PHF 36 AD and AS carburetors were fitted. These had accelerator pumps and a choke operated by a lever on the right, underneath the speedometer. One of the problems with the Pantah was the very restrictive air filter system. A pleated paper air filter situated in a plastic box between the upper frame tubes fed air through plastic ducts, the rear being rather tortuous. Running with the air filters the Pantah was jetted very rich, indicating that the factory expected the filters to be removed. An improvement over earlier Ducatis was in the inlet manifold sealing, with a large O ring located between the manifold and cylinder head as opposed to flexible plastic gaskets. Fuel lines were still the green plastic *Nava Granturismo* as used on all bevel-drive twin Ducatis to that date, retained by the same wire clamps.

Unlike the bevel-drive twins, the exhaust headers weren't retained by the problematic threaded ring nut, but by a superior system of two split bushes and a bolted ring nut. The exhaust header pipes were dual-wall to resist bluing, and the standard system included a large balance pipe underneath the engine. Standard mufflers were Conti, but these were a far cry from the bellowing units fitted to bevel-drive twins. With the standard pipes the 500 SL was the quietest Ducati ever.

The Pantah was also designed to be electric-start only. The electric-start motor fitted underneath the front cylinder and drove an intermediate helical gear connected to the ignition flywheel. This 15-tooth gear mated to a 55-tooth spur gear keyed to a 14-tooth gear driving the 69-tooth gear bolted to the ignition flywheel giving an overall gearing reduction of 18:1. Inside the flywheel was a freewheel bearing, the flywheel itself located on the crankshaft by two needle bearings. As it had on the 900 SD Darmah, problem with this starter clutch sprag bearing persisted on the Pantah. On the crankshaft near the main bearing was a 25-tooth helical gear driving the 50-tooth jackshaft to the camshaft drive. The quoted power figure for the first 500 SL, with standard intake and exhaust system, was 45 HP at 9,050 rpm with 4.1 kg/m of torque produced at 6,300 rpm.

Ignition, Electrical System, and Switches

Long a criticism of Italian motorcycles, and Ducatis in particular, by the time of the Pantah Ducati electrical systems had come a long way. With only provision for electric start, a Yuasa YB 14L/A2 YUMICROM battery was employed, along with a four-diode 12-volt regulator. The battery was located on the right, behind the rear cylinder, along with a three-fuse fuse box. Most of the time the electrical system was reliable but a perennial problem with Pantahs was often a slow trickle charge that could flatten the battery just enough to prevent the engine starting if the machine wasn't ridden regularly. This was due to a voltmeter that automatically controlled the switching of the *GEN* warning light. When battery voltage exceeded 12.35 volts the light was switched off. It would also switch on in the case of regulator failure and the voltage exceeded 15.7 volts. Unfortunately this voltmeter was an unreliable device, responsible for much heartache and push starts for owners of early Pantahs.

The flywheel on the left side of the crankshaft incorporated the ignition rotor, the two magnetic pickups located on a plate bolted inside the crankcase. Outboard of this on the end of the crankshaft was the 200-watt alternator. Ignition was a similar Bosch BTZ electronic type as used on the Ducati Darmah SD 900, consisting of two amplifiers, two high-tension coils and two resistors. The electronic amplifiers and resistors were Bosch, but the coils (0799.46.511) Nippon Denso. All these components, along with the regulator and relays, were rather inconveniently positioned under the steering head. Unlike the ignition for the larger twins, though, advance was only in two stages, 6 degrees until 1,600 rpm, and 32 degrees after 2,900 rpm. Champion L81 spark plugs were specified on early engines, with black ignition leads and the early rubber KLG spark plug caps. Starting was through a compact four-brush SJCE electric motor. Unfortunately the location of this, just behind the front wheel, could lead to failure from corrosion if the motorcycle was continually used in wet weather.

Other electrical components consisted of an Aprilia 170mm 55/60-watt halogen (*jodio*) headlight and a rectangular 12V-5/21-watt CEV taillight. The headlight rim was chromed with a black-painted shell, and European versions featured a 3-watt parking lamp. 12V-21-watt turn signal indicators were standard, the front being incorporated in the fairing. The instrument panel was similar to that of the 900 SSD, featuring seven warning lights, including a stand light for a non-existent sidestand, and a three-position ignition key. These warning lights were *Stand* (red), *Lights* (green), *High Beam* (blue), < > (orange flasher), *Gen* (red), *Neutral* (green), *Oil* (red). The left Nippon Denso handlebar switches were shared with the 900 SD. New for the Pantah was the twin-cable plastic Verlicchi

All the Pantah ignition components were tightly packed behind the steering stem, making general accessibility difficult.

throttle incorporating the electric-start button and on/off switch. Frame-mounted Nippon Denso instruments (speedometer on the left and tachometer on the right), and a Bosch horn completed the specification. Because the instruments were shared with the larger twins, these always had an 8,000-rpm redline, and an orange line from 9,000 rpm.

Frame and Cycle Parts

Ing. Fabio Taglioni designed a completely new trellis frame for the Pantah. Frame numbers for the 500 SL started at DM 500 SL 660001. The main part of the black-painted frame was constructed in Fe35 tubing, 25mm x 3mm. This frame, while not the most compact and stiffest, was still commendably strong, the engine hanging from the lower tubes and located by two M10mm x 252mm and one M10mm x 228mm bolts. Much of the design of the frame seemed to center around the requirement for space for an adequate air filtration system. The frame also drew on traditional Ducati steering geometry with its 30.5-degree steering head angle. The two 26mm x 52mm x 15mm tapered roller steering head bearings were as with the

The Pantah instruments and warning lights were standard Ducati issue of the early 1980s. The Nippon Denso tachometer was still redlined at 8,000 rpm.

larger twins. Completely different was the swingarm that pivoted in the engine cases on two bronze bushes, although the chain adjustment system was the Seeley type, pioneered with the 750 GT in 1971. All Pantahs featured a small foldout handle above the left rider's

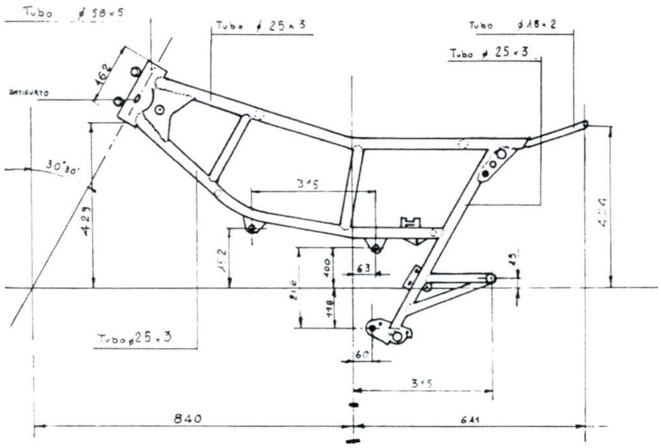

Fig. 127

The Pantah trellis frame that lasted for all the SL, TL, XL and Cagiva Alazzurra.

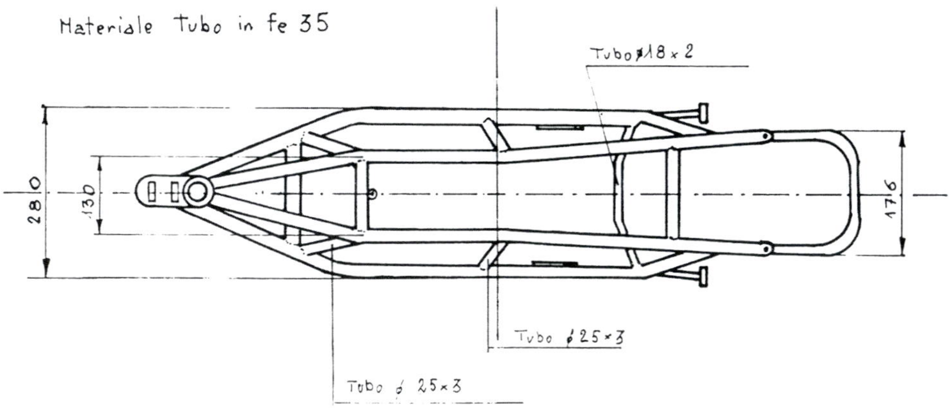

Fig. 128

footpeg. This frame would continue on all Pantahs (and the Cagiva Alazzurra) until the advent of the F1 in 1985.

The first 500 SL had rather flimsy 35mm Marzocchi forks, with polished aluminum fork legs, black-painted triple clamps and two bolt mounts for the front fender. Fork tube length was 605mm and a small red MARZOCCHI decal was fitted to the lower left fork leg. The twin shock absorbers were red Marzocchi AG Strada oleo-pneumatic remote-reservoir 310mm. These were nitrogen charged at 28 psi, but this was very difficult to check without loss of pressure. However, these units definitely performed better if charged even if some guesswork was required. The Pantah was also the first Ducati to feature dual six-spoke aluminum FPS wheels, a WM3 2.15 x 18-inch inch on the front and WM4 2.50 x 18-inch on the rear. These were gold with polished rims on the first series and fitted with Michelin tires; 3.25H18 S41 on the front and 3.50V18 M45 on the rear. The tires were a hard compound and not

One of the important considerations in the design of the frame seemed to be to provide sufficient air filtration and intake silencing.

particularly suitable for a sport bike such as the Pantah. Another unsuitable feature was the 38-tooth final-drive sprocket, giving the Pantah ridiculously high overall gearing. In standard trim, with the restrictive air filters and mufflers, the 500 SL was generally faster

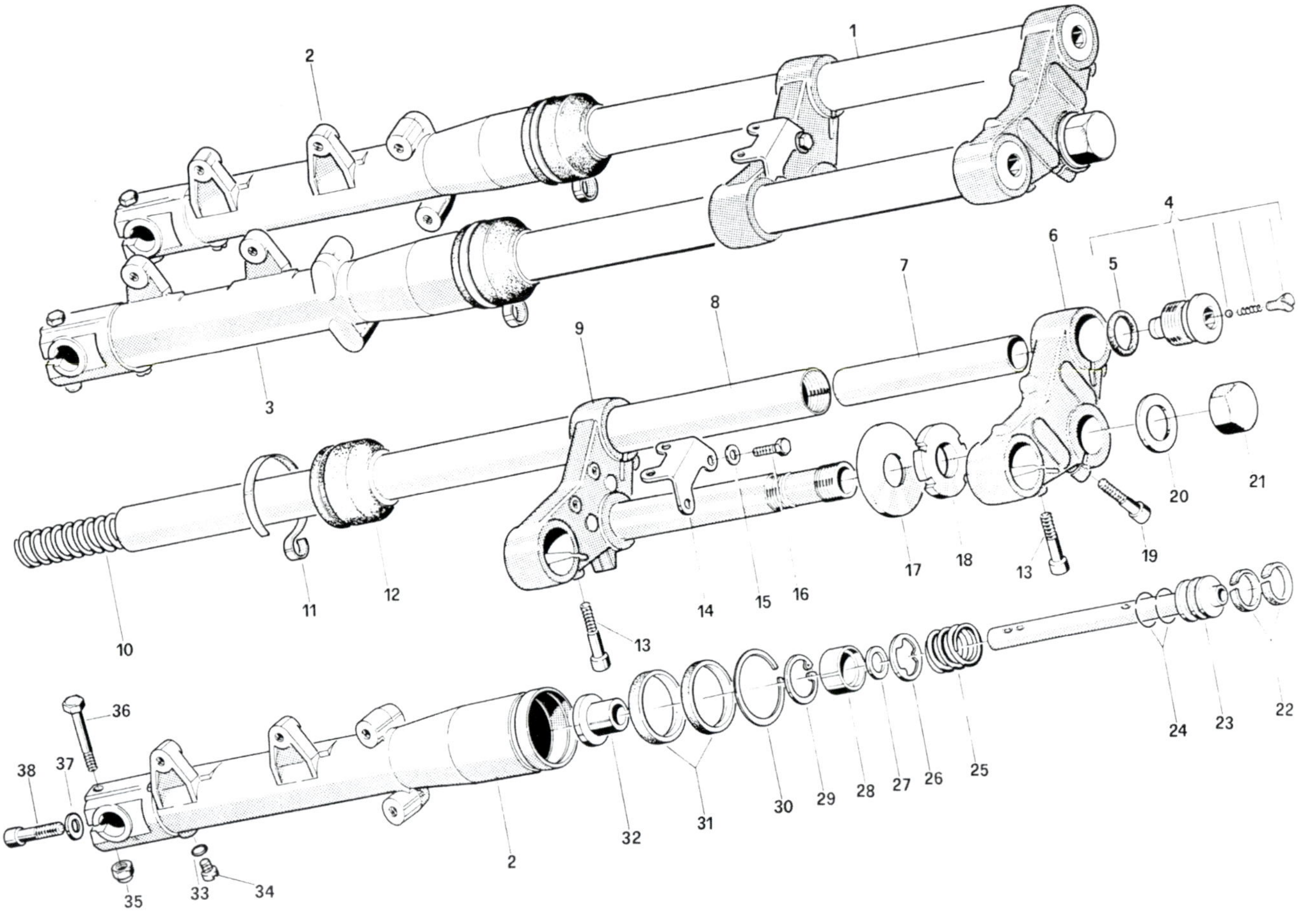

Early 500 SL Pantahs were fitted with 35mm Marzocchi forks with polished fork legs and black triple clamps. These were rather basic and flimsy units for the weight and performance of the motorcycle.

in fourth rather than fifth gear. The rear wheel featured the cush drive of the larger twins. Final drive was by a 94-tooth 5/8 x 3/8 inch Regina chain.

One of the Pantah's more satisfactory features was the Brembo braking system. Three 260mm drilled discs (with six-bolt location) with small 05 Brembo brake calipers were more than adequate for the 500 SL. The brake and clutch levers were polished aluminum, and the front brake calipers mounted in front of the fork legs. The front brake line was a 205mm rubber hose connected to a junction (with pressure switch), then to two 360mm rubber hoses and two metal pipes connecting to the brake caliper. The rear brake line consisted of one 435mm rubber hose. Standard brake pads were a rather hard compound Ferit I/D 346 GG.

Foot controls on the Pantah were similar to other Ducatis of the period. The folding steel footpegs were fitted with rubbers and the foot levers chrome-plated steel, the linkages including sloppy clevis pins and one ball joint only on the rear linkage for the gearshift. Such inconsistencies remained a peculiarity on all Ducatis until Cagiva bought the company in 1985. Passenger footpegs were from the 900 SD and Verlicchi handgrips from the 900 SS.

The first series of 500 SL featured a different seat and color scheme to later Pantahs. Both separate single and dual seats were available, the single seat also requiring a fiberglass rear section. The slab-sided fuel tank and

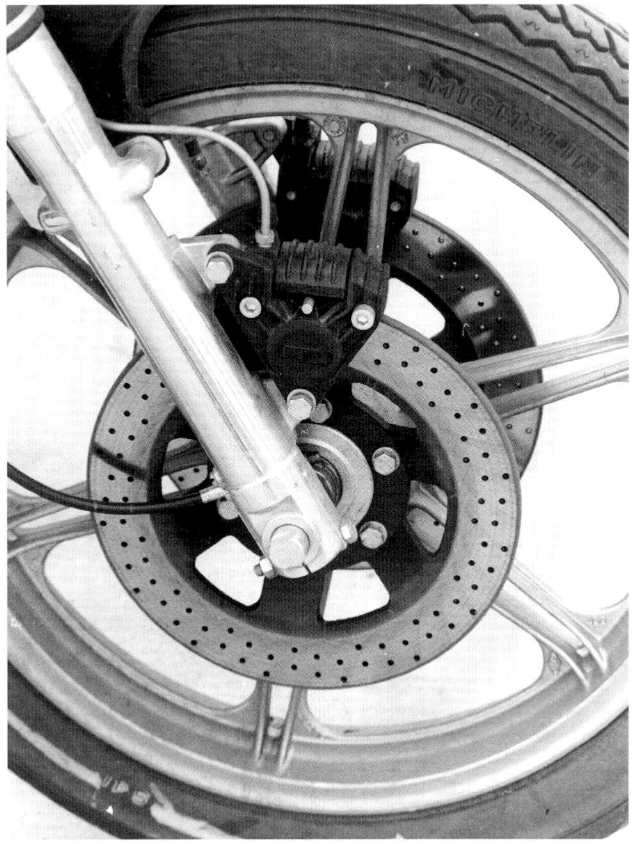

The standard front end of the early 500 SL. This 1980 machine has gold aluminum FPS wheels and a black plastic front mudguard. The Michelin S41 tire, polished Marzocchi forks, 260mm drilled discs, and 05 Brembo brake calipers were shared with the earlier version.

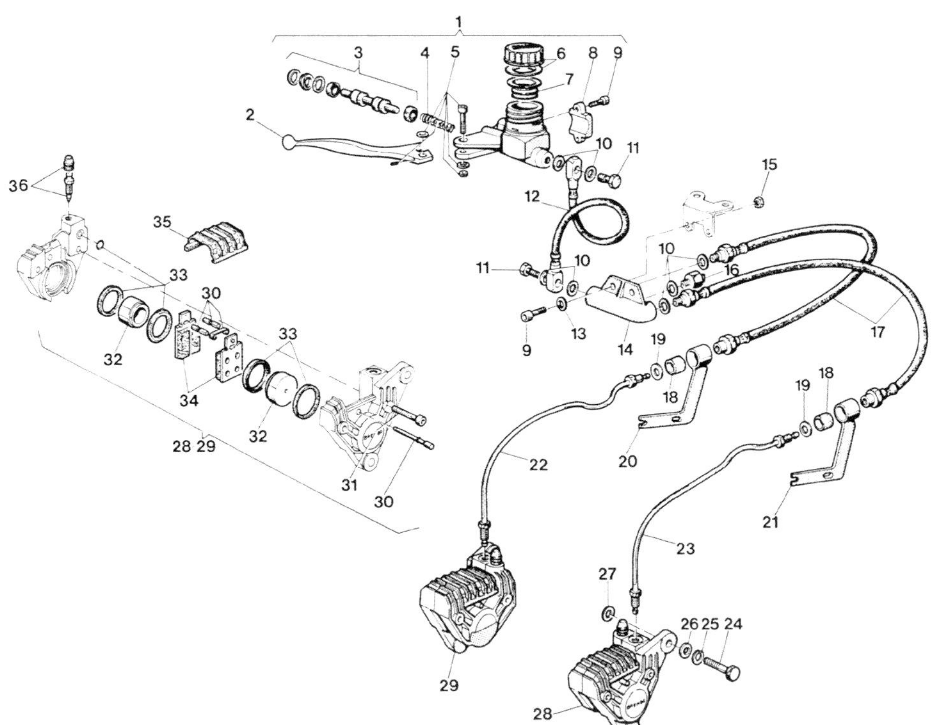

While using smaller calipers and master cylinder, the standard front braking system of the 500 SL was similar to that of the larger twins. Rubber hoses were used in conjunction with metal pipes.

NCR-inspired rear section were red with silver panels, and both the front and rear fenders were also red. Black and white DUCATI decals were located high on the fuel tank and on the front of the fairing. The tailpiece had a 500 decal on either side with a DESMO on the rear. Fuel taps were gray plastic Paioli and these would feature on all SL Pantahs. The red fairing also had a silver front section, and Pantahs still used individual keys for ignition, Neiman steering lock, and fuel cap. This fuel cap (0660.83.560) was a screw type, unique to the first and early production series of Pantah. It is probably fair to say that the Pantah wasn't one of Ducati's styling triumphs, but it did eventually evolve into a pleasant looking motorcycle.

1980

Soon after the first series appeared, the 500 SL went into series production. So sound was the design there were only a few alterations to the specification, mostly cosmetic. In some ways the 1980 500 SL represents the most satisfactory form of the 500 Pantah. A few early problems had been ironed out and the quality of many components was superior to those in some later machines. In the engine, the earlier six-dog gearboxes were much smoother shifting, if ultimately not as strong, as the later three-dog type, and the Marzocchi suspension superior to the later Paioli. Build quality was also better during 1980 than in subsequent years. As the first production bikes rolled off the assembly line, a factory racing kit also became available.

The 1979 500 SL dual seat was similar to that of the first series Mike Hailwood Replica. The conversion to a solo seat required a different seat pad. Also shown are the Conti muffler, Marzocchi AG Strada shock absorbers and gearshift control layout.

In 1980 a racing uprating kit became available for those wishing to race the 500 SL in Formula 2. This was offered as a complete kit to special order (0661.00.225) and included the following parts:

Racing Uprating Kit for the 500 SL Pantah. (until engine number 601653 and from 602238 until 602528).

Description	Part Number
Vertical Cylinder	0661.17.105
Horizontal Cylinder	0661.17.205
Piston	0661.47.405
Vertical Camshaft	0661.29.010
Horizontal Camshaft	0661.29.020
Main Jet #138 (x2)	0661.27.138
Main Jet #140 (x2)	0615.27.750

A rear view of the early 500 SL. The decals and decal placement differed to that of later versions, with a 500 and DESMO on the tailpiece. The same taillight lasted through until 1983.

An early series 500 SL photographed at the factory during 1979.

Main Jet #142 (x2)	0661.27.742
Main Jet #145 (x2)	0615.27.752
Main Jet #148 (x2)	0661.27.148
Main Jet #150 (x2)	0615.27.762
Main Jet #152 (x2)	0765.27.763
Main Jet #155 (x2)	0615.27.764
Silencer	0661.84.100
Tubes	0661.84.150
Lever	0661.69.515
Pinion Z=14	0660.16.095
Sprocket Z=39	0795.80.239
Sprocket Z=40	0795.80.240
Sprocket Z=41	0795.80.241
Sprocket Z=42	0795.80.242
Sprocket Z=42	0795.80.243

During 1981 the kit was modified to fit those 500 SLs with 600 crankcases (0661.00.228).

Changes to the Racing Uprating Kit for the 500 SL Pantah. (after Engine Number 601654)

Description	Part Number
Vertical Cylinder	0661.17.110
Horizontal Cylinder	0661.17.210
Piston	0661.47.400
Pinion Z=14	0660.16.098

Engine and Drivetrain

1979 series engines had experienced some gear-shift problems, so the selector drum was replaced for 1980 (0660.13.400). This no longer incorporated a retaining plate and screw, but a wire stop ring. At the same time the selector fork retaining pins were reduced in diameter to 7.7mm (from 7.7mm-8.0mm) and all parts were interchangeable with earlier types. Other gearbox modifications for 1980 included a new lay-shaft, countershaft sprocket and 27-tooth fourth driving gear (0619.16.040). A new countershaft sprocket oil seal (2547/7) was also used. From frame number 660901 (for some reason this modification was notified by frame and not engine number) the 27-tooth driven fourth gear was also changed (0660.16.085), as well as the driving fifth gear. This (0660.16.045) was now a 29-tooth rather than a 30-tooth, the slightly lower ratio featuring on all subsequent Pantahs.

Between the cylinder head and barrel the three 12mm-diameter bushes were found to be superfluous and no longer fitted, although the 115 VA 75 O ring was retained. Other small engine alterations included new crankshaft nuts, an M22mm x 1mm x 8mm for the primary drive, and a M20mm x 1mm x 7mm for the alternator.

Ignition and Electrical System

It wasn't long before Ducati became aware of the unreliability of the voltmeter controlling the dashboard

For 1980 there were new colors of light blue with dark blue and red flashes for the 500 SL. The first examples shared the FPS wheels with polished outer rims and earlier fuel filler cap of the 1979 model.

generator warning light and a new although still unreliable device (0660.38.453) soon replaced this. With the new device were red and blue cables connecting directly to the light and a revised mounting system. In addition to Champion L81 spark plugs, extended electrode L82Y or Bosch W7B plugs were also specified.

Frame and Cycle Parts

With series production the bodywork of the 500 SL was altered slightly. Although the shape of the steel fuel tank, fiberglass fairing and seat unit remained the same, the colors were changed to a light blue with dark blue and red decals. The DUCATI decals were now black, positioned much lower on the fuel tank. There was also a small black DUCATI on the rear tailpiece, the DESMO being incorporated with the 500 on the lower side of the seat unit. A black DUCATI on the front or the fairing completed the decals. Generally there was also a yellow Made in Italy decal near the fuel filler cap but this wasn't uniform. During 1980 the fuel cap was changed to one in line (0660.83.563) with those on other models. As with the 900 Mike Hailwood Replica that went into production simultaneously, the dual seat now became a convertible solo seat with a removable cowling. The plastic front fender and metal rear guard were now black instead of red. Marzocchi suspension was still a feature of the 1980 series, the fork legs still initially polished aluminum with black-painted triple clamps. Soon after the model went into production the fork's legs were painted the satin-black fleck finish shared with other Ducatis. A yellow Marzocchi decal was positioned on the lower left fork leg. There was also a new clutch cable. Early clutch cables had been found to be slightly too short and this was lengthened (0660.54.993). While the FPS aluminum wheels were also unchanged, these were soon painted gold all over. From frame number 660374 two additional 8mm-diameter dowels were added between the cush drive flange and wheel to overcome the problem of loose cush drive assemblies. The final-drive chain now became a 94-link Tsubaki 530 QR.

Most 1980 500 SLs received gold FPS wheels without polished rims. The filler cap was now the same as the larger V-twins.

1981

Even with the advent of the 600 SL, the 500 continued largely unchanged, but with several features of the larger model. The most noticeable was the 600 fairing, although the 500 colors were retained, and there were some further engine updates. Additional variation in specification occurred during this period as Ducati entered a time of inconsistency in production.

Engine and Drivetrain

During 1980 around 1,600 500 SL Pantahs were constructed, but for 1981 the engine cases were standardized with those of the 600. Thus after engine number 601654, 600 SL crankcases were used, with new 74mm cylinders and pistons. Effectively the 500 SL was now a sleeved-down 600. Mahle, instead of Borgo, now supplied the new cylinders and pistons. Possibly to use up surplus crankcases, a series of 290 500 SLs was also built with the earlier crankcases. Numbering from 602238 until 602528, these also used barrels and pistons by Mahle, but because of the smaller crankcase opening they were not interchangeable with the 600-type. From engine number 601866 there were new opening and closing rockers, as well as new camshafts. However, as these continued with the same part numbers, it was advisable to replace camshafts and rockers as a unit.

The cable-operated wet clutch was modified slightly for 1981 with one less steel driven plate, making a total of 16 clutch plates. The six-dog gearbox was as before (with a 29-tooth fifth driving gear), but from engine number 603246 this also became the three-dog 600 type. All the gears, layshaft, and mainshaft, were modified. Although the 600 used hydraulic operation for the clutch, the cable-operated clutch was unchanged on the 500 throughout its production life.

By 1981 the 500 SL was virtually a sleeved-down 600. Also shared with the 600 was the reshaped ABS fairing, though the 500 colors of light-blue with red and blue stripes was retained. The fork legs were painted black.

The author's new 500 SL shortly after delivery at the end of 1981. This still had Marzocchi forks.

Another problem with early 500 and 600 Pantahs was the oil filter retaining nipple dislodging from the crankcase with rather catastrophic results. I remember following a 600 SL in 1981 when this happened. The oil filter blew off, covering the engine (and hot exhaust pipes) in oil. The resulting cloud of smoke made a spectacular show, and the cause was due to the 2.5mm x 8mm split pin inside the filter nipple that was too short. During 1981 this was lengthened to 14mm, seemingly solving the problem. Another slight modification that enabled easier clutch removal was the replacement of the 7.6mm-diameter circlip on the end of the clutch control rod (0660.16.410) with a 6mm-diameter radial locking ring. This meant the clutch control was altered, although the part number was unchanged.

While the Dell'Orto PHF 36 A carburetors were as before, there were some small jetting changes. The accelerator pump jet was reduced in size from 38 to 35, and the idle jet for the left carburetor (AS-rear) increased to 70 (from 65). The right (AD) retained the 65 idle jet. Main jet size also decreased for the right (AD-front) carburetor. Down from 142 to 135, though the AS kept the 142 main jet. During 1981 alternative exhaust systems were sometimes fitted to 500 SLs. The Silentium system was slightly less restrictive and used shorter mufflers, with a connecting balance pipe that no longer attached to the lower crankcase.

Ignition and Electrical System

During 1981 an inferior Bosch plastic and metal interference-suppressing type spark plug cap replaced the KLG rubber spark plug caps. These were particularly prone to misfiring when wet. During 1981, from frame number 661763, a smaller 154mm-diameter Bosch headlight replaced the Aprilia halogen unit. This was at the same time as the incorporation of the 600 SL fairing although brackets and spacers were available to fit either the Bosch headlight to the earlier fairing or the Aprilia headlight to the later fairing.

Frame and Cycle Parts

1981 500 SLs received a new frame code-named the 500 SL/A (0660.91.203). Later there was also a 500 SL/B (0660.91.205). These frames only differed from the original in altered steering stops and brackets. The engine was now located slightly differently, the front engine mount now through two 10mm bolts that threaded into the crankcase halves and located by a lock washer. These replaced the long, 252mm bolt on the earlier engines and made for a more rigid assembly. As with the engine, there was also standardization of bodywork to that of the 600 SL. From frame number 661763 the earlier fiberglass fairing was replaced with an ABS 600 SL type with an additional lower crossbar, along with the smaller 154mm-diameter

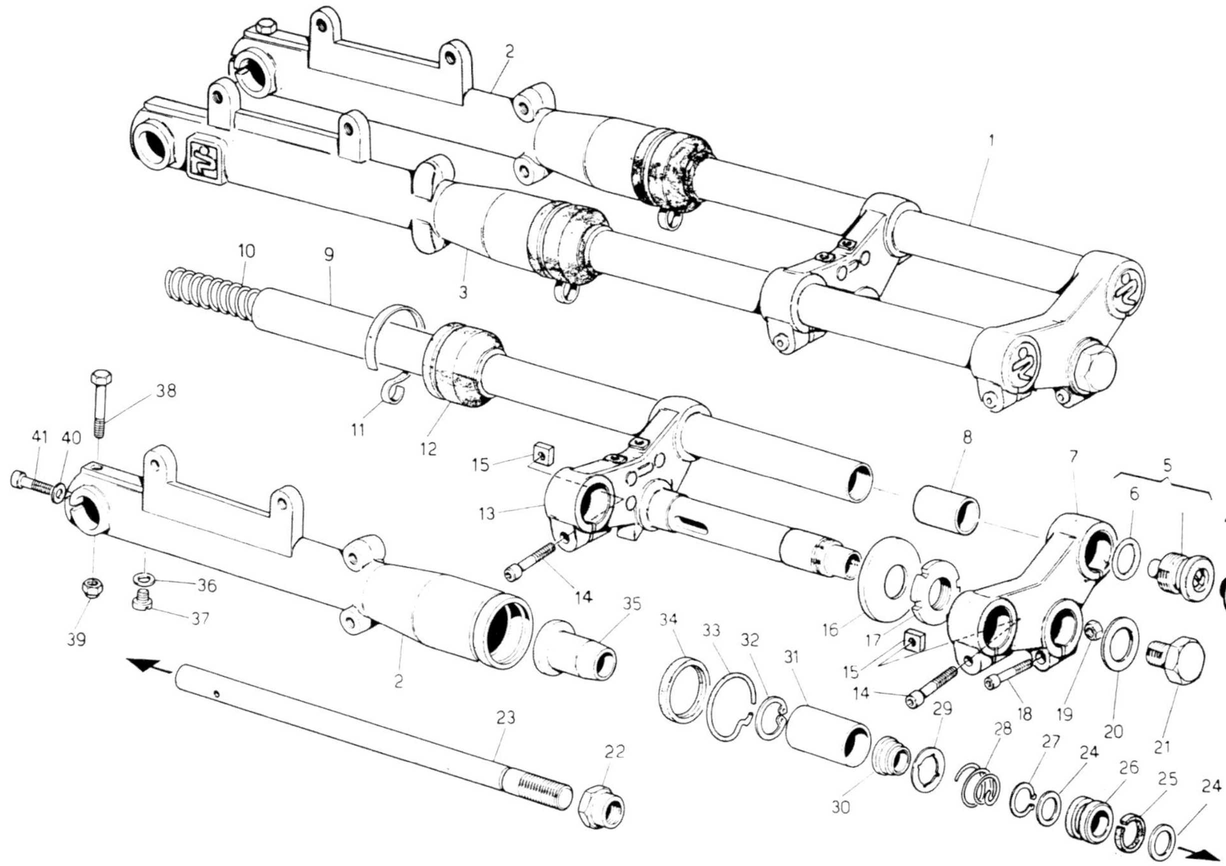

Most 1981 500 SLs came with Paioli forks and matching shock absorbers.

Bosch headlight. The fairing was constructed in two pieces, with a split down the middle. Colors remained as before, but with slightly altered decals.

In the quest to reduce costs, cheaper (and more primitive) Paioli suspension was often fitted to 500 SL Pantahs during 1981. The forks still featured 35mm fork tubes, black-painted fork legs, and forward-mounted brake calipers. Marzocchi forks were also fitted to 500 SLs during 1981. Although these carried the same part number (0660.37.100), they had black-painted fork legs and a revised fork spring retaining nut. Instead of the 12mm Allen head, these now had a 30mm hexagon nut.

With the Paioli forks came alternative oleo-pneumatic Paioli shock absorbers. These required the chainguard to be altered in order for them to fit, although surprisingly only one chainguard was still specified (0660.14.200). During 1981 a stronger sintered Tsubaki 530 HSL (94-link) final-drive chain was fitted to 500 and 600 SLs. Although it wasn't originally anticipated, swingarm pivot wear was a problem on early Pantahs, and for 1981 three oversized swingarm pivot pins became available (0.03mm, 0.05mm and 0.1mm). With the bronze swingarm bushes inserted in the crankcases it was easier to replace the pin rather than the bushes. The gearing was also changed on some Pantahs from 1981. A 39-tooth rear sprocket replaced the earlier 38-tooth, along with a 14-tooth gearbox sprocket. While this improved the problem of over-gearing, the 500 still benefited from an even larger rear sprocket. I used a 41-tooth rear sprocket on my 500 SL in 1983 and, with K&N air filters and an open two-into-one Conti exhaust, would pull to the redline in top gear.

1982-83

The 500 SL continued in production alongside the 600 SL during 1982 and 1983. However, as with the 750 and 900 Super Sport from 1975 until 1978, the smaller family member was overshadowed by the larger version. It was unfortunate that the two models were so similar because the 500 offered similar performance and the smaller 05 Brembo brakes were more than up to the task. With more interest in the 600, many 500 SLs were sold off at discount prices until 1983.

For the final series there was one small change within the cylinder head. New opening and closing

A few of the final 500 SLs were produced in white with red decals. Unlike most 1982 500 SLs these final examples were also generally fitted with Marzocchi suspension.

rockers (0660.92.173/183) were fitted, these being dimensionally different so earlier cylinder heads needed to be modified to accept them. Some final 500 SLs also came with white bodywork and red decals from the 600 SL. Typical of state of Ducati documentation during this period there was no official recognition or advertising of these white 500s and it is difficult to ascertain how many were manufactured. No parts list was ever supplied, and all those that I have seen had Marzocchi suspension and Conti exhaust pipes. Total production of the 500 SL from 1979 until 1983 was 3,835.

Restorer's Tip: Colors for the 350/500/600/650 SL, 350/600 TL, and 350 XL

Model and Year	Color
500 SL 1979	Red and Silver
500 SL 1980-83	Blue; Blue and Red decals
500 SL 1983	White; Red and Orange decals
600 SL 1981-83	Silver; Red and Orange decals
600 SL 1983-84	Red; Green decals
650 SL 1984-86	Red; Yellow decals
600 TL 1982-83	White; Red, Orange and Yellow stripes
600 TL 1983-84	Gray; Red, Orange and Yellow stripes
350 TL 1983-84	Red; Red, Orange and Yellow stripes
350 XL 1982-83	Red and Black
350 SL 1983-84	Red; Green decals

The prototype 600 SL had a full fairing and was based on the early 500.

600 SL

As the factory was already racing 600cc Pantahs in the Italian Formula 2 championship of 1980, it was no surprise to see the announcement of the 600 SL at the Milan Show at the end of 1980. As in the past, it was obvious that a simple overbore would be the first step in the development of the Pantah. Boring the 500 6mm to 80mm while keeping the 58mm stroke

Another prototype 600 SL as displayed at the Milan Show at the end of 1980. This varied from the eventual production version in a number of details, noticeably the hydraulic clutch cover, the 05 Brembo front brake calipers and aluminum centered discs.

gave 583cc. Early in 1980, a 600 Pantah with a Mike Hailwood Replica-style full fairing had been seen at the factory, and by September a 600 in 500 SL bodywork was tested. This version had Dell'Orto 38mm carburetors and a 9.5:1 compression ratio. Maximum power was 63 HP at 8,500 rpm. A normal cable-operated clutch was used, but by the time the 600 SL was featured at Milan it had a hydraulic clutch with new engine side cover, with a revised fairing, graphics and front fender. This early prototype also featured Marzocchi suspension with 500-style forward-mounted 05 Brembo brake calipers, but with aluminum-centered 260mm front discs. The 600 SL was displayed along with a prototype 86 HP turbocharged Pantah engine. Nothing came of the turbocharged version, but the 600 SL went into production in April 1981.

Engine and Drivetrain

The 600 SL received a new set of engine numbers, starting at DM 600L 700001. The relationship between the 500 and 600 was identical to that of the 750 and 900 Super Sport. In nearly every respect the engines were identical but for the 6mm increase in cylinder bore. With 80mm Mahle pistons and a 58mm stroke the capacity was 583cc. It was probably for historical reasons that 80mm pistons were used. This size had been that used on the 350 single and 750 bevel-drive twin. The TT2 featured 81mm pistons to give 597cc, almost the 600cc TT2 class limit. The three-ring 80mm 600 SL pistons had the same 59mm deck height of the 74mm 500 pistons, and identical piston ring thickness; 1.5mm, 1.75mm, and 3.947mm. Unlike the bevel 900 SS that had a wider squish band than the 750, the 600 SL shared its cylinder heads with the 500. Thus the compression ratio was raised from 9.5:1 to 10.4:1. Although carburetion and valve sizes were unaltered, the claimed power rose an astonishing 35 percent to 61 HP at 9,100 rpm. Claimed torque was up 26 percent, to 5.17 kg/m at 7,500 rpm. These were obviously fanciful figures from purely a slight increase in compression and an 84cc increase in displacement and were presumably quoted to aid in the sales of the more expensive 600.

The only change to the engine specification from the 1981 series 500 SL was a set of stronger clutch springs (661.16.550) and hydraulic operation via a handlebar-mounted master cylinder. The 16-plate aluminum clutch was the same as the 500. Also as with the 500 SL there were new opening and closing rockers and camshafts, from engine number 700102 on the 600 SL. Carburetor jetting was the same as for the 1981 500 SL.

Frame and Cycle Parts

Although the frame of the 600 SL was identical to that of the 500 SL, it carried a new part number (0661.91.200). Frame numbers started at DM 600 SL 700001. There was also a revised 600 SL/A frame

When the 600 SL went into production it had a new clutch cover and rear-mounted 08 Brembo calipers on Paioli forks.

For 1982 the 600 SL received a new clutch and clutch cover. This was now cable-operated. Period photo.

during the year (0661.91.203). The major change from the 500 was in the brakes and suspension. Unlike the Milan Show prototype, the 35mm Marzocchi or Paioli forks featured rear front brake caliper mounts. Most early 600s came with Paioli forks, generally with red oleo-pneumatic 310mm Marzocchi shock absorbers. The front brakes, although using the same 260mm drilled cast-iron discs of the 500 SL, were upgraded to the larger 08 Brembo calipers with a larger-diameter (and larger reservoir) master cylinder. These larger brake calipers increased the swept pad area from 48cm^2 to 80cm^2. The 485mm rubber brake hoses attached directly to the caliper without the metal pipes used on forward-mounted calipers.

The wheels and rear brake were identical to that of the 500, but the gearing was initially even higher, with a 36-tooth rear sprocket and 15-tooth gearbox sprocket. Along with a larger, 4.00H18 M45 Michelin tire fitted to many 600s, it was even more ridiculously overgeared than its smaller brother. Later the rear sprocket was changed to a more sensible 39-tooth. Earlier 600s featured a 92-tooth Regina chain, this becoming 94-tooth Tsubaki like the 500 with the lower gearing. The bodywork was identical to the 1981 500 except for a silver ABS front fender. Colors were silver with two-tone red decals, making the 600 SL one of the more attractive Ducatis of this period.

There were two color schemes available for the 600 SL for 1982. Most were in the Mike Hailwood Replica colors of red and green and featured Marzocchi forks and shock absorbers.

1982

There were only a few developments to the already proven Pantah 600 engine during 1982. From engine number 701650 the 600 SL received a completely new clutch, now cable-operated rather than hydraulic. Following experience with the TT2 racer, this now included a larger-diameter clutch drum, steel instead of aluminum, which was now incorporated with the primary gear. The inner clutch drum was also steel and the clutch plate arrangement altered. There were now seven steel

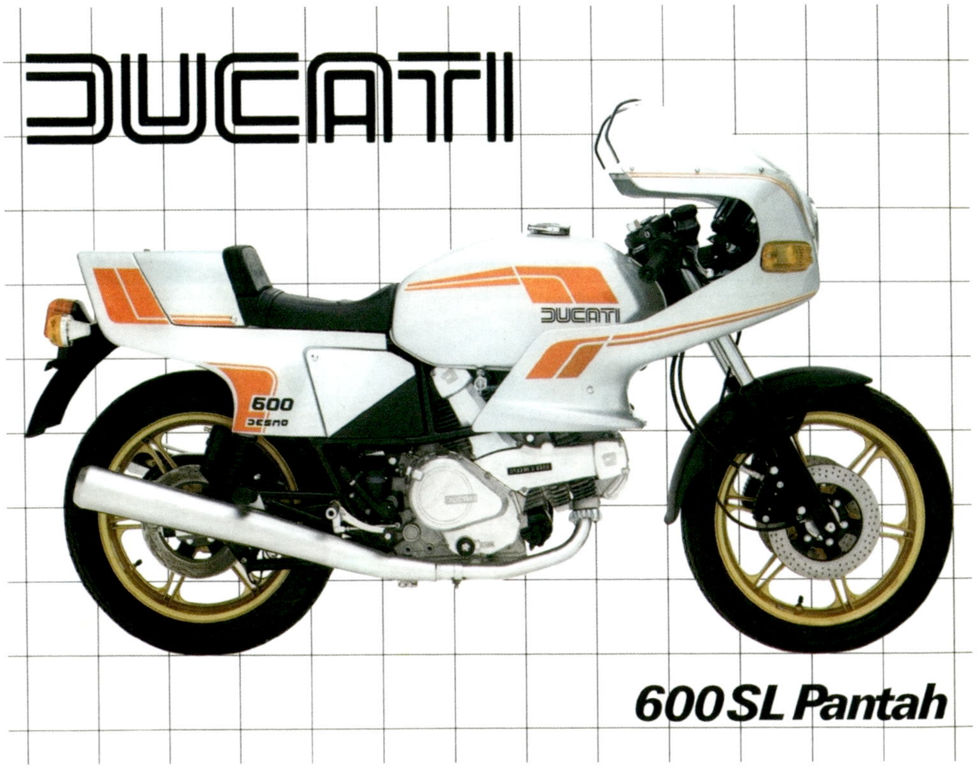

Continuing also for 1982 was the previous silver 600 SL, now with a black plastic front fender. This factory brochure displays a version fitted with Paioli forks and shock absorbers, and Silentium mufflers.

driven plates, seven fiber driving plates, and one outer driving plate, giving a total of 15 clutch plates. These were all new, with new part numbers (see Appendix). Removal of the revised clutch assembly also required a new tool (88713.0146). This clutch would carry though to the 350 XL and SL, 600 TL, and 650 SL. There was also a new clutch side cover, not interchangeable with that of the 500. Also added during 1982 were new pistons and cylinders (0661.17.503/603).

Further small refinements continued during the year. From engine number 702388 the ignition flywheel was altered, maintaining the same part number (0660.46.470). Instead of the previous two-stage advance, this now became three-stage, the flywheel receiving an additional step. Up to 1,700 rpm advance was now 6 degrees, from 1,700 to 2,600 rpm, 26 degrees, and full advance (over 2,600 rpm) 33 degrees. The air gap was initially maintained at 0.55mm-0.60mm but later closed to 0.50mm-0.55mm. As with the 500 SL, from September 1982 new opening and closing rockers were specified.

The front end of the 1982 600 SL. The brakes and wheels were as for the previous year though this red-and-green example has Marzocchi forks.

There were only small changes to the chassis specifications of 600 SL during 1982, one being the substitution of a black front fender for the earlier silver type. During the year the 600 SL was also produced in the Mike Hailwood Replica colors of red and green with a red-painted frame. The black DUCATI and 600 SL decals were now white but positioned as before. Most of these red 600 SLs had Marzocchi forks and shock absorbers, the oleo-pneumatic shock absorbers being painted black rather than red. The chainguard too was painted red. While they still used the earlier taillight and indicators (the front flush-mounted in the fairing), these had the black lockable flush-mounted fuel filler cap. This was from the 900 S2, a poor design that was notorious for allowing water to enter, eventually rusting the tank internally. At this time the steel brake and gearshift levers became aluminum, with DUCATI cast into the side and bolt-on end pins.

1983-84

The final 600 SLs of 1983 and 1984 were all red and green, but incorporated some small changes to the general specification. The engine remained as before but

The rear disc, Marzocchi shock absorber and Conti muffler on a 1982 600 SL.

From late 1982 the 600 SL featured Oscam wheels with tubeless tires and larger turn signal indicators and taillight.

for new synthetic timing pulleys (0660.29.070) and yet another alteration to fifth gear. Following experience with the TT2 racer this was lowered even further with two new gears, a 28-tooth driven gear (0659.16.125), and 29-tooth driving gear (0659.16.045). The carburetor jetting was again changed for 1983. The main jet in the Dell'Orto PHF 36 AD was reduced to 132, and in the 36 AS to 138. The 70 pilot jet in the AS carburetor too was reduced to a 65 and a K8 needle replaced the K4. During 1983 Motoplat coils (0769.46.250) replaced the Nippon Denso, and the two resistors eliminated. As with the contemporary 900 Mike Hailwood Replica, some 1983 600 SLs were fitted with a Conti two-into-one exhaust system exiting on the left.

Some final 600 SLs came factory-fitted with a Conti two-into-one exhaust system. This was significantly louder than the normal mufflers and boosted mid-range power.

In line with other Ducatis of the period, a larger CEV taillight and rectangular indicators were fitted, the front no longer flush-mounted in the fairing, but located on stalks. Also carried over from the 900 Replica was the new three-wire regulator (0805.46.758), replacing the six-wire type that had first featured on the 860 GT (0759.46.750). This three-wire regulator would also become standard fitment to the rest of the Pantah range of 1984 onward. Other changes carried through from the larger models were the gold-painted Oscam aluminum wheels that accepted tubeless Michelin A48/M48 tires. The sprocket retaining nuts were changed to those with an Allen head rather than a hexagon head with two locking plates, and the chainguard

Possibly the definitive Pantah was the 650 SL. In the factory racing colors of red and yellow this was quite similar to the final 600 SL.

was black rather than red. Marzocchi suspension was now universal, the rear black-painted shock absorbers having white MARZOCCHI decals. The final 600 SLs also included a 170mm Carello H4 headlight and

From the front the 650 was almost identical to previous Pantahs and made for a satisfying street machine.

black-anodized dogleg brake and clutch levers. Right through until the end the 600 featured the same instrument panel, still with the stand warning light. Very few of the final red-and-green 600 SLs were manufactured, by this stage it was superseded by the 650 SL. Total production of the 600 SL was significantly less than the 500, numbering 2,346.

650 SL

Engine and Drivetrain

This final sporting Pantah before the advent of the 750 F1 was also arguably the best, and certainly one of the rarest. The purpose of the 650 was to homologate the longer stroke so as to race the 750 TT1, both in Formula One and the World Endurance Championship. For 1984, this saw a drop in the capacity limit from 1000cc to 750cc, so a 750cc Pantah-based racer could once again see Ducati competitive in this class. No official parts list was available for the 650 SL and engine numbers started at DM 650L 610001. The 650 was created by boring and stroking the 600, and again it was a surprising choice of capacity because it could so easily have been a full 750. Lengthening the stroke 3.5mm to 61.5mm, plus a moderate 2mm overbore to 82mm, provided 649cc. Valve sizes remained as on the 500 and 600, 37.5mm inlet and 33.5mm exhaust. As with the 500 and 600, the three-ring pistons had a 59mm deck height. Compression ratio was down

The left side of the 650 SL.

slightly to 10:1, and power up to 63 HP at 8,500 rpm. Although the stroke was lengthened 3.5mm the same 124mm con rods were used, giving a rod to stroke ratio of 2.016:1. In all other respects the engine of the 650 was identical to the 1983-84 600 SL. This included the same cable-operated wet clutch, five-speed gearbox, and Dell'Orto PHF 36A carburetors. Conti mufflers were fitted to the 650, the restrictive type of the first 500 SL. In 1985 steel timing pulleys (0367.29.050) also replaced the synthetic type.

Frame and Cycle Parts

The chassis and bodywork was essentially identical to that of the final 600 SL. With a new number sequence starting at DGM 650 SL 065001, the frame was painted red, and the bodywork the red and yellow of the factory F2 bikes. The DUCATI and 650 DESMO decals were white. On some 650 SLs the black front fender was similar to that of the 1984 900 S2, solid on the leading side of the forks. All 650 SLs came with Marzocchi suspension, the fork legs, triple clamps,

Specific only to the 650 SL was this instrument panel with Nippon Denso instruments. Three of the warning lights were incorporated in the tachometer.

The taillight and rear turn signal indicators of the 1983-84 600 SL and the 650 SL.

and oleo-pneumatic shock absorbers painted black. By 1985 the 35mm Marzocchi forks were beginning to show signs of obsolescence, the skinny fork tubes and basic design harking back to an earlier era. 650 SLs shared the Oscam wheels, large rectangular CEV indicators and taillight with the 1983 MHR, 900 S2, and 600 SL. A Zadi Gege steering lock replaced the previous Neiman. The 650 SL also received the later passenger footpegs (0803.91.950). One area that showed considerable improvement over earlier Pantahs though was the final-drive gearing, which at 2.73:1 was much more realistic.

The most noticeable update for the 650 was a new instrument panel and instruments. The Nippon Denso instruments were only used on the 650 SL, a 220-km/h (no mph) speedometer and 12,000-rpm tachometer redlined at 9,000 rpm. The speedometer indicated 1 km/h per 1400 revs and the tachometer a 1:4.16 ratio. A rather ugly plastic surround supported the instruments, with three warning lights on the right. These were labeled with icons, < > (orange flasher), *Lights* (green), and *battery* (red). Three more warning lights were incorporated in the tachometer, *Neutral* (green), *Oil* (red), and *High Beam* (blue). The ignition key fitted to the left of the speedometer. The Nippon Denso switchgear and Verlicchi throttle was as on other SLs, and the 650 SL had a 170mm Carello 60-watt headlight and black dogleg levers.

Along with the instrument panel the other area where the 650 SL departed from the 600 was the use of a single vacuum fuel tap on the right, similar to that of the 900 and Mille MHR. This was also unreliable and leaky like those on the larger models and was better replaced by a manual type. With this fuel tap also came the black rubber fuel lines of the larger models. One of the rarest of all Pantahs, only 288 650 SLs were built, in late 1983 as 1984 models, production continuing until 1985. Even then the basic engine survived for several more years in the 650 Alazzurra.

600 TL

Occasionally Ducati releases a model that epitomizes the worst of Italian design, none more so than the 600 TL. Not since the Giugiaro designed the 860

This was the 600 TL displayed at the Milan Show at the end of 1981. It differed in a number of details from the production version, noticeably the fairing and body panels, footpeg bracket and bags and rack.

The pre-production 600 TL, with a Marzocchi front fork.

GT of 1974 had there been such an ugly and contentious Ducati design and, like that earlier model, the 600 TL suffered because of it. However, underneath the extreme bodywork of the 600 TL was an excellent and thoroughly reliable motorcycle. In many ways it was a superior all-round motorcycle to the SL, and represents bargain buying for those wishing to enter the world of two-valve belt-drive twin-cylinder Ducatis. First shown at the 1981 Milan Show, the 600 TL prototype differed slightly to the eventual production version. It was also shown with optional rack and bags. The bodywork on this show bike was similar to the production bike but for vertical grills near the shock absorbers and no horizontal slots under the fuel tank. In May 1982 the eventual production 600 TL was displayed, this becoming available in Italy during August, differing in only a few small details.

Engine and Drivetrain

Although the engine and five-speed gearbox (with the later lower fifth gear) of the 600 TL was shared with the 600 SL of the same period, the TL had a new set of engine numbers, starting at DM 600L 650001. Despite this, part numbers for the crankcases and other engine components were the same, and all 600 TLs featured the larger cable-operated 15-plate wet clutch. After engine number 650465 new 80mm piston assemblies were fitted (0661.47.403), and some 600 TLs were fitted with 500 SL crankshafts (0660.47.150). This was probably to use up surplus stock and may have adversely affected the engine balance. Unfortunately there is no official documentation stating which engines received 500 crankshafts. Early in the 600 TLs production life the aluminum timing pulleys were changed to a synthetic composition. Carburetor jetting was as with the 600 SL, with revised jetting for 1983. For some reason the choke lever was now located rather inconveniently between the front downtubes next to the Bosch horn. As on the 600 SL either Silentium or Conti exhaust systems were fitted, but most TLs had Silentium. While all the engine specifications were the same as for the 600 SL, claimed power was less, at 58 HP at 8,700 rpm. This was undoubtedly another case of the factory creating figures to suit the marketing profile of a particular model.

Ignition and Electrical System

Early 600 TLs featured Nippon Denso ignition coils, these becoming Motoplat during 1983. The two Bosch resistors (0801.38.080) were no longer required. With the Motoplat coils came new ignition cables and terminals (0661.46.270) connecting to the Bosch amplifiers. Spark plugs were either Champion L81 or L82Y. The 600 TL featured a number of unique electrical components. A rectangular 190mm x 132mm 60-watt Carello 616 halogen headlight was mounted in the fairing, along with rectangular 10-watt CEV indicators on stalks. The taillight was a rectangular twin 21/5-watt bulb CEV type. Similar Nippon Denso instruments to the SL were fitted, these now shrouded by a large black plastic dashboard with a different arrangement of warning lights. The eight lights were the same as before but for an additional red FUEL light in the center underneath the indicator light. The red STAND light was connected to the sidestand. The tachometer was now redlined at 9,000 rpm, with a new part number (0664.38.030). The 140-mph/240-kph speedometer also had a new part number (0664.38.600).

Frame and Cycle Parts

The basic Pantah frame was retained for the 600 TL, but now had provision for a sidestand on the left, underneath the lower engine mount. Two types of sidestand were supplied, either for Silentium or Conti mufflers. There was another series of frame numbers starting at DM 600 TL 060001 and the frame was painted black, and largely hidden underneath the new bodywork. Painted white on the first series, the 18-liter fuel tank featured a black flush-mounted locking fuel cap. An unusual fuel tap system was employed on the TL. On the right was an electrically operated solenoid type, connected to the dashboard warning light to indicate reserve. On the left was a manually threaded type, with an additional reserve tap located away from the left fuel tap. Fuel lines were still green plastic and the system seemed unnecessarily complicated.

This was how the 600 TL appeared when it went into production. Paioli fork and shock absorbers replaced the Marzocchis.

Large black DUCATI decals were located on the lower sides of the fuel tank, with red, yellow and orange stripes at the rear. The dual seat was a comfortable, thickly padded arrangement, with a white TL on each side, locked to the seat base by another key. Along with the steering lock and ignition, the TL thus featured four keys. There was also a large black-anodized aluminum handrail running from the shock absorber mounts. This, along with the footpeg brackets, had been polished aluminum on the 600 TL appearing in press releases. Completing the bodywork was a small handlebar-mounted fairing with angular Plexiglas screen, and vented lower panels. The screen was smoked on the pre-production model, but all 600 TLs featured a clear screen. Two M6mm x 20mm screws, later being changed to two black-knobbed screws, initially retained the lower panels. A black 600 decal was located on each lower cover, and another black DUCATI at the rear, above the taillight. DESMO decals were fixed to the fairing. During 1983 the color changed from white to gray, but the decals remained the same. All 600 TLs had black plastic fenders, the front shared with the 600 SL.

Although the official factory brochure shows a 600 TL with Marzocchi suspension, only 35mm Paioli forks were fitted to the 600 TL. These had black-painted fork legs and provision for rear-mounted brake calipers. Rear suspension was also Paioli, with a finned lower shock body and a pressure valve. Unlike the

The 600TL instrument panel was quite different to the 600SL. Notice how the clutch cable passes through the dash.

The last 600TLs were produced for the municipal police.

600 SL the front brake used twin 05 Brembo calipers, still with the drilled 260mm cast-iron discs, with single rubber brake lines connecting to the junction on the lower triple clamp. Front brake and clutch levers were initially polished aluminum, later becoming the black dogleg type. The rear master cylinder was now similar to that of the 900 S2 with a remote reservoir.

Wheels were gold-painted six-spoke FPS, becoming gold Oscam during 1983. Sizes were 2.15 x 18-inch and 2.50 x 18-inch-inches fitted with Michelin or Pirelli tires. With the Oscam wheels came tubeless A/M48 Michelins. The folding footpegs were shared with the 900 SD Darmah, located on a large black-anodized bracket, and the brake and gearshift levers aluminum.

The final 600 TL was grey with Oscam wheels and tubeless Michelin tires. The footpeg brackets and passenger grab rail were black. This is the 1983 brochure.

Alloy pins screwed into the levers, the rubbers becoming the heavier, ribbed 900 S2-type (0803.69.530) during 1983. Handgrips were the usual Verlicchi rubber type and the passenger grab rail was also black.

Later the 600 TL was more successful as a vehicle for the Italian municipal police. Here style was secondary and practicality more important. With side panels from the 1981 Milan show prototype, a solo seat, the blue-and-white 600 *Polizie Urbane* featured crash bars, panniers, radio, loud hailer, and a sidestand. Apart from forward-mounted 05 Brembo front brake calipers they were similar in specification to the regular 600 TL. 100 of these police versions were built, along with only 801 600TLs.

350 XL

Not generally available outside Italy, the 350 XL was first displayed in April 1982, going into production one month later. Designed for the 18 percent IVA tax rather than the 38 percent for motorcycles over 350cc, the 350 XL was another one of Ducati's parts-bin specialties; ostensibly a 500 SL with a 600 TL handlebar fairing and higher handlebars. More was sourced from the SL than the TL, including instruments, instrument panel, and rear-set footpegs.

Engine and Drivetrain

Engine numbers for the 350 XL started at DM 350L 030001 and the engine was a smaller version of the 500 SL. Still with Gilnisil cylinders, the 66mm bore and 51mm stroke provided 349cc. Compression was 10.3:1 and the valve sizes reduced from the 500's to 33.5mm for the inlet and 30.5mm for the exhaust. The included valve angle was still 60 degrees. With Dell'Orto PHF 30A carburetors and new camshafts (for valve timing see Appendix) the claimed power was 40 HP at 9,600 rpm. The lower end, including the five-speed gearbox and wet cable-operated clutch, was identical to the later series 500 SL. The crankshaft still utilized the 124mm con rods, although these were not optimum length for the smaller engine, giving a con rod to stroke ratio of 2.43:1. From engine number 030802 the three-step ignition and new flywheel (shared with the 600 SL) was also fitted. Silentium exhaust systems were fitted to the 350 XL.

Frame and Cycle Parts

Using a black-painted 500 SL frame and swingarm, all 350 XLs featured 35mm Paioli forks with polished aluminum fork legs. The rear suspension was also Paioli (shared with the 600 TL), with individual pressure valves located at the base. Braking was by the three 05 Brembo calipers of the 500 SL (with forward-mounted front calipers) but the 260mm cast-iron discs were generally solid and not drilled. The FPS wheels were painted silver and shod with either Pirelli or Michelin S-rated tires.

As an amalgam of body parts from the 600 TL and SL, the 350 XL was surprisingly successful. Only a dual

Generally only available in Italy, the red-and-black 350 XL was designed to circumvent increased tax on motorcycles over 350cc.

Replacing the 350 XL in Italy during 1984 was the red-and-green 350 SL. Only produced in limited numbers this was essentially a 500 SL with a smaller engine.

seat was offered (without a removable solo seat cowling), and the red-and-black paint was quite striking. The steel front fender was peculiar to the 350 XL and also black. Unlike other Pantahs there were no decals on the 350 XL, plastic badges used instead. The fuel tank, seat, and side covers were all from the SL, except for the new-style black locking fuel cap. Although the Nippon Denso instruments and warning light panel came from the 500 and 600 SL, the small fairing and rectangular Carello headlight was shared with the 600 TL. From the bevel-drive 900 S2 came the rectangular CEV indicators and large CEV taillight. Quite popular in Italy, 940 350 XLs were produced in 1982 and 1983.

350 TL

First displayed at the Milan Show of 1983, the 350 TL replaced the 350 XL. This took much of the existing 350 XL and 600 TL to create another machine essentially for the Italian market. This featured light- red TL bodywork, polished 35mm Marzocchi forks with forward-mounted 05 Brembo brake calipers, red steel XL-style front fender, and XL Nippon Denso instruments. Wheels were gold-painted Oscam and the 260mm cast-iron brake discs drilled. It offered little to entice the Italian buyer from the more attractive 350 SL, and only 275 were produced at the end of 1983, with a solitary example in 1985.

350 SL

As the sport-touring role of the 350 XL was modified during 1983 to become the 350 TL, full sporting duties saw the evolution of the 350 SL. Rather than a sport-touring motorcycle like the 350 XL this was now a full sport bike. The red-painted frame and red -and-green bodywork were shared with the contemporary 600 SL. The 350 SL also had the removable solo seat cowling and black plastic front fender of the 600 SL. From the earlier 350 XL came the silver FPS wheels and undrilled 260mm cast-iron discs. The front 05 Brembo brake calipers were now positioned behind the fork legs. Suspension was Paioli, and mufflers were Conti rather than Silentium. Rather strangely, while the taillight and rear indicators were from the 1983-84 600 SL, the fairing with flush-mounted front indicators was that of the earlier Pantah. 1985 engines had steel timing pulleys (0367.29.050) that also required a new tool for removal (88700.5644). Production, essentially for the home market, was 211 in 1983.

TT2 Replicas

It was expected that not long after the success of the factory TT2 the factory would capitalize on it, but this was typically very slow in eventuating. As the factory developed and raced their TT2, with only talk of a street version, many independent manufacturers went ahead and produced street versions. A number of TT-style frames were available, most common being the original Verlicchi, copies by Italian manufacturers Forcatelai and Icomek, and an English Harris. Two versions of the Verlicchi were available, the original a direct copy of the racing TT2 frame that didn't allow for belt covers and featured a steel swingarm. A second version of the Verlicchi frame could accommodate belt covers and used an aluminum swingarm. The Harris frame was easily recognized by additional bracing, notably above the clutch, and on some Harris frames chain adjustment was by eccentrics. Depending on cost constraints, it was almost possible to create an exact street version of the TT2, although difficulties in obtaining the original 35mm magnesium Marzocchi forks of the TT2 generally saw regular SL wheels and suspension used on these specials. As far as engine choice was concerned, all Pantah engines were suitable, most donors coming from the 600 TL or 650 Alazzurra. Aftermarket bodywork patterned on the original racer too soon became available, making the construction of a TT2 replica quite feasible. However, creating such a motorcycle was not for the faint-hearted, and required a great deal of patience along with one-off fabrication. Other frame kits were also available for Pantahs, notably a single-spine Egli-type with a De Carbon monoshock by Terry Prince in Australia.

Several TT2 replica frame kits were available for the Pantah engine. This is the English Harris version with rear axle adjustment by eccentrics and an additional frame brace above the clutch. Notice the location of the battery behind the engine, underneath the swingarm. Much effort has gone into creating this superb motorcycle.

Another Pantah frame alternative was this Egli-type monoshock.

Modifications to Pantahs

Engine and Drivetrain

Anyone with any experience of 500 and 600 Pantahs can testify that the engine performance, while smooth, was somewhat disappointing. To those brought up on the larger twins the engines seemed to produce no low-down or mid-range torque. In order to meet more stringent noise regulations the Pantah was virtually strangled and considerably over-geared. Fortunately this was easily rectified. The air filter system was simply removed and K&N pod filters or similar installed. The standard exhaust system in addition to being restrictive and quiet was very heavy. Generally any two-into-one system will be noisier than a two-into-two, but offers improved mid-range power.

Engine reliability for the Pantah was considerably improved over earlier bevel-drive twins. *Motorrad*, in November 1982, tested and stripped-down a 500 SL after 22,500 km. Apart from a faulty alternator and regulator leading to two battery failures, along with a broken freewheel starter bearing, the engine was totally reliable. The Pantah even went faster at the end of the test period. According to a Ducati service release in March 1983, the toothed belts also proved extremely reliable, as long as the belt was subject to an initial tension check around 300 miles. Delayed or missed checking, along with misalignment, could shorten the belt life considerably (to around 1,000 miles in extreme cases).

Owners of post-1981 500 SLs can easily convert their 500 to a 600 (except for engine number 602238 to 602528), but a common modification applicable to all 500 and 600 engines is the substitution of 86mm 900 Super Sport Borgo pistons (0759.47.407). This is a major undertaking and requires opening the crankcase mouths to accept the larger sleeves. The 86mm pistons need to have the deck height reduced from 5mm to 3mm, and the dome reshaped with larger valve cutaways. The skirt also needs to be shortened and the overall weight reduced so as to retain the same balance. The con rods too have to be machined to accept the 20mm wrist pin. The Gilnisil alloy cylinder needs to be bored out to accept a normal cast-iron 900 SS liner. This has to be shortened to the same 53.5mm sleeve protrusion of the stock 500 and 600. A 5mm spigot must then be machined onto the top of the liner so it will fit the 500 or 600 cylinder head. The resulting 86mm x 58mm engine gives 674cc with a noticeable increase in low and mid-range torque, but appropriate cylinder head modifications will need to be performed to increase maximum power substantially. More power can be obtained through cylinder head modifications with slightly larger valves, and the installation of either race-kit SL camshafts or those from the TT2. The maximum power is produced around 7,500 rpm. More extensive cylinder head modifications can allow up to 45mm inlet and 40mm exhaust, but this requires a reduction in the 60-degree included valve angle.

Ignition and Electrical System

One of the major problems with Pantahs is the continual trickle drain of the battery. As previously mentioned, this was due to a voltmeter that controlled the switching of the GEN light on the dashboard. The simplest solution to this problem was to disconnect the voltmeter. Even later versions with the new generator light switch device were prone to a slow continual battery discharge. Another problem emanating from the rather weak ignition system was poor starting and an appetite for spark plugs. This can be rectified by using a platinum type, NGK B6HVX or similar. The ignition switch also could give problems, again simply remedied by incorporating a relay. Other ignition problems can be traced to poor ignition coils, especially those models fitted with Motoplat units. The earlier Nippon Denso or a comparable Dyna can replace these.

Frame and Cycle Parts

Even retaining the standard trellis frame the Pantah was a respectable handling motorcycle. While it lacked the rigidity of a TT2 type, the frame was sufficient for up to 650cc. The weakest component was undoubtedly the 35mm Marzocchi or Paioli fork. Here lighter fork oil (10 weight) helped but they were simply not strong enough and very prone to flexing. I fitted a fork brace to my 500 SL but found this only increased stiction. Given that the Pantah didn't weigh much less than a 750 it was surprising Ducati fitted these flimsy forks when they could easily have used 38mm forks. Any serious modification should consider replacing the forks, either with 38mm Ducati units or possibly those from a similar sized Japanese motorcycle. Brian Catterson, former editor of *Motorcyclist* magazine, raced a Cagiva Alazzurra (essentially a Pantah) with some success in the early 1990s, and found that Yamaha FZR600 forks fitted relatively easily, even retaining the stock triple clamps after they were bored to accept the larger fork legs. The main problem with using alternative forks is adapting the Pantah wheel and brakes to fit. While the rear shock absorbers were adequate, improvement could be obtained with alternative units. The braking system was perfectly adequate as well, though using softer 64GG (or similar) compound brake pads and braided steel brake lines improved performance. The other beneficial improvement to the Pantah was the previously mentioned change in final-drive gearing. A common modification to Pantahs was the replacement of the stock fuel tank and seat with a one-piece fiberglass NCR type.

The factory used NCR-style bodywork on their 1980 racer.

CHAPTER THREE

750 F1, Montjuich, Laguna Seca, Santamonica, 350/400 F3

One of the more surprising things that happened at Ducati during the early 1980s was their reluctance to produce a street version of the all-conquering TT2. This was undoubtedly due to managerial indecision and the impending Cagiva takeover. Even in 1982 it was rumored that a street TT2 was on the drawing board and that it would appear at the 1983 Milan show. Typically this didn't eventuate. By 1984 Tony Rutter had won four World Championships, and already the factory was campaigning the 750cc TT1. 1984 saw yet another manager of the company, Dott. Ing. Mario Scandellari and it wasn't until June 1984 that pictures were released of a proposed 750 F1 street bike. There were even brochures printed of this prototype, but this machine was quite a long way removed from the eventual production F1.

This prototype 750 F1 engine set the scene for the eventual 1985 production model. As on the factory racers, an 88mm bore and 61.5mm stroke provided 748cc. With a compression ratio of 10.4:1, and either 36 or 40mm carburetors, claimed power was 70 HP at 9,000 rpm. At this stage there was still indecision in the eventual specification, and the carburetors breathed through open bell-mouths, with a Verlicchi two-into-one black-painted competition-type exhaust system. The bike was obviously not street-legal. The five-speed gearbox was similar to other Pantahs, but the clutch was new, also hydraulically operated through a handlebar-mounted master cylinder. Also featured was an oil cooler, mounted in the front of the fairing. This non-running prototype was boldly painted red, white, and light-green, with a red-painted cantilever frame similar to that of the TT2 but for a lower extension to allow for a centerstand. With a full fairing and huge DUCATI decals, it was almost a defiant statement in the face of the impending Cagiva purchase. Only a solo seat was fitted, this also styled similar to the TT2. The battery was intended to go in the tailpiece but there was no room for a battery on this prototype. Lighting included a rectangular CEV headlight, and a normal 600 SL taillight. No turn signal indicators were fitted and the instruments were the Nippon Denso type of the 650 SL, without the plastic surround.

Where this unusual prototype was unique was in the use of 16-inch Oscam wheels front and rear. Even

This was how the 750 F1 first appeared when it was displayed during 1984. It's doubtful if this was ever a running prototype but official brochures were printed.

The first production 750 F1 was shown at the Sydney show in early 1985, then used as a press demonstrator. Here is the author astride this first F1. Notice the tall fuel filler cap that was unlike those on subsequent production versions.

the tire choice was confused. These were either Michelin A/M48 100/90V16 and 120/90V16, or radial 120/60VR16 and 150/60VR16. The suspension was a red-painted 38mm Marzocchi fork on the front with a rear Marzocchi monoshock, while braking was by the usual Brembo 08 calipers with front 280mm discs. At the rear was a 260mm disc with a Brembo 05 caliper. This suspension and brakes would carry through to the eventual production F1.

750 F1 1985

With Ducati in the process of being purchased by Cagiva, the production 750 F1 was even further delayed, development continuing through until the end of 1984. While it had missed both the Cologne and Paris Shows, it had still been intended to display the F1 at the Bologna show in December. However, it wasn't until the Sydney Show at the end of February 1985 that the production 750 F1 finally made its debut. Incidentally no official factory literature ever distinguished the various models of F1 as being F1A, F1B, or F1S, this nomenclature probably coined by the U.S. distributor. As with many models of Ducati, identification of the 750 F1 by model year is the most reliable system. Although all 1985 750 F1s were designated as 7/85 in the factory production data, there were still two distinct series of 1985 750 F1. Frame numbers for the U.S. now included a 17-digit VIN number, causing further identification confusion.

Although it may not have been to the same specification as the factory racers in 1985, the first 750 F1 was the most race track-oriented production Ducati to appear since the original 750 Super Sport of 1974.

The engine of the 1985 750 F1 was black and there were two versions. This is the later version with the hydraulically actuated dry clutch and featured a new clutch cover. This second series of 1985 750 F1 also had small Malossi air filters on the carburetors. The oil lines to the bypass oil cooler were rubber with crimped fittings.

Engine and Drivetrain

The engine of the F1 was still basically that of a Pantah, as described in Chapter Two, but for a few modifications to allow for the larger capacity and corresponding increase in power. Engine numbers started at 7500001 and, for the first time for a Ducati, the engine crankcases were painted black. The three-ring 88mm pistons provided less compression than the earlier mock-up (9.3:1), but the cylinder head was largely unchanged from the 650 SL. Valves were identical to all earlier Pantahs, at 37.5mm inlet and 33.5mm exhaust, obviously a compromise on the larger engine. Even the bevel-drive 750 of 15 years earlier had used 40mm and 36mm valves. The valve guides were cast-iron, 38mm long for the inlet and 37mm for the exhaust. All the rockers were identical to earlier Pantahs, but for the F1 there were new camshafts, and a wider selection of opening and closing adjusters, now in 0.05mm increments. Opening caps were from 2mm-5mm and closing adjusters 5mm-9.6mm. Timing pulleys were again aluminum, but with new part numbers (0367.29.050).

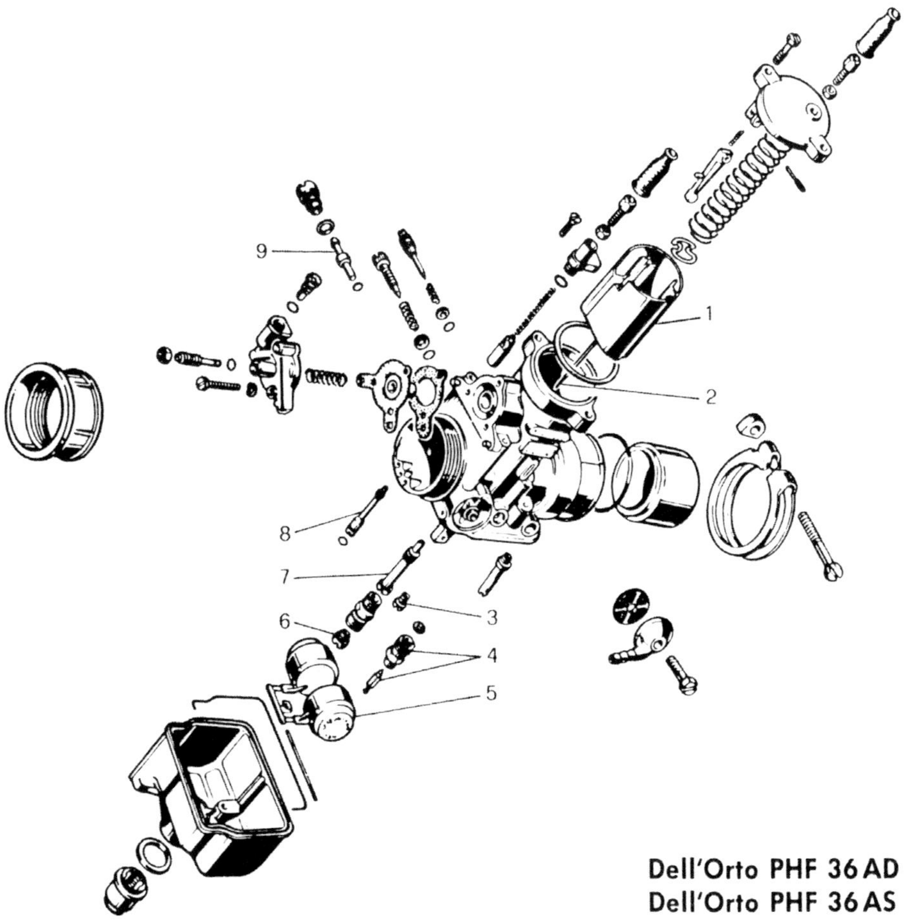

Dell'Orto PHF 36AD
Dell'Orto PHF 36AS

Carburetion for the 750 F1 was by two Dell'Orto PHF 36 A carburetors.

The 124mm con rods were identical to those of other Pantahs, although the crankshaft was rebalanced for the heavier pistons. The Pantah oil pump housing was retained, but the 11-tooth driving gear was now shared with the bevel-drive Mille. The five-speed gearbox was unchanged, but there were new primary gears, 36/71 (1.97:1), now straight-cut rather than helical. There was also a change to the wet clutch layout, with a new pressure plate and more clutch plates (16 plates). Clutch actuation was also hydraulic, with a new clutch cover to allow for the larger clutch basket. This also featured rather weak springs (066716550). For the second 1985 series, the clutch was changed to a multi-plate dry type, still with hydraulic actuation. This used a new clutch cover, with HC cast on it. This clutch was primarily a 1986 item and is detailed in the next section. The basic crankcases were shared with the later series 650 Alazzurra, with additional M8mm x 70mm engine screw between the crankshaft and layshaft, bringing the total number of crankcase screws to 13.

An oil cooler was mounted under the headlight with a takeoff point from the pressure switch, and two return lines to each cylinder head. The oil lines were a cheap rubber (Gr.tto) with crimped fittings, hardly befitting a motorcycle carrying a race replica status. The engine breather on the first F1 was a black plastic tube and flapper valve under the seat, a system long used by Ducati, but scarcely meeting impending emissions requirements.

Carburetion was the same Dell'Orto PHF 36 AD/S of the 650 SL, although the factory workshop manual specified 140 main jets in conflict with the spare parts list (132/138). Flip-up choke levers were mounted on the carburetors, and the first model had no air filtration, as one of the main problems with the F1 frame was limited space for air filters. Subsequent production runs saw small Malossi foam filters fitted. The F1 came with a new exhaust system, a black-chromed Conti two-into-one, exiting on the left. Claimed power for the 1985 F1 was a modest 62.5 HP at 7,500 rpm, with 6.2 kg/m of torque at 6,500 rpm.

Ignition, Electrical System, and Switches

Although the Bosch BTZ ignition system was carried over from other Pantahs, the Motoplat coils were now the same as those of the bevel-drive 900 and Mille MHR. Maximum ignition advance was 33 degrees, and spark plugs Champion L82Y. The F1 also received a new Nippon Denso 0.7HP electric-start motor, also similar to that of the 900 and Mille. There were several changes to the electrical system, most notable being a 300-watt alternator and the final removal of the troublesome generator warning-light device. Much of the electrical system was shared with the Mille. This included the three-wire 18-amp regulator, four-fuse fusebox (three connected), and starter motor relay. From the Pantah came the Yuasa YB 14LA2 12-volt 14-Ah battery. While the battery was positioned at the rear, all the ignition components and regulator were below the steering head in front of the fuel tank, with the fuse box under the seat near the engine breather outlet.

Other electrical equipment was either new or shared with the 900 and Mille Replica. The headlight was a rectangular H4 55/60-watt CEV 283, 168mm x 107mm, and the instruments, instrument panel and switches from the larger model. Thus the 220-km/h speedometer also read to 140 mph, and the tachometer redlined at 9,000 rpm. Although the instruments were the Nippon Denso that had been used on earlier Pantahs (not the 650 SL), there was a new set of warning lights, the colors incorporated in an opaque cover. These were *Neutral* (green), *Fuel* (red), *High Beam* (blue), *Lights* (green), *Oil*, *Gen* (red), <=> (orange). The CEV taillight was new, and specifically designed for the F1, as were the rectangular turn signal indicators.

Frame and Cycle Parts

The red-painted frame was modeled on that of the TT2 and carried numbers starting at 7500001. The F1 was also the one of the first series of Ducati to carry a ZDM prefix, in this case ZDM 750 R. This prefix was essential in order to identify individual models, as many used identical engine and frame number se-

The fit of the engine was so tight in the frame that the first 750 F1 was without air cleaners.

The red-painted 750 F1 frame was derived from that of the TT2, but with a different subframe and extension for a centerstand. The high rear location of the battery led to a kicked-up tail.

quences. U.S. versions featured a 17-digit VIN number (ZDM3AA3L0FB750xxx). Several alterations were required to adapt the pure racing TT2 frame for street use. The racing TT2 frame was so compact that there was no room for timing belt covers, essential on a street motorcycle, and there was also no provision for either a sidestand or centerstand. With a 26-degree steering head angle, an extra loop was added to the rear subframe to support the battery and seat. This was also lowered to reduce the seat height. The frame extended below the engine, providing an additional engine support as well as a centerstand mount. U brackets were located on either side behind the engine, the left bracket for retaining the exhaust system, relegating the right bracket unnecessary. The 650 SL Zadi Gege steering head lock, requiring a separate key, was also fitted, and later versions also featured a helmet lock on the left front frame tube.

Where the F1 seemed to be hastily conceived was in the styling and bodywork. Although the aluminum fuel tank was similar to the TT2, fitting inside the frame tubes with neat grooves underneath on the right side to allow for the front carburetor cables, the solo seat unit was overly large and square, also strangely angled upwards at the rear. The seat pad was detachable, covered in plain black plastic. A rubber strap retained the fuel

Early 750 F1s had the filler cap mounted on the right of the aluminum fuel tank. Instruments were Nippon Denso, and there were red plastic end-plugs in the handlebars.

The solo seat and decals of the 1985 750 F1.

tank, this with a plastic screw-on filler cap situated on the right side of the tank. The first production machine had a taller metal screw-on filler cap, and the final 1985 750 F1s (for the U.S.) had a central flush-mounted, aircraft-style aluminum fuel filler cap, neither of these appearing in the parts list. The two-piece hand-laid fiberglass fairing was more successful aesthetically, as was the small clear screen. An aluminum cross brace located the fairing to the top triple clamp, and the 6mm screws retaining the fairing and seat were black. On the first series, the lower fairing featured cutouts for the exhaust system, the second series having a wider bell-pan with no cutout. Black fairing-mounted mirrors were also standard on the F1. The front fender was red, with three horizontal slots on each side. Strikingly painted diagonally in red, white, and green, the 1985 750 F1 was the final Ducati (at least until Pierre Terblanche's Mike Hailwood *Evoluzione* of 1998) to feature the distinctive Giugiaro graphics. These were boldly displayed in white, DUCATI on the fairing and fuel tank, and DESMO 750 F1 on the seat. A later style light-gold MADE IN ITALY decal was located on the left side of the plastic fuel filler or beneath the aircraft-style filler cap. Fuel lines were the black braided rubber type used by Ducati at that time, as were the fuel taps; a manual tap on the right and the leaky vacuum tap on the left. These were the same as for the Mille Replica and it was advisable to replace the vacuum tap with another manual type.

The 38mm Marzocchi front forks with red-painted fork tubes and triple clamps were shared with the Mille Mike Hailwood Replica and S2 (0905.37.100). Each fork leg featured an air cap, and the lower left fork leg a yellow MARZOCCHI decal. The front black P2F08N Brembo brake calipers were mounted behind the fork legs, with two rubber brake lines connecting to a

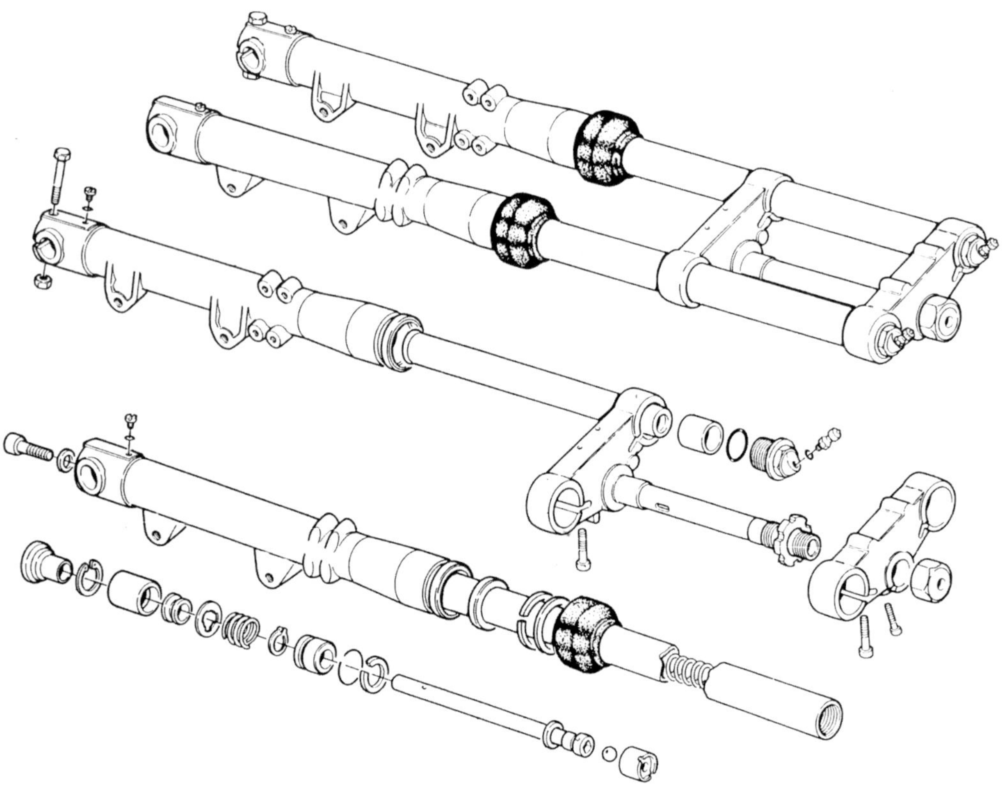

Air-assisted 38mm Marzocchi forks were fitted to the 1985 750 F1.

All 1985 750 F1s featured a gold-painted 16-inch Oscam wheel with Michelin 120/90V16 A48 tire. Only the very earliest examples used these 280mm fixed discs with aluminum centers.

junction box with pressure switch on the lower triple clamp. The earliest examples had non-floating 280mm Brembo cast-iron discs with aluminum centers, along with a solid 260mm rear disc. However, most 1985 F1s featured fully-floating 280mm front and 260mm rear discs. The rear P2F05N Brembo brake caliper was located underneath the swingarm. The rear wheel was controlled by a single oleo-pneumatic Marzocchi PVS 4 shock absorber. With a 58mm stroke giving 110mm of wheel travel, this was generally underdamped and oversprung, and not the best quality component available.

Wheels were gold-painted Oscam, a MT 2.50 x 16-inch on the front fitted with a 120/80V16 A48 Michelin tire. The rear MT 3.00 x 18-inch was shod with a 130/80V18 M48 Michelin. These tires were quite unsuitable for a motorcycle with the sporting capability of the F1, and the wheels almost unacceptably heavy. The front wheel/disc/tire weighed around 14kg (30 pounds), and the rear wheel with sprocket around 17kg (37 pounds), all of this unsprung weight. One area where the F1 was considerably improved over earlier Pantahs was the more appropriate final-drive gearing. A 15-tooth countershaft sprocket was used in conjunction with a 40-tooth rear sprocket, an even lower 43-tooth also being specified. Final drive was by 96-link 530 Regina 136 OR chain.

Handlebars were the Verlicchi multi-adjustable offset type of the 900 and Mille MHR, with red plastic end-plugs. Handlebar levers were the black dog-leg type, and the twin-cable plastic Verlicchi throttle identical to that of other Pantahs. The F1 did receive new rubber handgrips (067554800). The folding footpegs and foot levers were the aluminum type of other Pantahs, although the foot control rubbers were shared with the 900 and Mille. A rather poor-quality hydraulic steering damper attaching to the right fork leg and the lower right frame tube completed the F1 specification. 591 1985 750 F1s were constructed, making them one of the rarer production street Ducatis. Although they didn't offer tremendous engine performance, the 750 F1 was a commendably light and compact motorcycle, befitting a machine descended from a pure racer. *Motorcyclist* in April 1986 weighed their 1985 model 750 F1 at 423 pounds wet.

The rear wheel and cast-iron 260mm disc of the early 1985 750 F1. Most 1985 F1s had a fully-floating rear disc.

The machine that inspired the 750 F1 was the magnificent TT2 of 1981-85. While there were always a handful of super special racers built each year for factory riders, this machine also went into limited production for privateers during 1982. Because they were a limited-production motorcycle they, and the later TT1, deserve specific mention. Modeled closely on the factory TT2, the production version also featured a 597cc engine using special two-ring 10.2:1 81mm Borgo pistons (weighing only 408 grams) with a Gilnisil cylinder. Valve sizes were 41mm and 35mm, with a corresponding increase in port diameter over the stock Pantah. Racing camshafts gave 11mm of intake valve lift and 10.5mm of exhaust valve lift (valve timing figures are in the Appendix), though as always these were milder than the factory camshafts that offered even more valve lift (12mm inlet). The bottom end consisted of a highly polished standard 600 SL crankshaft and con rods, with a new steel clutch and straight-cut primary gears with a higher (36/70) ratio. Unlike the factory racers though, the clutch was a cable-operated wet type similar to the street bike. The five-speed gearbox was identical to the 600 SL but for a lower fifth gear that soon found its way to the production version. 1982 TT2s received Dell'Orto PHF 36A carburetors to give a claimed 76 HP at 10,500 rpm. 1983 versions were fitted with Malossi-modified Dell'Orto 41mm carburetors for a claimed 78 HP at 10,500 rpm. All TT2s were fitted with a fairing-mounted oil cooler, the 1982 version with a cylinder head bypass. On the 1983 TT2 the oil cooler was a full-flow system with braided steel lines tapped into the primary cover. A steering damper was also fitted to 1983 versions. Somewhat surprisingly for a racing machine, all TT2s came with an electric start, and ignition was the usual Bosch BTZ, the battery situated in the tailpiece.

The compact red-painted Verlicchi frame with cantilever rear suspension was shared with the factory bikes. The frame was so tight around the engine there was no space for the camshaft timing belt covers. Also

For 1982, 20 TT2 racing machines were produced. These were spectacular machines, but unfortunately, apart from TT2 events in Europe, there wasn't really a suitable class for them to participate in.

The 1982 TT2 has Dell'Orto PHF36A carburetors and a bypass oil cooler. The wet clutch was cable-operated and there was still an electric starter.

shared with the factory bikes were the 35mm racing Marzocchi forks with magnesium fork legs and adjustable rebound damping. The Marzocchi rear PVS 1 unit had a remote reservoir and adjustment for both compression and rebound damping. Wheels were magnesium Campagnolo, 2.15 x 18-inch and 2.50 x 18-inch in 1982, with a wider 3.50 x 16-inch front and 3.50 x 18-inch rear for 1983. Brakes were 05 Brembo Gold

For 1983 the TT2 had a 16-inch front wheel, 41mm Malossi carburetors, a full-flow oil-cooling system and hydraulic steering damper.

A small number of 750 TT1s were produced during 1984.

Line, with fully-floating 280mm front discs and a non-floating 260mm rear disc. Painted red and yellow, the TT2 weighed a claimed 286 pounds (130kg) and a total of 50 were produced, 20 in 1982 and 30 in 1983.

For 1984 a factory 750 kit became available to transform the TT2 into a 750 before a limited run of TT1 replicas was constructed. These were ostensibly the earlier TT2 fitted with a 748cc (88mm x 61.5mm) engine. With identical valves to the TT2 the claimed power was a modest 80 HP at the rear wheel. These catalog racers were heavily based on the Tony Rutter 1984 TT1, but for a cable-operated NCR dry clutch, and unlike the factory TT1 there was no rising-rate rear suspension or special magnesium engine covers. The Verlicchi frame was as before but for a wider aluminum cantilever swingarm to accommodate wider wheels. The 35mm magnesium Marzocchi forks and 05 Brembo brakes were also from the TT2, but an outboard countershaft sprocket allowed for the larger-section 18-inch rear tire, with an endurance-style quick-change assembly. This allowed the disc and caliper to stay in the swingarm as the wheel and sprocket were removed. Front wheel was still a 16-inch, but most were raced with an 18-inch front. The 1984 TT1 was painted red and blue, and as with the TT2, 25 were produced.

750 F1 1986

Due of the purchase of Ducati by Cagiva in 1985, 750 F1 development was delayed and compromised. Thus some aspects of the 1985 750 F1 disappointed many enthusiasts expecting a race-replica in the style of the revered 1974 750 Super Sport. Difficulties at the factory during the transition to Cagiva control unfortunately saw the 1985 F1 as a half-hearted race replica, with disappointing performance and many substandard components. The 1986 version went some way to address these shortcomings, and in nearly every respect was an improvement over its predecessor. Before the release of the 1986 750 F1 however, several hybrid 1985/86s were created by the factory and tested by several magazines, primarily in Italy. One was a 1985 750 F1 with the normal graphics plus an additional CAGIVA decal on the fairing. Some of these had the new Cagiva-inspired graphics in the 1985 chassis and bodywork, but with 40mm Marzocchi forks. Another was also painted the red and silver of the later Montjuich and fitted with the open Verlicchi racing exhaust system. Because these one-off F1s were produced for promotional purposes, it is important that they are not used as a guideline for restoration. The 1986 750 F1 was built in two series, described as the 12/1985 and Kokusan ignition.

Engine and Drivetrain

Production of the 1986 series 750 F1 commenced in late 1985 (as the 12/1985 series), 33 built toward the

The 1986 750 F1, now with red wheels, a steel fuel tank, and new Cagiva-inspired decals with elephants on the tank and fairing.

end of the year. Engine numbers for this series began at 7500595. The influx of capital from Cagiva was evident immediately with the improvement in specification of the 1986 750 F1. The Pantah engine was modified slightly to accept the larger displacement, and for the first time was not merely an oversized 500. Following experience derived from racing F1s, the black-painted crankcases were strengthened with additional webbing between the driveside main bearing and gearbox mainshaft bearing. Until engine number 7501494 these bearings were the same as before, but after engine number 7501495 the F1 engine was standardized with that of the Montjuich. These Montjuich crankcases featured larger gearbox bearings, an updated gearbox mainshaft, and new second driving gear.

There were also important changes to the cylinder head. Larger valves, a 41mm inlet and 35mm exhaust, were more appropriate for the 88mm cylinders. The cylinder head casting was new, with more metal around the ports and allowing the new engine to be more suitable for tuning. There were also new camshafts (although carrying the same part number as

The author's 1986 750 F1 photographed in late 1986. Non-standard is the fully-floating rear disc and engine breather. This is a 12/1985 series, bought at the factory in January 1986.

Some 1985 750 F1s were updated with new graphics and used as publicity by the factory. Generally these bikes were not readily available.

before) opening and closing the larger valves, with less aggressive valve timing but increased lift. Initially the earlier cast-iron valve guides were unchanged, but these were soon updated to bronze. Although the inlet ports remained unchanged, there were new intake manifolds for the Dell'Orto PHF 36 MD/MS carburetors, these including an alloy reducer between the carburetor and inlet manifold. The rocker pins now became available in 0.02mm oversize. The black-chromed two-into-one exhaust system with Conti muffler was carried over from the 1985 F1.

Higher compression (10:1) H-section three-ring pistons were used in the 1986 series 750 F1. These had a deck height of 55.4mm. Although the 124mm con rods carried the same part number as before (0660.47.350), these were thicker in section, especially around the little end. There was also a new forged crankshaft with more metal around the big-end journal. Significantly, the 1986 F1 received a revised gearbox, still with the same ratios as before but the gears were 30 percent wider and undoubtedly stronger. With the new gearbox came new selector forks, these also stronger than the earlier type. The dry clutch was new, with a steel inner clutch drum. The layout followed that of the earlier 600 SL dry clutch, but with a larger-diameter outer drum. There were seven driving discs and seven driven discs (see Appendix). Another improvement was a change to stronger clutch springs (065916703).

A significant improvement over the 1985 model was in the oil-cooling system. The oil radiator was still located on two brackets below the headlight (new brackets), but the oil lines were a more durable matted rubber type. Rather than returning oil to each cylinder head, the cooled oil returned to the right crankcase, just above the outlet. This system ensured that cool oil was supplied to the lower end of the engine, in addition to the cylinder heads. The 1986 F1 also received a proper engine breather catch tank, situated on the right next to the rear carburetor. Not only was the 1986 engine a stronger design, the claimed power too was considerably improved over the previous year, to 75 HP at 9,000 rpm, with 7.2 kg/m of torque at 7,000 rpm.

Ignition, Electrical System, and Switches

While the Bosch ignition system with Motoplat coils was carried over from the 1985 F1, the larger valves required smaller-diameter, Champion RA6YC spark plugs. From engine number 7501496 the entire ignition system was shared with that of the Montjuich and included Kokusan pick-ups, coils and ignition amplifiers. There was no difference in specification between the two systems, both featuring a two-stage advance idle to 1,700 rpm with maximum advance at 2,600 rpm, but the Kokusan system comprised higher quality components. Although the ignition pickups and wires were also continually submerged in engine oil, the Kokusan ignition wires were less subject to rotting. With the Kokusan ignition came a new wiring loom. The 300-watt alternator and Nippon Denso starter motor were also unchanged.

For the 1986 F1 the entire headlight and instrument panel was revised, although the taillight and rear

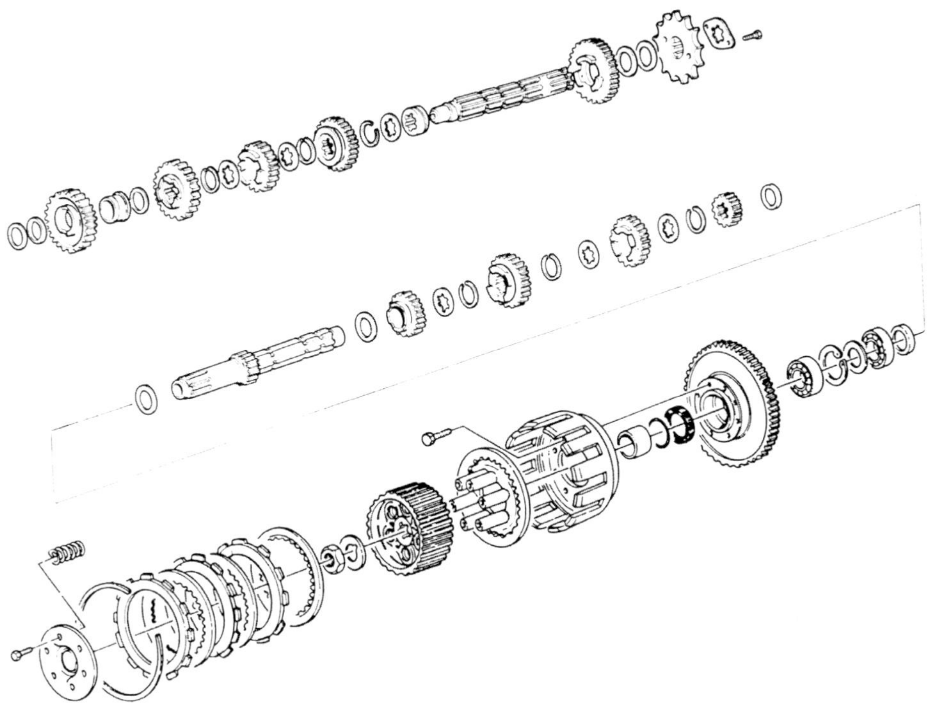

All 1986 750 F1s received a new gearbox, although the dry clutch and straight-cut primary gears had appeared on some of the final 1985 750 F1s.

indicators carried over. The headlight was still the same rectangular H4 55/60-watt CEV 283, but carried a new part number (0670.38.200). More significant was the new instrument panel, the basic layout lasting on 750 Ducatis through until 1998. Two white-faced Veglia instruments with a set of eight LED warning lights mounted in a gray foam surround. The left Nippon Denso handlebar switch and right-side plastic Verlicchi throttle were unchanged.

Frame and Cycle Parts

The red-painted frame was essentially unchanged for 1986, with numbers starting at ZDM 750R 7500595. Provision for brackets to locate an engine oil breather tank, new fuel tank, and revised under-seat battery tray were the main differences. There was no longer the usual Ducati-style steering head lock that required a different key, this now incorporated with the ignition. There was also the helmet lock on the left-front frame tube that had featured on the final 1985 series. While in many respects the 1986 750 F1 was an improvement on the earlier model, the steel fuel tank wasn't as nice an item as the 1985's hand-beaten alloy unit. With the steel fuel tank came a revised locating system (two bolts to the frame). It also held considerably less fuel at 18 liters (4.76 gallons). The fuel filler was the flush-mounted alloy aircraft-style that had featured on some of the final 1985 F1s, and the combination of manual and vacuum fuel taps was as before. Decals on the fuel tank were now the first of the new Cagiva-style (white with black surrounds) with an elephant graphic incorporated above the DUCATI. There was also the usual yellow Made in Italy decal underneath the filler cap.

The rest of the bodywork was similar in style to that of the 1985 model. The seat shape was still rather large but more attractive, as it was lower at the rear, and the red front fender was as before. The only difference to the two-piece fairing was the change in decals, a taller Plexiglas screen, and a slightly different air intake near the exhaust on the left. On the fairing for 1986 were large Cagiva-style DUCATI decals, with elephant graphics. The seat featured new 750 F1 and DESMO decals in the new-style lettering.

A major advancement over the 1985 F1 was the replacement of the non-adjustable Marzocchi forks with 40mm Forcelle Italia (formerly Ceriani). Although not featuring air-assistance, these excellent units provided adjustment for compression damping at the base of the fork leg, and rebound damping by a knob on the top of the fork. It was also important to use a lighter oil than that of a comparable Marzocchi, SAE5 weight being specified. A similar oversprung Marzocchi single shock absorber controlled the steel cantilever swingarm. The Brembo braking system was identical to that of the previous year, with full floating 280mm front disc rotors, but at the rear was a solid 260mm cast-iron disc. Also unchanged were the Oscam wheels, but these were now

Two 750 F1s about to be tested at the factory in January 1986. The basic frame was unchanged, but for several locating brackets and a relocated battery. The second battery is for testing only. The revised oil-cooling system can be seen, as can the solid rear disc and white-faced Veglia instruments.

painted red. Only a 40-tooth rear sprocket was fitted, and tires remained the rather unsuitable Michelin A/M48 combination.

All the footpegs and levers were as with the 1985 F1, as were the black dogleg handlebar clutch and brake levers. The only change was in the multi-adjustable clip-on handlebars, replaced by a more basic offset black clip-on. Red plastic end-plugs were still used. Although there were only a few alterations to the specification, the 750 F1 of 1986 was a considerably more appealing motorcycle than its immediate predecessor. The red wheels and slight restyle of the seat improved its appearance, and functionally the front forks were superior. Only with the steel fuel tank and solid rear disc did the F1 disappoint, but these were rectified with the Montjuich. Production of the 1986 series was 826 units with the Bosch ignition plus 84 for the U.S., still a small number in terms of modern production levels. The Kokusan-equipped versions were also built in 1986, but can be considered 1987 models.

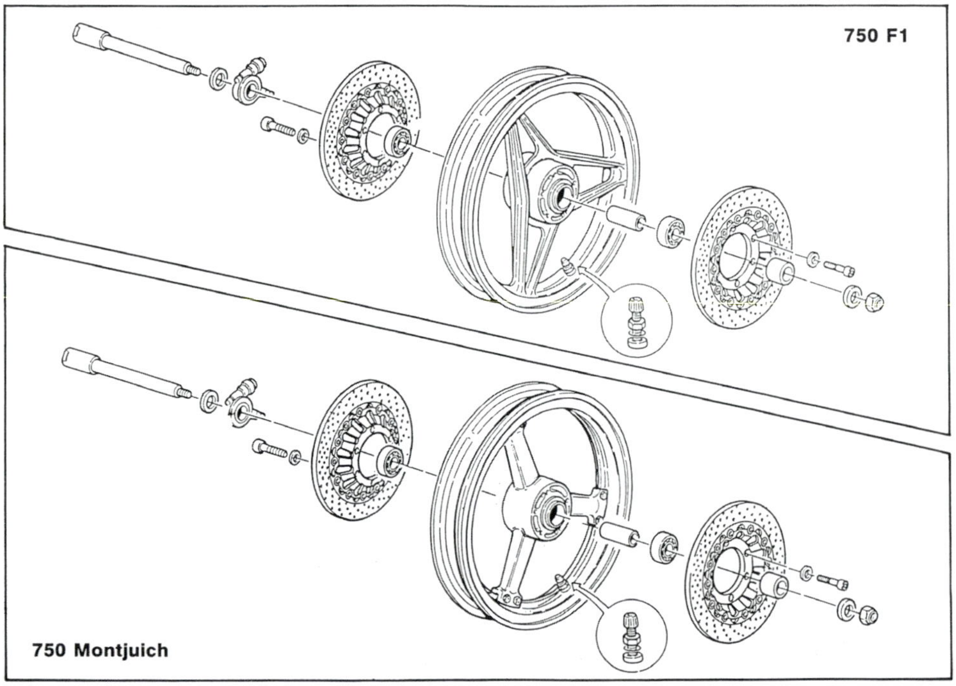

While the 750 F1 continued with a 2.50 x 16-inch Oscam front wheel, the Montjuich came with a lighter 3.50 x 16-inch Marvic/Akront composite front wheel.

Bimota Db1

As part of Cagiva's expansion plans, the Castiglionis entered into an agreement with the Rimini company, Bimota, in 1985 to supply them 500 750 F1 engines during 1986, with additional units in subsequent years. These were to be used in a motorcycle to be called the DB1, designed by Federico Martini, an engineer who had worked at Ducati from 1978 until 1983. Martini first penned the DB1 in February 1985 as a racing bike, this successfully raced in F1 events by Massimo Matteoni and Maurizio Rossi during the year. When it appeared as a street bike, it was very closely based on the racer, much more so than Ducati's own 750 F1.

The DB1 used a standard 1986 750 F1 engine (engine numbers starting around 7500950), but for a relocated oil cooler and a different air filtration system. The air cleaner element was tucked away in the rear section, requiring a long intake to the front 36mm Dell'Orto carburetor. This resulted in inferior carburetion than that of a standard 750 F1, as well as diminished performance. Also contributing to less power than a standard F1 was the two-into-two exhaust system. It was mainly in the chassis and bodywork that the DB1 differed to the F1. Although still utilizing a tubular-steel frame, Martini's DB1 was significantly more compact than the Ducati, and rather more beautifully executed. With a steering head angle of 25 degrees the red-painted frame consisted only of straight tubing, formed in a series of triangles, but not supporting the engine at the lower mount. This left very little room for ancillary components, the battery, regulator, and ignition sitting above the engine, underneath the black molded, foam-filled, plastic fuel tank. Arching over the top frame tubes to improve weight distribution, a small connecting tube between the left and right sides was also responsible for some fuel starvation problems. The lack of a lower section of the frame also required the

The first Bimota to be powered by a Ducati engine was the DB1 of 1986. The full-coverage bodywork set the DB1 apart from the 750 F1.

The details on the DB1 were superb. Early versions featured brake and clutch reservoirs on top of the fork legs and all had machined triple clamps. The instruments were mounted very flat and were difficult to read.

alloy sidestand to mount on the exhaust balance pipe underneath the engine.

Instead of the F1's round-section steel swingarm, the DB1 featured a rectangular-section steel swingarm that operated the single adjustable Marzocchi PVS4 shock absorber through a rising-rate linkage. Shock absorber damping was by a cable and knob attached to the swingarm, and chain adjustment was by eccentrics at the axle. Front suspension was 41.7mm Marzocchi M1R forks, state-of-the-art racing equipment for the day, with triple clamps machined from solid billets of Avional 14. Rolling on 16-inch Bimota composite alloy wheels front and rear (3.25 x 16-inch front and 4.25 x 16-inch rear) meant the DB1 was an extremely short and low motorcycle. The wheelbase was a mere 1,380mm (54.3 inches), and the seat height only 714mm (28.1 inches). Claimed dry weight was only 160kg (352 pounds) but wet weight according to *Cycle* magazine in May 1986 was 406.5 pounds, still significantly lighter than a standard 750 F1. The tires were a newgeneration 60-series Pirelli MP7S radial, also shared with the contemporary Ducati 750 Paso; a 130/60-VR16 front and 160/60-VR16 rear.

Underneath this bodywork was a compact tubular-steel frame with all components tightly packed together. The panel over the exhaust pipes was designed to maintain air flow to the rear air intake.

As with the F1, the front brakes were fully-floating 280mm cast-iron Brembo, but the DB1 featured Brembo Gold Series 08 brake calipers. The rear brake caliper was located by a torque rod. Other equipment was similar to the F1 but also of higher quality, in particular the milled and forged aluminum handlebars, footrest brackets, levers, and master cylinder reservoirs on the tops of the fork legs. Only the first series of DB1 had these alloy reservoirs, later versions featuring the normal plastic Brembo type. The instrument panel also included the same white-faced Veglia instruments of the 1986 750 F1, but with an additional oil temperature gauge.

Probably the most striking feature of the DB1 was the totally enclosed fiberglass bodywork that not only fitted perfectly, but unlike most original Ducati equipment, designed to come apart easily through a combination of Dzus-type fasteners and 12mm Allen screws. Included in the white bodywork was a lower panel running over the exhaust pipes and removal of this had a detrimental effect on carburetion. The DB1 was undoubtedly one of the best handling motorcycles available in 1986, this confirmed in contemporary road tests. So successful was the model that 453 were constructed (frame numbers 00.001-00476), including five as kits. 360 were sold to Japan. The DB1 was followed by a further 63 DB1 S in 1986-87 (frame numbers 00.477-00.538), and finally 153 of the higher performance DB1 SR from 1987-89 (frame numbers 00.539-00782). The S looked visually identical to the DB1, but for an S on the fairing, and was otherwise identical but for a set of 40mm Dell'Orto carburetors. The SR featured red and white bodywork, four-piston Gold Series Brembo front brakes, and Marvic/Akront 16-inch composite wheels. Engine changes included higher-compression 10.4:1 pistons, Montjuich camshafts, Malossi 41mm carburetors, and a Ducati-NCR two-into-one exhaust system. The claimed power for the DB1 SR was 80 HP at 9,000 rpm. The DB1 was also available in Japan in 1989 as the DB1 J, with a six-speed 400 F3 engine (frame numbers included in the DB1).

Montjuich

The Barcelona 24 Hour-endurance race held at Montjuich Park had long been a successful event for Ducati, and July 1983 saw the first major victory for the 750cc TT1 in the now non-championship 24-hour race. Limiting the revs to 8,000 rpm, and 83-84 HP, in front of 250,000 spectators Grau, de Juan and Reyes completed 708 laps on a factory prototype to the second-place French Kawasaki's 690 laps. The following year a locally prepared customer TT1, this time ridden by Juan Garriga, Grau and Reyes, again won the Montjuich 24-hour event, although this time only in front of 130,000 spectators. These successes prompted Ducati to name their first limited-edition 750 F1 street bike the Montjuich when it was displayed at the Milan Show at the end of 1985. However, like many prototypes, this show bike also differed in many details from the eventual production version, notably in the use of 16-inch red-painted cast-alloy wheels, and the fitting of a centerstand. Another prototype Montjuich was sent to Australia for production racing that also had one-piece wheels and a centerstand. When displayed at Bologna in December, the Montjuich was closer to its final form (with Marvic composite wheels and a sidestand) but still with Bosch ignition.

Engine and Drivetrain

Engine numbers were shared with the 750 F1, but the Montjuich engine, although ostensibly similar, included different crankcases to accept larger gearbox mainshaft bearings. There was also a different mainshaft and second driving gear. Although the Montjuich clutch was the same as the 750 F1, the outer clutch drum was aluminum and the external cover vented. Also shared with the F1 was the entire crankshaft and piston assembly. Thus the Montjuich didn't follow in the earlier tradition of the limited-edition race replicas featuring stronger con rods, though they did have stronger cylinder head studs (0377.49.270). There was also a different outer sprocket cover, and countershaft sprockets came in either 14- or 15-tooth.

There were several changes in the top end. Although 41mm inlet and 35mm exhaust valves were retained, they carried new part numbers (0377.92.110/120). The Montjuich also received different cylinder heads, with larger inlet ports and a larger-diameter rubber inlet sealing gasket. New camshafts with very aggressive valve timing (see Appendix) were probably the most significant contributor to the improved performance of the Montjuich over a standard F1, and continue to be the performance camshaft profile for two-valve belt-drive twins. These provided 11.3mm of intake lift and 10.3mm of exhaust lift. Carburetion followed that for all previous high-performance Ducatis, with Dell'Orto 40mm carburetors, only in this case they were PMH 40 ND/NS that provided attachment to a rubber inlet manifold. These came with open bell mouths and no filtration like the F1. A very loud Verlicchi *Riservato Competizione* exhaust was fitted on the Montjuich.

The prototype Montjuich as displayed at the Milan Show at the end of 1985. A modified 1985 750 F1, this differed from the production version by having one-piece Marvic 16-inch wheels and a centerstand. There were no Montjuich decals on the fairing.

This is an early unnumbered example imported into Australia by the distributor for production racing. Differences to the regular Montjuich included one-piece Marvic wheels and a centerstand, but all the other specifications were identical.

The Montjuich in its eventual production form was one of the classic production Ducatis.

While undoubtedly aiding engine performance, these were certainly not street legal. The sum of these engine modifications boosted power to a claimed 95 HP at 10,000 rpm.

Ignition, Electrical System, and Switches

One of the most significant improvements offered by the Montjuich over a standard F1 (until engine number 7501496) was the Kokusan ignition system. This included a different flywheel, pickups and pickup support plate, coils, electronic amplifiers, and mounting plate. All other electrical equipment was identical to the normal F1.

Frame and Cycle Parts

Sharing more with the street 750 F1 than the pure works racers, the Montjuich featured a new frame number sequence, starting at ZDM750M 001. Although

The Montjuich engine was quite similar to that of the 750 F1, but featured a competition exhaust system.

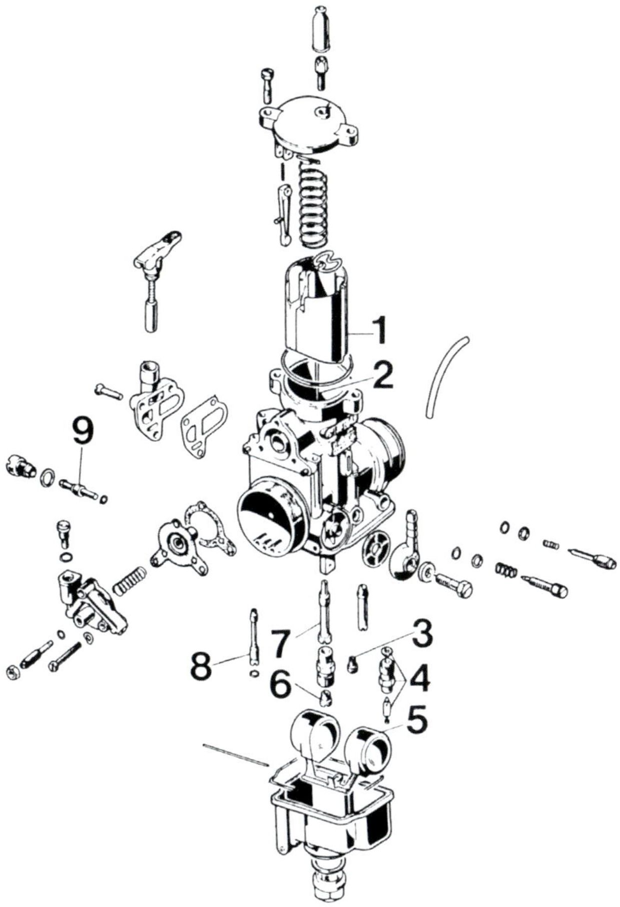

The Dell'Orto PMH 40N carburetors of the 750 Montjuich.

the red-painted Verlicchi frame was identical to that of the F1, on all production versions there was no centerstand, the sidestand mounting on a small bracket attached to the left-hand centerstand mount. The swingarm was aluminum, patterned on that of the racing monoshock TT1. The bodywork was that of the F1, except the Montjuich was painted the traditional racing Ducati colors of red and silver. All the decals followed the pattern set by the 1986 F1, but for the addition of Montjuich decals on the fairing. The fuel tank was aluminum, but not the same as the 1985 F1 tank, as it was retained by two bolts like the 1986 steel tank. To allow for the wider front tire a racing-style two-piece red front fender was fitted. A strange feature for such a motorcycle was the normal F1 helmet lock situated on the left front frame tube.

While the front forks were the same 40mm Forcelle Italia of the 1986 F1, a higher-quality rear Marzocchi shock absorber was specified. However, the biggest changes in specification occurred in the wheels and brakes. Composite Marvic/Akront magnesium/aluminum 16-inch wheels were fitted, a 3.50 x 16-inch on the front and 4.25 x 16-inch on the rear. With polished aluminum rims and three red-painted magnesium spokes these were much lighter than the aluminum Oscams of the F1. On the Montjuich they

The Montjuich frame was very similar to the 750 F1.

were shod with Michelin intermediate racing tires, a 12/60-16 and 18/67-16. Unlike the 750 F1, a fully-floating 260mm cast-iron disc featured on the back, otherwise the rear braking system being identical. It was the front brakes that were significantly upgraded. Racing Brembo P 432 D Gold series four-piston calipers with specific adapters and a larger-diameter handlebar master cylinder featured on the Montjuich, though somewhat surprisingly the brake lines were the same 750 F1 rubber type with a junction on the lower triple clamp. To clear the wider rear tire a narrower, 5/8- x 1/4 inch, chain was used, still with a 40-tooth rear sprocket (though a 43- tooth was specified in the workshop manual).

Only 200 Montjuichs were built, 20 coming to the U.S., in many ways epitomizing the race replica Ducati. Each came with a numbered plaque on the fuel tank. They were loud and uncompromising machines, but unfortunately could have been more if they had been more closely related to the factory TT1 racers of 1984 and 1985. Astonishingly the claimed weight was only 155 kg (341 pounds), a figure difficult to believe considering the basic 750 F1 was underneath, but *Cycle World* weighed their test bike in at a respectable 396 pounds wet in August 1986. In every respect the Montjuich was a considerably faster and more effective sports motorcycle than a stock 750 F1.

1986 750 F1s and Montjuichs were fitted with superior 40mm Forcelle Italia front forks, but the Montjuich had composite Marvic wheels.

Distinguishing the Montjuich from the F1 was an aluminum swingarm.

750 F1 1987

By 1986 Cagiva was committed to a new lineup of Ducatis built around the Paso, with a reversed rear cyl-

The Montjuich was undeniably one of the most desirable production Ducatis.

inder head and Weber carburetor, the traditional F1 no longer having a place. Thus toward the end of 1986 the final batch of 300 750 F1s (excluding the limited-edition Laguna Seca and Santamonica) was constructed, beginning at number 7501505. Fifty of these were intended for the U.S., and for the first time there was a specific U.S. market F1. This was essentially identical, but differed in a small number of details. Unfortunately they were also much heavier than before (*Cycle* magazine weighed a test 1987 model 750 F1 in at 449.5 pounds wet) and this hurt performance. The final F1s were also quite slow to sell, still being available well into 1988 in the U.S.

Engine and Drivetrain

By now all 750 F1 engines were standardized with the higher-performance Montjuich and Laguna Seca. This included shared crankcases, gearbox, clutch, cylinder head studs, and entire lower end. All engines received the new-style smooth and lower-crowned rocker covers of the 750 Paso, but no F1 ever had the clip-type opening rockers with gold rocker covers. All F1s for 1987 featured a new 58-tooth oil pump gear, up from 44-tooth in 1986. From engine number 7502169 there was a revised outer clutch actuation system that included a larger-diameter thrust bearing and plunger, with improved sealing. There was also a small change to the clutch plate combination with two 1.5mm grooved driving plates instead of one, although the number of plates was unchanged at 14. Only the Kokusan ignition featured on this series of 1987 F1s. The same Conti two-into-one exhaust system as before was generally fitted, except for a heavier and quieter two-into-two system for the U.S.

Frame and Cycle Parts

Identical to the 1986 750 F1, the red-painted Verlicchi frame with steel cantilever swingarm started at frame number ZDM750R 7501505 for 1987. Only a sidestand was fitted for 1987, with a stronger spring, although the centerstand lugs were retained. The steel fuel tank was unchanged but for a new lockable fuel tank cap with Cagiva elephant logos. U.S. versions were fitted with a different fuel filler cap. While the elephant graphics were still incorporated on the fuel tank decals, they were now absent on the fairing sides.

Other bodywork updates included a two-piece Montjuich front fender, and a dual seat with grab handles and a replaceable solo seat cowling. Passenger footpegs were also fitted, making the extra right-side support at least appear useful with a two-into-one exhaust system. There were no other changes to the specification, although U.S. versions received a different left switch block (with hard-wired headlamp).

Laguna Seca

During 1986 the 750 F1 had a moderately successful racing year, particularly in the United States. Marco

For 1987 the 750 F1 received a rather ugly dual seat and the Montjuich front fender. There were now no elephant decals on the fairing. Behind are two 1986 750 F1s.

The 750 F1 dual seat without the cover.

Lucchinelli won the Battle of the Twins race at Daytona in March, and later went on to win the Battle of the Twins race at Laguna Seca. This prompted Ducati to name the next series of limited edition 750 F1 the Laguna Seca, and provide each with a Marco Lucchinelli decal autograph on the fuel tank. Production of the Laguna Seca occurred with the final 750 F1 toward the end of 1986, with 200 built with a solo seat and a further 96 with a dual seat. Fifty solo-seat Laguna Secas made it to the U.S. Even by this stage Ducati had learned the economic advantages of producing limited editions in moderate quantities.

Engine and Drivetrain

But for slightly different cylinder heads the engine of the Laguna Seca was ostensibly identical to that of the Montjuich, also offering equivalent performance. Small updates included a steel, rather than aluminum, inner clutch drum, and changes to the clutch actuation system. This included a new clutch slave cylinder and

With the Laguna Seca of 1987 several details were inferior to those of the Montjuich. The wheels were shared with the 750 Paso, the steel tank with the F1 and a larger muffler with aluminum can. The only decals on the seat were 750.

The Laguna Seca also featured a slightly altered fairing with a narrower air intake under the headlight. Although the non-floating brake discs came from the Paso, the Laguna Seca still used racing four-piston Brembo brake calipers on the front.

bearing, although the vented clutch cover was retained. There were also new clutch springs (065916558). As with the 1987 F1 the Laguna Seca had a 58-tooth oil pump drive gear. In an effort to reduce noise levels the Laguna Seca featured a new muffler with a larger canister and riveted aluminum cover. U.S. versions received a different muffler again, a Conti similar to that on the 1986 F1.

Frame and Cycle Parts

Yet another frame number sequence was used for the Laguna Seca, beginning at ZDM750LS 750001, although the red-painted frame was identical to that of the Montjuich except for revised and reshaped footpeg/muffler brackets. There was also a different Verlicchi alloy swingarm to the Montjuich. This included a plastic rear wheel guard with an additional clip to locate the rear brake line. In many respects the Laguna Seca reflected the cost cutting that was now evident at Ducati under Cagiva. The hand-beaten aluminum fuel tank made way for a normal 18-liter steel type, but now included a Marco Lucchinelli signature decal. A feature of the Laguna Seca that wasn't shared with the F1 was the replacement of the troublesome left-side vacuum fuel tap with a manual type. The red-and-silver fairing was also revised slightly, with a narrower front oil-cooler air intake and lower Plexiglas screen. As on the 1987 F1

Each Laguna Seca came with a Marco Lucchinelli decal on the fuel tank.

96 Laguna Secas were produced with a dual seat, this the same as that on the 1987 750 F1. The footpeg brackets were also different for the Laguna Seca.

there were no elephant logos on the large DUCATI fairing decals, although these still featured on the fairing front and fuel tank. While most Laguna Secas (200) were built with a solo seat, 96 were also produced with a dual seat. This was identical to that of the regular F1 except painted red and silver with 750 decals, not 750 F1 like the Montjuich. All Laguna Secas came with a new front fender shared with the 750 Paso.

Different 40mm Forcelle Italia forks were used for the Laguna Seca. These had revised hydraulics that included a new damping rod and fork spring so as to limit the stroke to 110mm (4.3 inches) rather than the 140mm (5.5 inches) of the F1 and Montjuich. This was in response to complaints that the F1 fork was too soft and offered too much travel for racing. At the rear was a new Marzocchi oleo-pneumatic shock absorber. Another area where cost cutting was evident was the wheels and brakes. Instead of the light, but expensive, composite Marvic/Akront wheels of the Montjuich, the Laguna Seca took its wheels straight off the 750 Paso. These aluminum Oscam wheels had wider rims, a 3.75 x 16-inch on the front and 5.00 x 16-inch on the rear, and allowed the fitting of wider and lowerprofile Pirelli radial tires. The wheels had red spokes and polished alloy rims and non-floating 280mm brake discs that bolted directly to the wheel without a disc center. At the rear the 270mm Paso solid disc was also used.

The same four-piston Brembo racing Gold series front brake calipers as the Montjuich were used, but now with a rectangular reservoir handlebar master cylinder. There was also a matching rectangular clutch master cylinder. Because of the use of Paso wheels, the rear brake caliper was also shared with the Paso, this now a Brembo P2108N, with a new caliper bracket. It was unfortunate that the Laguna Seca was burdened with these few Paso items because they detracted from the purity and purpose of the Montjuich and compromised the performance and handling. When tested by *Motorcyclist* in October 1987, the Laguna Seca weighed in at 418 pounds wet, a considerable increase over the Montjuich, and most of it unfortunately unsprung due to the wheels.

The final limited-edition 750 F1 was the red-and-white Santamonica. Production versions differed slightly to this publicity model. The exhaust was that of the Laguna Seca, and the normal street-type front four-piston brake calipers replaced the gold-series racing type.

Santamonica

By 1987 the racing days of the F1 were almost over, as the air-cooled two-valve engine was barely competitive in any international open class. One of the most astounding victories late in its racing life, however, was at Misano at the Autodromo Santamonica in April 1986, when Lucchinelli won the opening round of the World TT Formula 1 Championship. This prompted Ducati to name their final limited-edition 750 F1 the Santamonica. Displayed at the end of 1987, and going into production before the end of the year, 204 Santamonicas were produced, essentially for the Japanese market, at the time the most important for Ducati. The Japanese always had a fondness for the F1 (and F3) series. The Santamonica engine was identical to the Laguna Seca. Although publicity photos showed the Santamonica with a Verlicchi competition muffler, the production Santamonica shared the Laguna Seca's muffler.

Frame and Cycle Parts

Continuing the number sequence of the Laguna Seca, Santamonica frame numbers began at ZDM750LS 750303. They were very similar to the dual-seat Laguna Seca apart from the white-and-red paintwork. Decals were as with the Laguna Seca, although the front DUCATI on the fairing lost the elephant logo. A small Santamonica decal was situated on the fairing on each side. Everything was as with the Laguna Seca except for the wheels and brakes. It seemed that Ducati almost acknowledged they had made a mistake with the Laguna Seca, as the Santamonica came with the beautiful Marvic/Akront wheels of the Montjuich. This also saw the return of the front 280mm and rear 260mm fully-floating cast-iron brake calipers. Although publicity photos show the Santamonica with Gold series P432 Brembo calipers fitted, these were not a feature of the production version. In their place were the newly developed black street P4 calipers that would also be fitted to the 1988 851. The production Santamonica also came with braided steel brake lines. Tires were Michelin radials, in the same sizes as the Laguna Seca.

Modifications To F1s And F3s

As the final Ducati of the pre-Cagiva era, the F1 series left Bologna as a confused combination of excellence and mediocrity. Prior to the Cagiva purchase, economics and conflicting politics dominated the management and influenced the decision making at Ducati. As they were the most expensive component, the construction and development of engines always took precedence and often other parts were substandard. While by 1985 this situation had improved, the original F1 was still burdened with 500cc cylinder heads, poor suspension and unsuitable tires. The 1986 F1 redeemed itself slightly but was still flawed in its execution. However, to the traditionalist these are endearing features, and as the F1 is one of the rarest of all Pantahs and the closest to the racing TT1 and TT2, modifications should be performed keeping the essential soul of the motorcycle intact. In many ways the F1 was the end of an era for Ducati, the last pre-Cagiva motorcycle from Bologna. Subsequent two-valve Ducatis, while often being less well developed, seemed to have been produced with a different ethos, and often with even more emphasis on cost cutting.

As far as engine performance was concerned the standard F1 was disappointing, especially the 1985 version with small valves. However, a freer exhaust system was beneficial, particularly the Verlicchi *Riservato Competizione*. My own experience with a 1986 750 F1 found that with this exhaust system engine perfor-

A nicely modified 1986 750 F1. Tastefully executed, this maintains the spirit of the original, but is an improved motorcycle. Modifications include Marvic/Akront wheels, still in 16 and 18 inches, a Verlicchi exhaust, 40mm Dell'Orto carburetors, and four-piston front brake calipers with braided steel brake lines.

mance was increased, particularly at the top end, but the noise may be unacceptable. 1987 versions with the restrictive two-into-two system would definitely perform better with an alternative system. What the F1 really needed was a Montjuich or Laguna Seca engine, complete with hotter camshafts and 40mm carburetors. All this is possible but relatively expensive. The same applies to bigger-bore kits and bottom end modification to include Carrillo con rods. 1985 F1s suffered even more because of 28mm inlet ports that didn't match the 32mm inlet manifold. A common modification with racing F1s was to run an additional oil line through the blanked-off hole behind the gearbox for additional gearbox lubrication. The Motoplat coils on 1985 and early 1986 750 F1s were weak, and ignition can be improved by substituting these for Dyna coils or similar.

While the engine could use more power, more beneficial modifications can be made to the suspension, particularly the rear. Here I used a Koni gas-hydraulic type 3012 shock absorber and found the handling transformed. Others have found an Öhlins Type 4 equally successful. Undoubtedly any similar quality unit (Works Performance, White Power, etc.) would have the same result. At the front, the 38mm Marzocchi fork of the 1985 F1 could be substituted for 41.7mm M1Rs, but these require softer springs. The Forcelle Italia forks of later F1s are also a little softly sprung, effectively remedied by some 500mm Öhlins springs. The brakes also benefit from braided steel or Frentubo brake lines. Other improvements to the F1 also follow those the factory supplied with the Montjuich, Laguna Seca, and Santamonica. These include four-piston front brake calipers and a Verlicchi aluminum swingarm. The standard hydraulic steering damper has been known to lock solid, causing accidents, so should be replaced. The 16-inch Montjuich/Santamonica Marvic/Akront wheels are also much lighter but still present a problem regarding tire choice.

One of the problems with the 750 F1 is the 16-inch front wheel. Not only does this produce rather unusual steering characteristics, but finding suitable tires for such a narrow rim these days can be problematic. An easy, and effective, modification is to fit an 18-inch front wheel from a later model Cagiva Alazzurra. The Alazzurra 650 GT of 1986 featured Oscam wheels that accepted tubeless tires. The hub width was the same as the 16-inch Oscam so the only modification required is to the front fender. An 18-inch wheel not only improves the aesthetic balance but makes for more stable handling, especially over bumpy roads. In many ways it is only restoring the bike to the way it was originally intended, as the 16-inch wheel was very much a passing fashion fad in the mid-1980s. This still doesn't solve the problem of excessive wheel weight, but changing to lighter wheels is a more expensive solution.

Tire choice is restricted on both the F1 and limited edition models. For the F1 with 16 and 18-inch wheels it seems that Metzeler 120/80 V 16 M/C (60V) TL Lasertec and 130/80 V 18 M/C (66V) TL Lasertec is one of the more satisfactory setups. For 16-inch wheels front and rear either Metzeler 130/70 ZR 16 M/C (61W) TL Sportec M3 front and 150/80 VB 16 M/C (71V) TL Lasertec rear, Pirelli Sport Demon, Bridgestone BT 56 tires (in the same sizes) seem to work well. These are taller than the standard tires and may require the front end to be lowered. This tire choice also applies to 16-inch-wheel Pasos and 750 Sports.

350/400 F3
1986

As there had always been a limited number of 350s built for the domestic market, it was inevitable that a 350 F3 would also appear at some stage. Along with the 350 for Italy there was also the similar 400 F3 for Japan. With 470 350s and 506 400s built in 1986 they also accounted for a significant proportion of the total series. Taking the basic frame and bodywork of the F1 and installing a 350 SL engine, along with more basic suspension, saw the creation the 350 F3. The 400 was virtually identical but for the larger pistons, but incorporated a number of unusual features that have often been typical of Japanese-market Ducatis. First displayed at the Milan Show in November 1985, the 350 and 400 F3 went into production in April 1986.

Engine and Drivetrain

Although now painted black, the 350 F3 engine was identical in specification to the final 350 SL. This included the smaller valves, a cable-operated wet clutch and Bosch ignition. The 400 F3 used the same engine, but with a 70.5mm, 10.4:1 piston. Both shared Dell'Orto PHF 30M carburetors without air cleaners.

Visually similar to the 1986 750 F1, the 350 F3 featured smaller (05) brake calipers and an aluminum fuel tank. No air cleaners were fitted as standard.

The 400 also featured an oil cooler, not the full-flow 1986 750 F1 version, but the partial-cooling of the 1985 F1. Claimed power for both the 350 and 400 was 42 HP at 9,700 rpm.

Frame and Cycle Parts

The red-painted frame of the 350 was shared with that of the 750F1, but the 400 frame no longer featured the two rear curved brackets for muffler location. Instead it had a single straight tube on the left only. Painted red and white, the first series of both 350 and 400 featured a 22-liter (6.31-gallon) aluminum Montjuich fuel tank. No steering damper was specified.

While the 350 was in many ways a mini-F1, sharing the instrument panel with the white-faced Veglia instruments, the Japanese market 400 was a unique model. The instruments on the 400 were the Nippon Denso from the 1985 750 F1, along with the same warning lights. Another unusual feature of the 400 was the use of black non-dogleg brake and clutch levers when all other Ducatis were using the dogleg type (including the 350 F3). The biggest difference between the 750 and its smaller brothers was in the brakes and suspension. Non-adjustable 35mm Marzocchi forks were fitted to both the 350 and 400, these having red-painted fork legs and triple clamps. The brakes were non-floating 260mm cast-iron front and rear, with Brembo P2F05N calipers.

1987

As with the 750 F1, the 1987 400 F3s differed from the earlier versions in much the same way. Visually the easiest way to tell the two apart was the lack of elephant logos on the fairing on the later bike, and a sidestand instead of a centerstand. The F3 continued to use the earlier 750 F1 front fender, but with four bolt mounts instead of two. A solo seat was still fitted, and the 18-liter steel F1 fuel tank replaced the earlier aluminum one. While the 750 F1 went to Kokusan ignition, the smaller versions retained the Bosch BTZ. The 400s from 1987 also used the white Veglia instruments and had 260mm fully-floating cast-iron front discs. 206 1987-specification 400s were built in September 1986, with a further 94 during 1987.

1989

It was indicative of the influence of the Japanese distributor Murayama that he persuaded Ducati to build a further 300 400 F3s at the end of 1988. These were of a higher specification than the earlier variety, and were styled as a mini-Santamonica with white-and-red paintwork and a dual seat. 150 were produced with a red fuel tank and 150 with a white fuel tank.

The Japanese-market 400 F3 for 1986 was a unique model.

The instruments were Nippon Denso on the Japanese 400 F3.

A 1987 specification Japanese market 400 F3, now with a steel fuel tank and fully floating cast-iron brake discs.

The engine was as before, but now featured a six-speed gearbox and Dell'Orto PHF 36 carburetors. Ignition was still Bosch and no oil cooler was fitted (though it was on the comparable Bimota). Power was increased to 47 HP at 10,000 rpm. The 16- and 18-inch Oscam wheels and front brakes with 260mm fully-floating discs and Brembo 05 calipers were as for 1987. The red-painted 35mm Marzocchi forks now had air caps, and the earlier 750 F1 front fender was still used. It was almost as if these were being produced to use up surplus spare parts, but they remain a unique, and quite desirable, model.

The very final 400 F3 for the Japanese market had a six-speed gearbox.

CHAPTER FOUR

750/906 Paso, 907 I.E., ST2

The purchase of Ducati by Cagiva in 1985 resulted in an immediate change in the direction of product development. Cagiva's first Ducati was the 750 Paso, and this represented a significant departure from any previous model. Although it may have come under criticism from the traditional Ducati enthusiast, the Paso was really an important step forward for the company. For the first time this was a Ducati designed to have an appeal beyond the world of the diehard Ducatisti. Cagiva realized that for Ducati to survive and sell more than a few hundred hard-edged idiosyncratic sportbikes a year, a new generation of Ducatis was required. These needed to be broader-appealing in concept and also more user-friendly. Real attempts were made to simplify servicing and create a totally balanced motorcycle with quality components throughout. The Paso was well sorted out of the crate and there was now no need to change the rear suspension or fit better tires. Unfortunately, while the concept was sound, the execution left something to be desired, and despite glowing press reports the Paso wasn't readily accepted. As it was the first Ducati in which the engine was completely covered, and was particularly ugly with the bodywork removed, it only appealed to a new buyer. These buyers were thin on the ground in the mid-1980s.

750 Paso

Designed by Massimo Tamburini, who had been wooed from Bimota by the Castiglionis, both a 350 and 750 Paso were first displayed at the Milan Show of 1985. The 750 was red and the 350 white, and they differed slightly to the eventual production version by having mufflers with aluminum end-cans and no rear-view mirrors incorporated in the fairing. As with many Ducati models it was some time after it was first displayed that the Paso went into production, the first versions produced in July 1986. The name Paso came from that of the Italian racer Renzo Pasolini who was killed at Monza in 1973. Pasolini had a long association with Aermacchi, before Cagiva acquired the Aermacchi plant at Varese in 1978.

Pre-production show Pasos differed in several details to eventual production versions. On this white model there were different mufflers and decals, as well as an absence of mirrors and passenger grab handle.

The first production 750 Paso of mid-1986 was red with black lower bodywork. There were now PASO decals, and mirrors incorporated in the fairing.

Clutch-side view of the 750 Paso engine. While the general engine was as with the 1986 750 F1, the rear cylinder head was reversed with the downdraft Weber carburetor feeding both cylinders.

With the Weber carburetor came equal-length inlet tracts, though these were longer than for the twin Dell'Ortos.

Engine and Drivetrain

Using the 1986 750 F1 engine as a basis, the 750 Paso incorporated a number of significant updates. With a new series of numbers starting at ZDM 750 LP 750001 the most noticeable difference was a reversed rear cylinder head to allow the installation of a dual-throat automotive-style Weber carburetor and large single air cleaner. The crankcases, crankshaft, primary-drive and gearbox were as for the 1986 model 750 F1, but the 14-plate clutch was the later (1987) F1 type, along with the later clutch springs. Initial U.S. versions were between numbers 751081 and 751480. From engine number 751448 the primary drive gears were changed to those of the 1987 F1 and Laguna Seca. Soon after production commenced the Paso received a revised belt-pulley bearing set-up that now included a bearing sleeve and circlip.

Although the design of the cylinder head was similar to the F1, (still with 41mm and 35mm valves) and the camshaft profile the same, the camshaft timing was retarded 8 degrees. This had the effect of improving top-end horsepower, but at the expense of the lower end. Valve lift was unchanged at 9.35mm inlet and 8.50mm exhaust. A significant development occurred after March 1988 when the opening rocker system of the desmodromic valve layout was redesigned to allow for easier servicing. Here Luigi Mengoli, who had assisted Taglioni in the original design of the Pantah, designed a removable clip that allowed a shortened rocker to be slid sideways to allow access to the opening cap. No longer did the opening rocker pin need to be removed for the adjustment of valve clearances. Engines with this system also received gold-anodized rocker covers.

Due to the expected increase in heat for the rear exhaust valve in particular, the oil-cooling system on the Paso was also much more elaborate than on the F1. Twin oil radiators, with a temperature switch, were fitted on either side of the engine, inside the fairing. Early Pasos (until engine number 751447) received the smaller (44-tooth) oil pump gear of the earlier F1. After engine number 751448 the 55-tooth gear of the Laguna Seca was used.

In an effort to obtain almost straight, equal-length inlet tracts, and to incorporate the large single air filter, the Paso was fitted with a single twin-choke down-draft carburetor. With an embargo on certain Japanese products at that time, Cagiva went to Weber and adapted an automotive-style 44DCNF 107 carburetor. Bored to 44mm at the throttle butterflies, this necked down to 36mm at the venturis. U.S. versions initially received different jetting to those in other markets, but all versions were standardized after July 15 1987. The Weber, although theoretically a suitable carburetor for the Ducati engine, and despite several factory updates, never really worked as well as the separate Dell'Ortos. It also required a fuel pump that was located outside the fuel tank. One of the reasons the Weber didn't work as well as the Dell'Ortos was the fuel pump provided excessive pressure, causing richness and flooding. The exhaust system was also considerably more complex than that of other Pantahs, with a large four-way swirl-type collector underneath the engine. It also saw an end to the distinctive finned exhaust header retaining nuts that had featured on all previous Pantahs. For the first time a Ducati engine actually produced respectable horsepower, despite effective silencing. Claimed power was 72.5 HP at 7,900 rpm, with 7.7 kg/m of torque at 6,350 rpm. From October 1988 the 750 Paso was also designed to use 95 octane unleaded fuel. Until number 750130 the final drive was by Regina 3/8- x 5/8-inch DA-OR 136 chain, becoming a DA-OR 135 1/4- x 5/8-inch, with new sprockets, after number 750131.

Ignition, Electrical System, and Switches

Much of the electrical system was also derived from the 750 F1, but with increased complexity. Ignition was

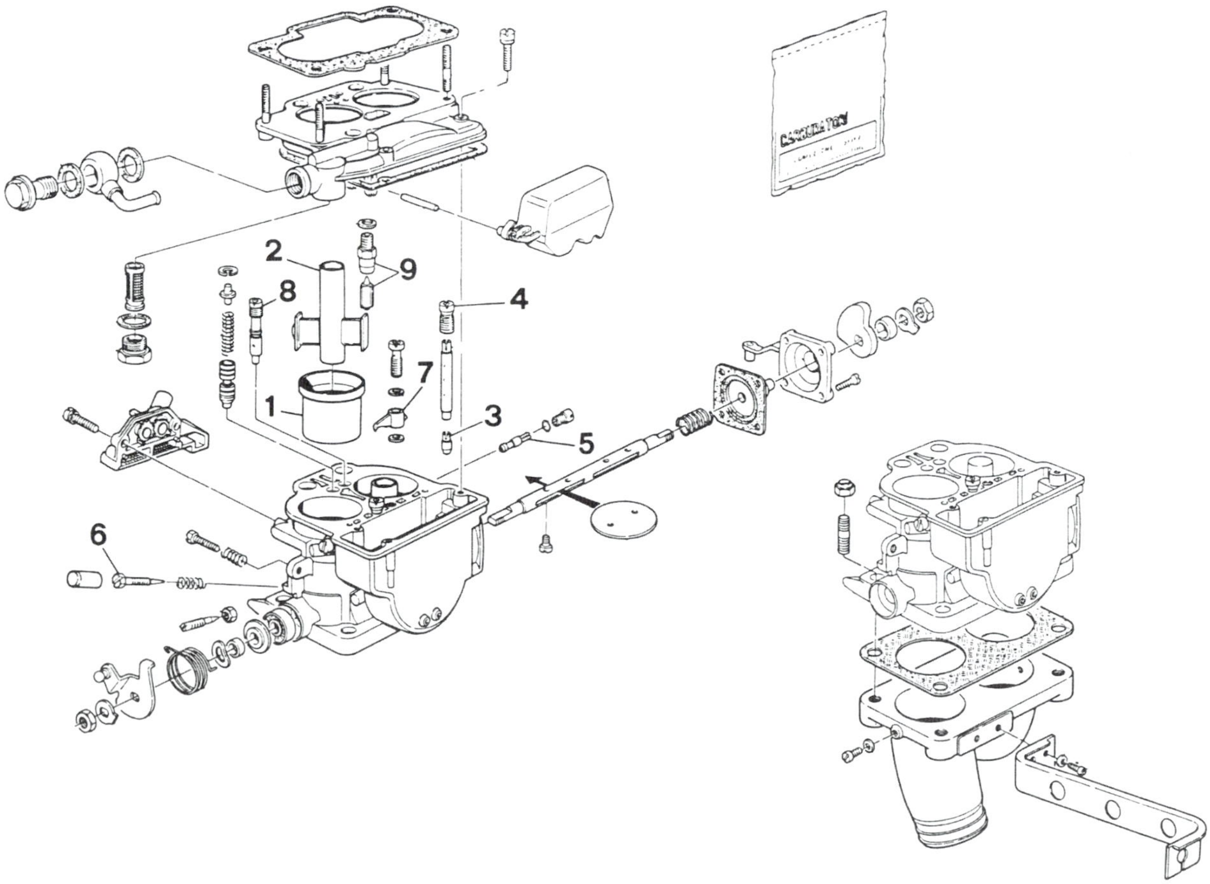

The Weber 44DCNF 107 carburetor as fitted to the 750 Paso. While good in theory, adapting the automotive-style unit to a motorcycle proved problematic.

the two-stage Kokusan of the 1987 F1, 6 degrees of advance up to 1,700 rpm, with a progressive advance up to 32 degrees from 1,700 to 2,600 rpm. The coils were mounted on the outside of the front frame downtubes, contributing to the generally ugly look of the 750 Paso with the bodywork removed. After frame number 750056 there was a new wiring harness (and handlebar switches).

Where the 750 Paso did deviate from other Ducatis was in the headlight, handlebar switches and instrument panel. Two types of H4 55/60-watt headlight were fitted, both measuring 271 x 125mm. All right-dip models had a CEV 319, while left-dip models featured a superior Japanese Koito unit. The instrument panel featured a plastic cover, and Veglia instruments: a 160-mph (240-km/h) speedometer, 9,000-rpm-redline tachometer, fuel level and oil temperature gauges, and an analog clock. There were also eight warning lights. Unfortunately the instruments were prone to failure, particularly the speedometer and clock, and it wasn't until 1991 that Veglia-Borletti modified the components to prevent electrical interference. All-new Japanese switches were used on the Paso, these also used on the next generation of Ducatis. The general expansion in the level of electrical equipment was

A new instrument panel and switches were used on the 750 Paso. Details such as the milled aluminum triple clamp and handlebars were superior to those of earlier Ducatis.

The Paso's large rectangular headlight dominated Tamburini's full-coverage bodywork.

With integral indicators and taillight, the rear end styling treatment of the 750 Paso was very tidy.

reflected in the addition of an ignition-operated electric fuel pump, necessary for the Weber carburetor.

Frame and Cycle Parts

While the 750 Paso engine was largely derived from the 750 F1, when it came to the chassis and running gear the Paso was unlike any previous model of Ducati. The impetus for the design of the Paso came more from the Bimota DB1 than the F1, although with square-section steel tubing rather than the tubular space frame. In another radical departure for Ducati, the frame was a traditional double-downtube, full-cradle design, conveniently leaving the rear cylinder head exposed for easier servicing.

Frame numbers started at ZDM 750 P 750001, with U.S. models having frame numbers 751081 to 751480 in 1986-87. Compared to the F1, the frame had a steeper rake (25 degrees), and a 60mm (2.36 inches) longer swingarm. The three Pantah engine mounting bosses were used as stiffening members and the lower cradle tubes unbolted to aid servicing. It was in the design of the rear suspension that the Paso exhibited most advances over the F1. The aluminum swingarm (with eccentric chain adjusters) no longer pivoted solely in bronze bushes in the engine crankcases, but was additionally supported on outside frame plates by two needle roller bearings. Three linkages operated the single shock absorber, these also being supported by needle roller bearings. This Soft Damp system was considerably more sophisticated and effective than that of the F1, if contributing to weight and complexity.

The early 750 Paso also came with high-quality suspension components. Front suspension was by the new racing-inspired Marzocchi 41.7mm M1R forks. These used the left fork leg to control compression damping and the right to control rebound damping. A knob at the base of the fork leg controlled the rebound damping, and a tapered inner rod in the left leg also provided progressive compression damping. While these forks were very sophisticated for the mid-1980s, the M1Rs were soon superseded by more advanced designs. At

Underneath the bodywork, however, the Paso was unlike any previous Ducati. The steel frame was constructed in rectangular-section tubing. The 750 had twin oil radiators on each side.

the rear the first 979 750 Pasos were fitted with an Öhlins CA 508, with an external hydraulic spring-preload adjuster along with adjustable rebound damping. After frame number 750980 a Marzocchi Supermono shock absorber was fitted, this an inferior unit to the Öhlins. With the Marzocchi it was very important to keep the shock absorber charged at 10 Bar, otherwise the unit will feel very underdamped.

Integral to the design of the 750 Paso were the 16-inch wheels. These were aluminum Oscam, a 3.75 x

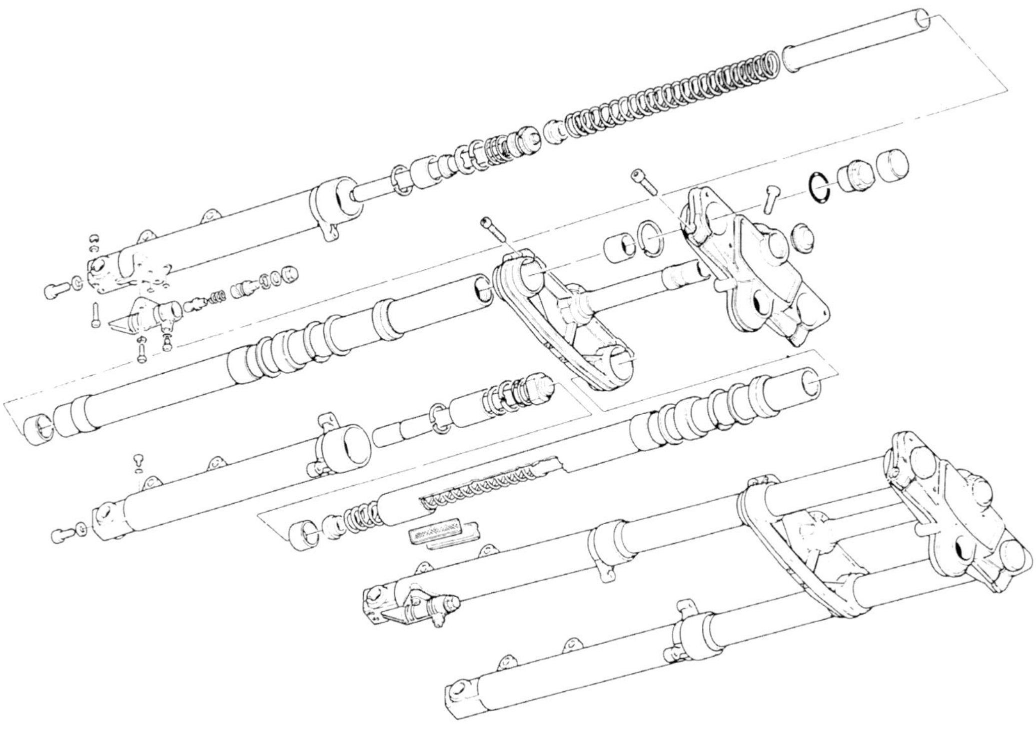

The 41.7mm Marzocchi M1R forks as fitted to the 750 and 906 Pasos, as well as the 907 Ie, represented a significant step forward from earlier designs.

Also new for the 750 Paso were the 16-inch Oscam wheels and 280mm discs. Tires were a new-generation low-profile Pirelli radial.

There were many superior details on the 750 Paso. The aluminum swingarm featured eccentric chain adjusters and the footpeg brackets were milled aluminum.

16-inch on the front and a 5.00 x 16-inch on the rear. Tires fitted were a new-generation radial, until frame number 750499 these were Michelin A59PLTL and M59PLTL. After frame number 750500 tires were Pirelli MP7S. The brakes were also new for the Paso, the 280mm front and 270mm discs mounted directly onto the wheel, without disc centers. Calipers were twin Brembo P2F08N on the front and a P2108N on the rear. The front master cylinder was a new type with a rectangular reservoir (along with a similar clutch master cylinder), with a remote-reservoir rear master cylinder. Much of the other equipment represented a departure from Ducati's traditional equipment. The Paso had completely new footpegs and levers, and enclosed fiberglass bodywork. For the first time on a Ducati, heim-type ball joints were used on both ends of the gearshift and brake levers, and the footpeg brackets were cast aluminum. Yet this was nothing compared to the styling of the Paso. With its solid screen and integral mirror/indicators, the 750 Paso was such a radical departure from previous Ducatis it took some time to be accepted. Initially only in red for 1986, for 1987 the Paso was also available in blue and white. In the U.S. this was a limited-edition model sold at a premium price ($7,195 instead of $6,695), also identified by Limited decals on either side of the fairing. There were also 100 of a more-powerful red 750 Paso for the U.S. However, in all guises the 750 Paso was never very successful in America, with many of the total of 2,562 being re-exported to Europe in 1991.

1988-90

While production of the 750 Paso ended in late 1988 with 405 red and 155 blue models for the U.S., stocks were such that the model was offered through until the 1990 model year. The final versions started at frame number 752608. Prior to that, from frame number 752155 there was a new exhaust system, with 40mm exhaust headers and new mufflers. U.S. models received a different exhaust system from European versions. California models also received the Marelli Digiplex MED 441-442 ignition system of the 906 Paso. These required resistor-type Champion RAY6C spark plugs, otherwise the ignition could lose synchronization and cause misfiring. Also for 1989-90 floating 280mm front discs (492 4007 1A) became available, fully homologated, and a bolt-on alternative to the earlier type. Although it was only produced for two years total, 750 Paso production was considerably more than the F1 at 4,863.

Up-Rating Kit For 750 Paso (699 2 005 1A)

In August 1988 the factory released a racing up-rating kit that allowed a 10-12 km/h (6-8 mph) top speed improvement. For pre-July 15 1987 750 Pasos it was also necessary to install the updated Weber carburetor jetting (see Appendix). This is also a useful general modification kit for improved road performance.

Qty	Part	Part no.
1	40 Horizontal exhaust pipe (up to Frame no. 752124)	0370.84.023
1	40 Vertical exhaust pipe (up to Frame no. 752124)	0370.84.033
1	R.H. Muffler	573 1 003 1A
1	L.H. Muffler	574 1 003 1A
1	Ignition flywheel 36 degrees advance (up to Frame no. 752756)	0370.46.470
2	Air corrector jet 175	0370.27.052
2	Main jet 155	0370.27.082
1	Engine cover gasket, flywheel side	0660.49.135

906 Paso

The evolution of the 750 Paso continued in late 1988 with the 906. Most of the changes between the 750 and the 906 occurred in the engine, which was now based on the new 851 large crankcase four-valve engine. Thus, with a six-speed gearbox rather than the 750's five-speed, the new bike was called the 906 — the 6 to indicate the six speeds. Actual capacity of the 906 was 904cc, for while the bore of 92mm was shared with the 851, an extra 4mm of stroke, to 68mm, gave additional displacement. The other new development was water-cooling.

Engine and Drivetrain

Engine numbers for the 906 started at ZDM 904SC 000001, and despite an increase in engine length and height of 10mm, it still fitted the 750 Paso frame. The top end was quite different to the 750. Not only were the valves larger (43mm inlet and 38mm exhaust), but there were new camshafts with higher valve lift (11.10mm inlet and 10.56mm exhaust). The valve timing was the same, but with steeper ramps. Although the valves were still inclined at 60 degrees, the combustion chamber on the 906 was a new tri-spherical design. This was called tri-spherical because the cylinder heads were now machined in three stages by centering milling machines first in each valve guide, followed by the spark plug seat. The result was a more consistently shaped combustion chamber, the ridges formed at the intersection of the three machining operations ensuring a reasonable compression ratio, even with flat-topped pistons. Turbulence was also increased through

The 906 Paso wasn't the first water-cooled Ducati. This modified Pantah was spotted at the factory as far back as 1981.

Although the 906 Paso looked superficially similar to the 750, underneath there were a large number of differences.

the large squish band, historically a typical Ducati feature that contributed to excellent fuel consumption and combustion. The flat-topped three-ringed 92mm pistons were also H-section, but used a 19mm wrist pin (up from 18mm on the 750, while the similar 92mm 851 piston featured a 20mm wrist pin) and provided only 9.2:1 compression. From engine number 001313 completely new pistons, rings and cylinder assemblies were fitted. The top piston ring was now L-shaped and these pistons and cylinders were not interchangeable with the earlier type. As on the 851 Desmoquattro the piston crowns were cooled with oil sprayed from nozzles underneath. The lower end was also stronger. With an extra 6.5mm of stroke over the 750, con rod length grew from 124mm to 130mm. Because of the necessity to keep the engine as short as possible, this gave a con rod length to stroke ratio of 1.91:1. An ideal 140mm con rod would have led to an increase in engine height of another 10mm, compromising weight distribution and requiring a different frame. Big-end bearing size increased to 42mm from the 40mm on the 750, while the main bearing shafts were still 35mm.

The 906 was no beauty unclothed. Here are the clothed and unclothed 906 outside the factory at Bologna.

The riding position of the 906 Paso was moderately sporty, the larger engine boosting overall performance over the 750. This is an early red-and-white example.

The crankcases, primary drive and gearbox were shared with the 1989 series 851. In every respect these were stronger than those of the 750 (and the earlier 851), particularly around the cylinder base where the contact area was increased to give a more stable base to the cylinders. This was as a result of problems with excessive oil blow-by out of the crankcase breather, eventually solved by the installation of a reed valve at the end of the breather. There were also larger ball bearings fitted to both primary and secondary shafts in the gearbox. On the clutch side the bearing was increased to 62mm (from 52mm), as well as on the output drive side behind the front sprocket. This meant that the gearbox shafts were relocated on the crankcase for a greater center-to-center clearance, requiring new tooling for the larger crankcases. It also resulted in fewer lower-end parts that were now interchangeable between the Pantah (up to 750cc), and the 904. The gears of the six-speed gearbox were also wider to handle the increase in torque, and to reduce the

While most 906 Pasos were red, some were also blue and black. This is a later blue example, with LIQUID COOLED decals on the fairing.

torque and speed up the clutch there was also a new set of straight-cut primary-drive gears with a ratio of 2:1 (62/31). This seemed a strange choice of ratio as there was no hunting tooth to spread the load and they sometimes broke. Surprisingly, this primary-drive ratio would be used for the next ten years in large-crankcase engines. The hydraulically operated dry clutch (14 plates) was the same as the 750 Paso, (and 1988 851). For 1990 there was an important change to the clutch when the actuation assembly was moved to the left side of the engine (as with the 1989 851), well away from the clutch plates. While this solved some of the bearing and sealing problems of the earlier type, the 1990 851 Strada received a modified clutch control piston and second sealing ring that for some reason wasn't fitted to the 906. All these clutch slave cylinders were problematic. Another development with the larger engine was the new timing belt covers that allowed

Weber Carburetor Heater Kit: 750/906 Paso 750 Sport, 900 Supersport 1990 (699 2 034 1A)

In February 1992 the factory released a Weber carburetor heating kit in response to carburetor icing in severe and wet weather conditions.

Ref.	Code	Qty	Description
1	802 2 002 1A	2	Hot air intake pipe
2	061992595	2	Clamp 32mm-50mm
3	0000 44099	1	Flanged spacer
4	0000 41583	1	Flanged spacer
5	771 5 073 2B	1	Socket head screw M6mm x 40mm
6	734006N01	1	Spring washer 6.2mm
7	0000 41582	1	Vibration damper
8	0000 63150	1	M5 threaded insert (750 Sport and Paso)
8A	036499020	1	M6 threaded insert (900 SS and 906 Paso)
9	771 5 043 2B	1	Socket head screw M5mm x 20mm (750 Sport and Paso)
9A	60N102509	1	Socket head screw M6mm x 20mm (900 SS and 906 Paso)
10	60N115548	1	Flat washer 5.3mm x 15mm x 1mm (750 Sport and Paso)
10A	075549310	1	Flat washer 6.2mm x 16mm x 1.5mm (900 SS and 906 Paso)
11	484 1 018 1A	1	Hot air conveyor duct

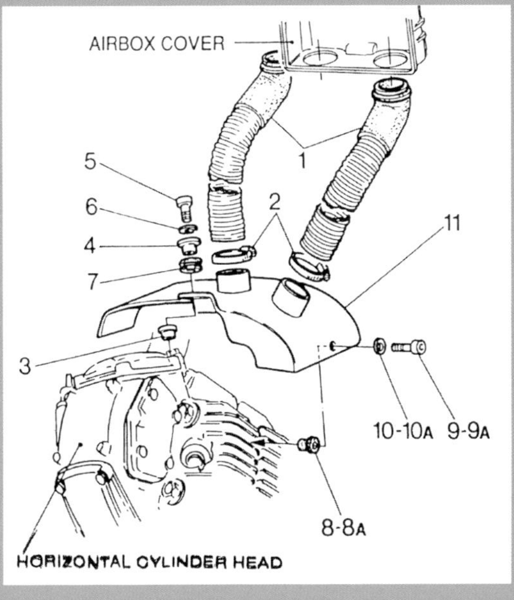

The factory Weber carburetor heating kit ducted warm air from the front cylinder to the airbox.

for the adjustment and checking of belt tension without removal of the complete cover. The belts and pulleys were stronger, now with round rather than square teeth, with an updated tensioner. Final drive was by Regina 135-OR 1/4- x 5/8-inch chain with 15- and 40-tooth sprockets. During 1989 the gearing was also raised to 15/38.

The cooling system was shared with the 851, and included the water pump driven off the left side of the camshaft driveshaft, the cylinders and radiator. The dual oil coolers of the 750 Paso were no longer fitted. Carburetion was by a Weber 44DCNF 116 twin-choke downdraft carburettor, with slightly revised jetting, and because of the improved engine cooling the carburetion was finally improved. However, although the intakes were between the base of the two cylinders in an attempt to minimize carburetor icing in cold weather, this was only moderately successful. The claimed power for the 906 went up to 88 HP at 8,000 rpm, and all 906 Pasos were designed for 95 octane unleaded fuel.

Ignition, Electrical System, and Switches

Along with water-cooling, another advance was the installation of Digiplex Magneti Marelli digital electronic ignition. With this unit ignition advance was monitored by crankshaft rpm in addition to inlet manifold vacuum, in accordance with throttle valve opening. Five mapped ignition advance curves for different manifold pressure and rpm were programmed into an EPROM inside the Digiplex electronic unit. This also included an input for electronic analysis. With the Digiplex ignition came new Marelli coils, the vertical cylinder coil located on the left frame downtube and the horizontal cylinder coil under the fuel tank. There was also a new flywheel (5 teeth) and pickup, with a crucial air gap of 0.5mm-0.7mm, and it was important to use a resistor-type spark plug like the recommended Champion RAY6C. Non-resistor types could cause voltage surge to the electronic unit, affecting the ignition timing. The equivalent NGK was a DPR8EA-9, and Nippon Denso a X24EPR-U9. With the 906 came a new regulator (540 400 11A) with an improved connection to the regulator body, less susceptible to failure from vibration. After March 1989 this regulator was standardized on the rest of the range. Apart from a 350-watt alternator and larger 12 V-19-Ah battery, all the other electrical equipment, lights, instruments and switches were shared with the 750 Paso. All 906s came with the CEV headlight.

Frame and Cycle Parts

Frame numbers for the 906 Paso started at ZDM 906 PC 000001, but the frame was unchanged from the 750, with the same 25-degree steering head angle. The reduction in trail, from 103mm (4 inches) to 96mm (3.8 inches) was achieved through a slight increase in fork offset and ensured the front wheel didn't hit the front cylinder with the forks on full compression. This required a 20mm-longer Marzocchi M1R 41.7mm fork, providing 15mm (0.6 inch) less travel. The Soft Damp rising-rate rear suspension was identical to the 750 Paso, initially with a Marzocchi 38mm Duo-Shock, providing 135mm (5.3 inches) of wheel travel through an 80mm (3.15 inches) stroke. This allowed external compression damping along with rebound damping adjustment, but spring preload was by a normal threaded collar. The shock was the same unit as fitted to the 1989 851 Strada and it was important that the gas pressure was set at 8 kg/cm^2. From frame number 001303, the 906 Paso was fitted with a simpler Marzocchi Supermono shock absorber. Providing 136mm (5.35 inches) of rear wheel travel, this had an external hydraulic spring preload adjuster (similar to the early 750's Öhlins), a rebound adjuster at the base of the shock absorber, but no compression damping adjustment.

The white-painted 16-inch Oscam wheels and Michelin radial tires were the same as the 750, as were the Brembo brakes. The passenger grab handle was now black anodized aluminum. Unfortunately, despite the power increase, the downside to all this extra engine sophistication was in the claimed increased weight to 205kg (452 pounds). This figure was quite optimistic, *Cycle* magazine in November 1989 weighing the 906 Paso in at a rather heavy 518 pounds wet. Colors of the 906 Paso were either red and white, or dark blue and white. Along with 906 PASO, LIQUID COOLED decals on either side of the fairing also distinguished it from the 750, though this only appeared on later 906s, as most early bikes didn't have these decals. The elephant logo was no longer included with the DUCATI decals. Production of the 906 Paso commenced in 1988 in red, blue, and metallic black for Europe. For the U.S. 250 red and 100 blue 906 Pasos were built in late 1988, these being sold through 1990. The Swiss market received a different version, and there were a further red and 100 black built for Europe in 1990. Total production of the 906 Paso however was considerably less than for the 750 at 1,802.

Modifications To The 750 And 906 Paso

With the Paso, Ducati endeavored to mate the automotive Weber twin-choke downdraft carburetor with a motorcycle engine, a concept theoretically viable but less than satisfactory in practice. Notwithstanding several factory jetting updates, the Weber always seemed to produce a flat spot between 4,100 and 4,500 rpm, and lacked the easy adjustment offered by the earlier Dell'Ortos. Another problem with the Weber was that regular maintenance was essential to ensure consistent performance, and the Weber was a more complex carburetor to service. A problem caused by excessive fuel pressure saw fuel overflow down the venturi into the front cylinder. This not only resulted in fuel infiltrating the engine oil but also damaged the float chamber gasket. These problems could be alleviated by the installation of a fuel pressure regulator and setting it at 3 psi. The size of the idle jet also affected the fuel pressure, and after July 1987 a smaller (57) jet was used. While the Weber undoubtedly worked better on the water-cooled 906, it was still inferior to the electronic fuel injection of the 907 I.E. and ST2.

Many owners opted to replace the Weber carburetor altogether. Malossi offered a bolt-on 40mm carburetor kit, but 36mm Dell'Ortos could also be fitted, albeit with some difficulty. Both these required the replacement of the stock airbox with separate K&N filters. A K&N filter was also available as a replacement for the stock air filter. The Dell'Orto conversion could also be affected by excessive fuel pressure, but the Dell'Orto overflow was through external vent holes. Another alternative was to fit the Mikuni carburetor setup from a post-1991 750/900 Supersport or a Keihin FCR conversion. With either of these alternatives the stock airbox will need to be replaced by individual K&Ns, or similar, air filters. Installation of the racing kit flywheel (0370.46.470) giving 36 degrees of advance can also improve the general rideability of earlier 750 Pasos.

There were also some problems with the lining up of the engine and rear wheel sprocket, causing chain misalignment on some 750 and 906 Pasos. If not rectified this could result in the chain breaking. The factory realized this and supplied an alternative countershaft sprocket plate (827 1044 1A). Water-cooled bikes benefit from the fitting of protective mesh over the radiator. On the 906 (and 907 I.E.) the radiator is Japanese and already fitted with brackets for a protective grille. These models also lend themselves to a capacity increase to 944cc through a 2mm overbore, to 94mm, as the cooling is not the problem it can be with air-cooled models.

A useful modification to all Pasos (and the 907 I.E.), is the substitution of the CEV headlight with the Koito as fitted to the left-dip 750 Paso. This is also the same unit as fitted to the 1985-86 Yamaha FZ750. All engines responded well to slip-on replacement mufflers, and several alternative exhaust systems were also available for all models. A problem associated with the 16-inch wheels and low-profile tires fitted to the 750 and 906 Paso was limited ground clearance. Fitting higher-profile tires (130/70 and 150/80) could rectify this, but often caused problems with front fender clearance and ride height. Raising the ride height of the Paso steepened the already steep steering head angle, creating a tendency for the front wheel to tuck in. Despite contemporary reports stating the Paso was an improvement in handling over the 750 F1, in standard trim both the 750 and 906 were quite disappointing. There was a tendency toward understeer that was associated with the wheel size and tire profile, and they exhibited a noticeable tendency to stand up while braking in corners. It is possible to install the 17-inch wheels from a post-1991 750 Supersport or 900 CR on both the 750 and 906 Paso. However, this will require new brake caliper brackets and a spacer for the speedometer drive. With 120/60-17 and 160/60-17-inch tires the correct geometry can be maintained. The standard rear Marzocchi suspension unit worked satisfactorily but it was important to maintain the gas pressure at 6 Atmospheres. At the front the forks worked better with 5-weight rather than 10-weight fork oil.

907 I.E.

After only two years the significantly improved 907 I.E. replaced the 906 Paso for 1991. Gone was the Paso name and the 907 I.E. (*Iniezione Elettronica*) drew even more on the technological improvements seen on the 851, not only in the engine, but also the chassis. Finally, with the 907 I.E., Ducati seemed to have created a homogeneous sport-touring motorcycle that could compete with anything on offer from Germany or Japan.

With the 907 I.E. there were a number of significant improvements over the 750 and 906, and the 907 was amongst the best sport-touring motorcycles available. This 1991 example has non-standard Staintune mufflers and a rack for Givi luggage.

1991 Model Year

Engine and Drivetrain

Essentially the water-cooled 904cc, six-speed unit of the 906 carried over to the 907 I.E. but for 1991 all large-crankcase models had new crankcases, along with a new number sequence. This began at ZDM 904 W2 000001. Following the rather dramatic series of crankcase failures Raymond Roche suffered on his way to winning the 1990 World Superbike Championship, the crankcases were updated with more extensive internal webbing and ribbing, especially around the cylinder support base. The crankcases were black, as was the clutch cover. Most other engine specifications were as for the 906, the pistons and rings the modified set as fitted to the 906 Paso after engine number 001313, still with the 9.2:1 compression ratio. While the 1990 906 hadn't received the modified clutch control piston and second sealing ring of the 1990 851 Strada, the 907 I.E. had this modification. The clutch was also revised for 1991. Previous larger belt-drive twins used a 14-plate clutch, but the 907 I.E. (like the 1991 900 Supersport) had a 16-plate unit. Seven driven plates (2mm thick), seven driving plates (3mm), one curved plate (1.5mm), and one inner driving plate (3.5mm). As with other large-crankcase models, a close-ratio racing six-speed gearbox was also available. The cooling system too was slightly revised, with the water temperature sensor located next to the thermostatic switch for the fan rather than on the front cylinder head. Final drive was by 15- and 40-tooth sprockets, with a 108-link Regina 135-OR 1/4- x 5/8-inch chain.

It was to the intake system of the 907 I.E. that most of the changes took place. The air intakes were repositioned up by the steering head, drawing in colder, denser air. Early models suffered from interference between the air filter fasteners and the fuel tank, but this was rectified in May 1991 with new screws and bushes. Because electronic fuel injection replaced the troublesome Weber carburetor all the problems with carburetor icing and poor low-speed running disappeared. With black canister-style mufflers from the 1990 series 750 Paso, claimed power for the 907 I.E. increased to 90 HP at 8,500 rpm.

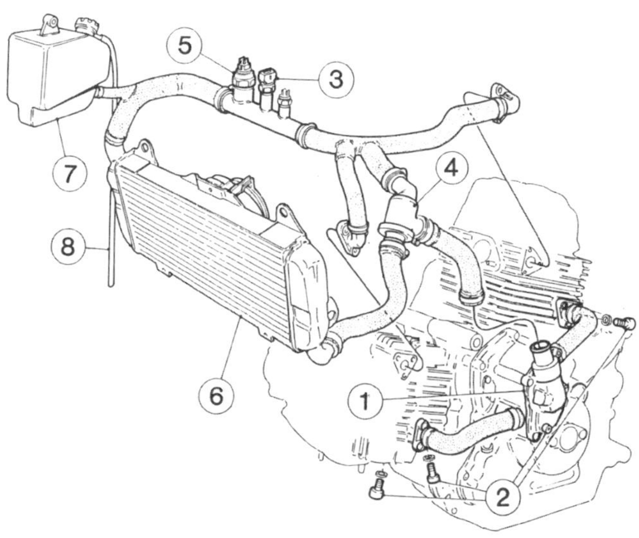

The cooling system of the 907 I.E. was similar to that of the 906 Paso with the water pump on the left side of the engine.

Without the bodywork the 907 I.E. was hardly a beautiful machine. This has the standard mufflers.

Ignition, Injection, and Electrics

By adapting the single-injector P7 Weber I.A.W. electronic fuel injection system of the 851 Strada to the two-valve 906 engine, the engine not only produced more power, but also ran more cleanly. The throttle bodies were 42mm (down from the 50mm of the 851), with the single injectors coming from the dual-injector 851 SP. The 023 EPROM was also changed from the 851, with the U.S. receiving yet a different, 023U EPROM. As the P7 electronic unit also controlled the ignition, the flywheel and pickup were similar to those used on the 906 Paso. There was an engine pickup mounted in front of the flywheel reading the four teeth around it, with a cam pickup mounted in front of the timing gear reading the tooth above it. This provided an exact reference for the relationship between phase and rpm for both ignition and injection timing. Other sensors included a throttle position potentiometer, air temperature sensor, water temperature sensor, and air pressure sensor. Spark plugs were Champion RA4HC. While the instrument panel was carried over, the 907 I.E. received modified Veglia instruments that were

The injection system consists of the following components:

1) Electronic device
2) Power module (one each cylinder)
3) Relays with fuses
4) Battery
5) Coil (one each cylinder)
6) Electro-injector (one each cylinder)
7) Air temperature sensor
8) Absolute pressure sensor
9) Pressure adjustment
10) Throttle potentiometer
11) Phase sensor
12) Timing driven gear
13) Motor flywheel
14) Revolution number sensor
15) Water temperature sensor
16) Fuel pump
17) Fuel filter

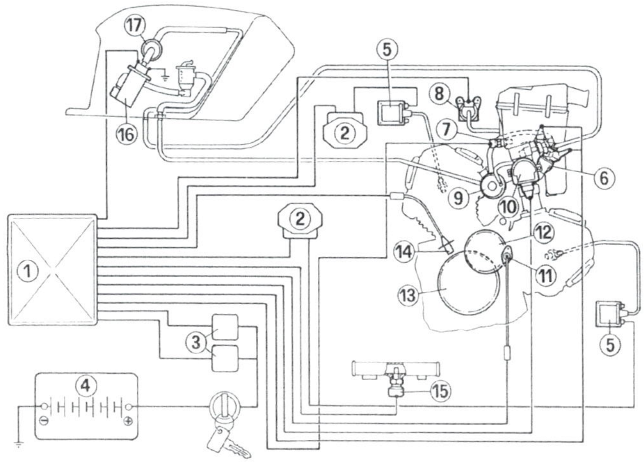

The electronic fuel injection system of the 907 I.E.

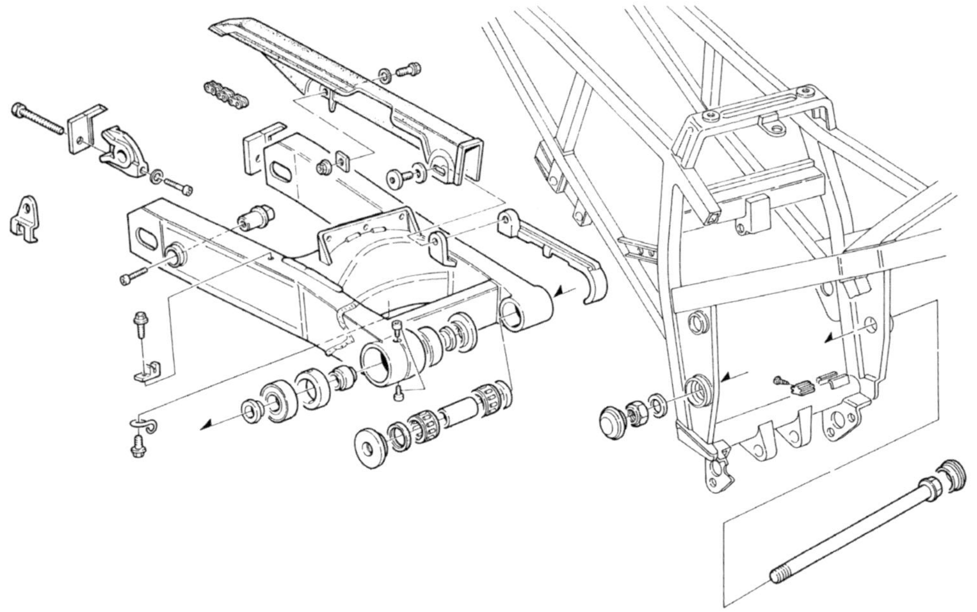

The 907 I.E. swingarm was similar to that on the 851 Strada and well supported by additional frame-mounted needle bearings.

more reliable. All other electrical equipment, including switches, was shared with the 906 Paso.

Frame and Cycle Parts

There were new frame numbers for the 907 I.E. starting at ZDM 906 PI 2 000001, and while the basic rectangular-section steel double-cradle frame with a 25-degree steering head angle was that of the 906, the longer aluminum swingarm and axle adjusters came from the 851 Strada. Rear suspension was still the Soft-Damp system, but saw a return to the more adjustable 38 Marzocchi Duo-Shock Remoto, now with only a 66mm stroke. This translated into 122mm (4.8 inches) of rear wheel travel. Pressure for the gas-charged Marzocchi shock absorber was 8 Atmospheres, and for good performance it was essential that this be maintained. The front suspension was as before, but with 10mm-longer fork legs so that the larger wheel/tire combination would clear the engine on fork compression. This also required less, 125mm (4.92 inches), of wheel travel from the 41.7mm Marzocchi M1R forks that incorporated anti-dive. The biggest changes were to the wheels and brakes. White-painted three-spoke Brembo 17-inch, a MT3.50 x 17 on the front and MT5.50 x 17 on the rear, replaced the 16-inch wheels. This allowed for Michelin TX11 ZR17 tires, although this compromised the height of the front of the motorcycle, as the front wheel was 40mm taller than before. The only street specification front tire available at that time was a 120/70 x 17-inch tire, although a 60-series would have been preferable.

The brakes were also upgraded with 300mm stainless steel front discs with Brembo four-piston P4.32d calipers. At the rear the disc was reduced in size to that of the 851, 245mm, and a smaller P2.105N Brembo caliper used. The front rectangular Brembo PS16 (16mm) master cylinder was retained, with a Brembo

Amongst the most noticeable improvements over the 906 Paso were the 907's 17-inch wheels and four-piston Brembo calipers. This 1991 model has 300mm discs.

The fairing on the 907 I.E. incorporated a NACA duct to smooth the airflow.

PS11 (11mm) at the rear. The larger wheels (and longer swingarm) led to an increase in both wheelbase (1490mm/58.66 inches), and trail (107mm/4.21 inches), but overall the steering and handling characteristics were vastly superior to those of the 906 Paso. All the footpegs and levers were similar to the 906, and while the style of the bodywork was similar to the 906, the solid 907 I.E. screen incorporated a NACA duct, supposedly to smooth the airflow. Much larger DUCATI decals were on the tank than on the 906. Colors for 1991 were red only, and while there was one show example built in 1989, most for 1991 were produced toward the end of 1990.

1992 Model Year

The 907 I.E. continued for 1992 with only minor changes. From April 1992, the clutch was revised. Still with 16 plates, another 2mm driven plate replaced the previous 3.5mm inner driving plate. The composition of the plates was also altered so the 1.5mm curved plate was now inserted after the first driving plate. The exhaust system now included aluminum-covered exhaust canisters instead of black. Final drive was now by a DID 520 VL2 5/8- x 1/4-inch chain. General engine specifications were unchanged, although power was now quoted at the rear wheel, 78 HP at 8,500rpm.

There were also a few updates to the chassis, notably the braking system. At the front, larger, 320mm front discs, were fitted, along with gold Brembo P4.30-34

For the final 907 I.E. of 1992 black was an alternative color to red. Other changes were to the mufflers and brakes. The front discs were 320mm with gold Brembo P4.30-34 brake calipers.

brake calipers. Later these became P4.30-34C, distinguished by a blue paint mark. Standard tires were now Michelin A/M59X on white-painted Brembo wheels. Along with red, the 907 I.E. was also available in black for 1992. For some reason the 907 I.E. wasn't as popular as anticipated. Although it offered improved power and reliability, plus more sophisticated rear suspension than the Supersport models, sales were disappointing. The 907 I.E. was also a very well developed all-round motorcycle, with excellent handling and comfort. After reasonable numbers being produced for 1991, only 500 were initially built for the 1992 model year, including 221 black examples. During 1992 only red 907 I.E.s were produced, and with slowing sales the 907 I.E. was discontinued. There wouldn't be a replacement sport-touring Ducati until 1997.

ST2

The first new model to be released after the Texas Pacific Group buyout of Ducati in September 1996 was the Sport Touring 2. Styled by Miguel Galluzzi for Cagiva, the ST2 was really a remnant of the Cagiva era and had been ready for production sometime earlier. However, this sport-touring Ducati was not a continuation of the line first begun with the 750 Paso, even though the engine drew heavily on that of the 907 I.E. First displayed at the Cologne and Bologna Shows at the end of 1996, the ST2 went into production in April 1997. Compared to the 907 I.E., the ST2 represented another step forward by incorporating color-matched hard bags by Nonfango. In other respects, though, the ST2 was a more modern rendition of the sport-touring concept first exhibited by the 750 Paso back in 1985.

1997 Model Year

Engine and Drivetrain

While drawing heavily on the 906 and 907 I.E., the ST2 featured more displacement and an updated Weber electronic fuel injection system. Engine numbers began at ZDM 944 W2 000001, the W indicating water-cooling, and the engine cases were gray. The capacity increase was achieved through a 2mm overbore, to 94mm, and the familiar tri-spherical combustion chambers retained. However, taking advantage of the benefits of water-cooling allowed the compression ratio to be increased to 10.2:1. Valve sizes remained at 43mm and 38mm, but there were new desmodromic camshafts (for timing see Appendix). These provided 11.8mm of inlet valve lift and 11.4mm of exhaust valve lift. But for a heavier flywheel and alternator rotor, the lower end, including the six-speed gearbox, was as before, although the clutch composition was different. Carrying part number 19020013A, this 16-plate arrangement was shared with the 900 Supersport from

The first series of ST2 of 1997. Some were like this example, in red, although black and silver versions were also available.

Modifications To The 907 I.E. And ST2

With the 907 I.E. and ST2, a replacement EPROM was needed with any change to the exhaust or inlet system. In March 1999 the U.K. distributor issued a recall on the ST2 to replace the front sprocket retaining plate with one of stronger steel. In an extreme case the retaining plate could wear out, allowing the sprocket to work its way off the countershaft.

A wider range of accessories are available for the ST2, not only for increased engine performance, but also alternative Plexiglas screens (either taller or lower), and rear luggage racks and hard luggage. For the 750, 906, and 907 I.E., Givi luggage was available. Popular additions for all these sport-touring Ducatis are also handlebar raisers, or higher handlebars, and Corbin seats. For the 750 and 906 Paso, along with the 907 Corbin offered the Gunfighter and Gunfighter and Lady with backrest. The Corbin seat for the ST2 was a Dual Sport. Useful additions to the ST2 can be fitting the adjustable brake and clutch levers from the 900 Supersport, although these require a small modification to the ST2 mounts to fit.

1992. It comprised two 2mm driven plates, one 3mm driving plate, one 1.5mm convex plate, and six 2mm driven plates alternating with six 3mm driving plates. A significant improvement after many years was the increase in primary-drive ratio to 1.84:1 (32/59). This finally alleviated the breakage problems that sometimes occurred with the 2:1 ratio without any hunting tooth. Some earlier ST2s also had DUCATI cast in the right-side engine cover. Final-drive ratio was 15/42, with a 102-link D.I.D. 525 HV 5/8- x 5/16-inch chain with 10.16mm pins. The cooling system was similar to that of the earlier 906 and 907 I.E., although the radiator was a curved type. The electric fan activated at 103-degrees Celsius, controlled by the central processing unit. Claimed power for the ST2 was 83 HP at 8,500 rpm, now at the crankshaft rather than the rear wheel.

Ignition, Injection, and Electrics

The Marelli I.A.W. 1.6M injection system was shared with other electronically fuel injected Ducatis of that era. The ECU was a 1.6M-A0 with a Motorola 68HC11 chip and 067 EPROM. Unlike the P7, this 1.6M unit was a single channel, specifically designed for single-injection systems. This system used five sensors (without the rpm trigger on the crankshaft of the 907 I.E.), the phase and rpm determined by the ECU from the cam-drive jackshaft. Unfortunately there was also a byproduct of this system that could lead to a misfire around 3,400 rpm on constant throttle. Because the rpm sensor was now reading off the cam-drive shaft instead of the crankshaft, the variability of gear backlash could initiate a slight stumble as the computer tried to determine whether the engine was accelerating or decelerating. Unfortunately there was no software solution, the only remedy to re-shim the jackshaft or replace the jackshaft bearings. For the ST2, throttle bodies were increased to 44mm. As with the 907 I.E., spark plugs were Champion RA4HC. The general electrical system was upgraded with a 420-watt alternator and 12 volt/16-Ah battery. All the instruments and switches were new for the ST2. Along with traditional analog instrumentation, there was also a digital display indicating fuel consumption, fuel reserve, water temperature and a clock. The instrumentation was inspired by the Hypersport 916 range more than the Paso, with the 11,000-rpm tachometer taking pride of place and mounted in polyurethane foam. From number 000001 to 003343, there were problems with the fuel pump mount, causing problems when the fuel level was low or the operating temperature high. A new flexible fuel pump mount rectified this problem.

The instruments on the ST2 were inspired by the 916, but included a small digital display.

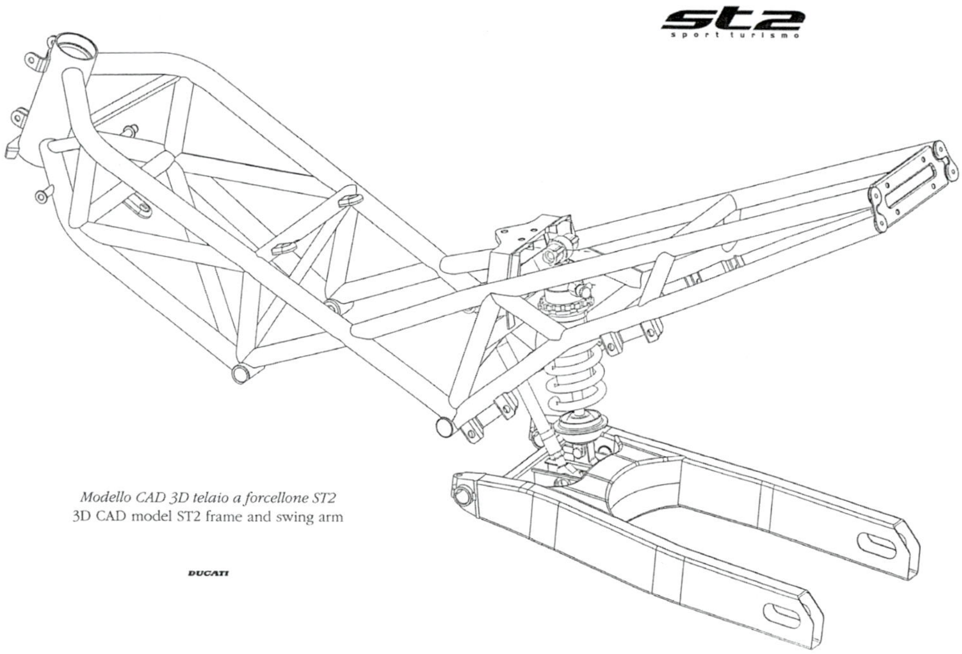

Modello CAD 3D telaio a forcellone ST2
3D CAD model ST2 frame and swing arm

With a tubular-steel frame and aluminum swingarm similar to that of the 888 and Monster, the ST2 featured a 916-style linkage for the single shock absorber.

Frame and Cycle Parts

If the ST2 engine appeared to be a development of the 907 I.E. unit, the frame and cycle parts bore no relationship to the earlier models. The Paso rectangular-section steel frame was consigned to the scrap heap and replaced by a trademark Ducati 916-gold tubular-steel unit constructed of ALS 450. This was based on that of the 851/888 and 900 M Monster, and more suited to 17-inch wheels than the Paso item that was designed back in 1985. Frame numbers started at ZDM S1 00AA 7 B 0000001 and the frame provided 24 degrees of steering head angle and 102mm (4 inches) of trail. Unlike the 907 I.E. that featured an aluminum swingarm, the ST2 had a steel swingarm, with a 916-style rear suspension linkage. Consisting of a rocker arm and adjustable tie-rod, the ride height was easily altered. Compared to the 916 the leverage ratio was changed, with more of a rising rate, and a

The ST2 unclothed, quite different to the earlier 907 I.E. and 906.

A production ST2 of 1997. This had the awkward curved side stand and short gearshift lever.

stiffer rate in the final half of the shock travel. Unlike the Paso, the swingarm now pivoted solely in needle bearings in the engine crankcases, but was undoubtedly not as well supported. Ing. Andrea Forni, Ducati's chief test engineer, justified the less rigid frame on the grounds that chassis stiffness was a compromise between rigidity and weight. Thus the ST2 frame was less torsionally rigid than the 916, but more so than the Supersport. Compared with the Paso, the suspension was superior. From the 916 were the 43mm Showa upside-down GD081 forks and 320mm stainless steel front disc brakes. One of the main advantages of the Showa forks was the larger-diameter 25mm (1 inch) axle, which was more rigid. Wheel travel was 130mm (5.12 inches). The front brake calipers were gold Brembo P4.30-34, with a PS16mm master cylinder. Compared to the 916 brakes the front P4.30-34 Brembo calipers had a wider bolt spacing for greater rigidity, and there were new lower fork legs to accommodate this spacing. At the rear was a remote-reservoir Showa GD082 shock absorber, the 65mm (2.56 inch) stroke translating into 148mm (5.82 inches) of wheel travel. The rear brake was a 245mm disc with a Brembo P32 caliper and PS11mm master cylinder. There were also new bronze-painted Brembo three-spoke wheels for the ST2. The rim sizes were unchanged from the 907 I.E. (3.50 and 5.50 inches), and specified tires were Metzeler TL MEZ4 or Michelin Macadam.

The bodywork and general level of equipment of the ST2 was unlike any earlier Ducati. The aspheric fairing-mounted mirrors were far superior to earlier offerings, and the option of side panniers contributed to the general practicality of the ST2. To accommodate the panniers the mufflers could be lowered, although this compromised ground clearance. Colors were red, black, or silver. There was also a safety recall on ST2s in January 1998, affecting bikes from 003040 to 003729, and requiring replacement of fuel lines inside the fuel tank. Production of the ST2 was quite healthy, numbers exceeding earlier Pasos in 1997 alone with 4,319 units. Only 800 ST2s were available in the US in 1997 due to delays in obtaining certification for the necessary emissions standards, and all these were 1998 model year specification.

The ST2 was the first Ducati with optional factory fitted luggage.

The silencers were adjustable to accommodate the panniers.

1998 Model Year

Because the ST2 went into production mid-model year, there were only a few changes for 1998. Most notable of these was the change in graphics to the new DUCATI logo, this no longer appearing on the tank, but only on the fairing. Other changes included a longer gearshift lever (from 003337), and a more accessible threaded shock absorber spring preload adjuster. Some later 1998 examples had a ramp-style preload adjuster. Following the introduction of the fuel-injected 900 Supersport, the forks and front brake calipers were shared, although they looked externally similar to before. The front Brembo calipers had a new piston surface treatment to reduce stiction, and different internal fluid passages. The colors were red, silver, and black, with the dull-gold frame and wheels, although red didn't appear to be available in the U.S. Model year 1998 production (until October) was 2,960 (10 percent of total production), 800 in Italy and 2,160 in the rest of the world. Interestingly, market research confirmed that 76 percent of ST2 purchasers were first-time Ducati purchasers.

Fully adjustable Showa forks and a Showa shock (threaded preload adjuster) were used, although it seems the ramp-style preload adjuster made it onto some of the later 98 models.

1999 Model Year

As this year saw the introduction of the ST4, for 1999 there were only small modifications to the ST2. Most of these were to the frame and cycle parts. From the 900 Supersport came a three-phase 520-watt alternator, and there were also new oil seals for the neutral light switch and oil pressure switch. An important improvement was a new side-stand, and there was yet another gearshift lever, this time from the Monster (45620091A). The headlight design was altered and a new Plexiglas cover included ventilation to prevent the fogging of the lens. There were also new wheels constructed of a new alloy with less silicon (GA/Si7), these being stronger and lighter, particularly around the wheel rim. 400gm was removed from the front rim, along with 900gm from the rear rim, reducing gyroscopic effect as well as unsprung weight.

There were also a few changes to the specification of the brakes for 1999. Both the PS16mm front brake master cylinder and PS13mm clutch master cylinder featured remote reservoirs, but not an adjustable lever. At the rear the Brembo P 32 brake caliper was upgraded to a P 34 (with 34mm piston). Initial plans called for the ST2 to receive higher handlebars, but this didn't eventuate. All Showa shock absorbers had a ramp-adjustable preload. Colors were expanded, with an additional metallic-blue available for 1999.

2000 Model Year

While basically as for 1999, there were a few additional refinements to the ST2 for the 2000 model year. There was now a SPORTTOURING logo on the fairing, as well as on the fuel cap, and protective treatment on the fairing to reduce damage from stones. At some stage during the year the plastic tank guard received an ST logo. Finally the automatic returning sidestand was eliminated, the new stand featuring a full-extension lock and anti-start sensor. There were new front disc rotors, these 320mm x 4mm with semi-floating aluminum carriers, and sintered high-friction brake pads. The PSC 16 master cylinder used technology developed from racing radial master cylinders, and braided steel brake lines were standard. The clutch master cylinder was revised, the smaller PSC 12mm master cylinder reducing lever effort by providing an increased hydraulic ratio. Other features included the removal of the rear splash guard and a specially made Kryptonite anti-theft padlock housed in a recess under the seat. To fully cater its role as a sport-tourer, there was now an electrical power output point to supply accessories or a special battery charger that reversed the current flow. This took a plug similar to that of the BMW. The frame and wheels were bronze, with colors of blue, red, or silver (red or blue in the U.S.). Color-matched luggage was also standard this year.

The ST2 continued largely unchanged for 1998 but for the new-style decals on the fairing. There was a new gearshift lever but not a new sidestand for this year. The ST2 was the first Ducati to come with the option of factory-fitted hard luggage.

2001 Model Year

The ST4S joined the range this year, so the ST2 was now the entry-level model in the sport-touring lineup. The engine featured new timing belt rollers, with stepless adjustment on the hub for more accurate valve timing. This also aided compliance with emissions standards. A redesigned, sealed, clutch slave cylinder was also included for 2001. This superior design used an O ring and longer housing to seal the slave cylinder against the engine casing. The suspension was the most basic in Ducati's lineup, the 43mm Showa fork, with inverted chrome-plated legs, only featuring spring preload adjustment. At the rear a fully adjustable Sachs shock absorber replaced the higher-spec Showa. Larger,

The 2000 Model ST2 came standard with luggage.

Some specifications of the ST2 were downgraded for 2001, as it became the entry-level model in the sport-touring lineup.

12mm engine bolts contributed to increased frame rigidity, and a lighter sealed-for-life battery improved maintenance. Color changes included a gunmetal gray frame and wheels, with a metallic-silver-gray engine. Bodywork was either silver, red, blue, or yellow this year.

2002 and 2003 Model Years

The ST2 engine was largely unchanged for 2002. An aluminum clutch housing and discs replaced the previous steel, and (except for the U.S.) the silencer incorporated a Euro 2-compliant catalytic converter. Colors were also unchanged this year.

With the three-valve ST3 waiting in the wings, 2003 was the final year for the ST2. Updates this year included a redesigned and improved gear selector drum. The new drum improved shifting action and precision, eliminating false neutrals between the gears. No longer available in the U.S., all versions were catalyzed, and again the range of colors was unchanged.

The final ST2 was for 2003. Largely unchanged, and about to be superseded by the ST3.

CHAPTER FIVE

750 Sport, 900 Supersport 1989-90, 400 Supersport Junior 1989

With the 750 F1 being phased out of production, and the 750 Paso becoming the sport-touring model in the new Cagiva-inspired Ducati lineup, the door was open for a new budget sporting Ducati in 1988 to complement the expensive new Desmoquattro 851. Titled the 750 Sport, Cagiva's replacement for the 750 F1 was cleverly intended to recall one of Ducati's most famous and desirable early 750s, the yellow 750 Sport of 1972-74. When released it was also sold for a price about half that of the 851 so it was an affordable Ducati. Unfortunately, because it was built to a budget, the *nuovo* 750 Sport suffered from insufficient development and poor quality components. On top of this it was beset with small problems throughout its limited production life. These included fuels tank splitting from vibration, and swingarms cracking.

750 Sport
1988

Released in June 1988, the 750 Sport was one of the first Ducatis conceived as an amalgam of existing parts. This parts-bin process had been evident a few years earlier with the bevel-drive 900 S2, but the 750 Sport took this idea further. Unlike the Paso, which was a completely new concept, the 750 Sport strove to expand the traditional Ducati sporting motorcycle approach that began with the 750 F1. In the process it moved away from the hard-edged race replica of the F1 toward a more refined product, and to keep costs down the 750 Sport combined many existing parts. The result saw a 750 Paso engine, wheels, and brakes, in a modified 750 F1 steel trellis frame with a Verlicchi aluminum swingarm. Also from the F1 came the more sporting instrument panel. Thus most specific

Although it was intended to continue the sporting spirit that epitomized the 750 F1, the 750 Sport was really quite a different machine. Here is a first series red-and-blue 1988 750 Sport.

details of the engine and running gear are covered in earlier chapters.

Engine and Drivetrain

The black-painted engine, along with the entire exhaust system, was shared with the 750 Paso, all 750 Sports featuring the new valve-adjusting arrangement and gold valve covers. For the 750 Sport, though, there was a new set of engine numbers starting at ZDM 750 LS 750001. The hydraulically activated dry clutch and 5-speed gearbox were the same as the 750 Paso. The Weber 44DCNF twin-choke downdraft carburetor was a slightly different type 113. While there was no difference in specification, claimed power was marginally less, 72 HP at 8,500 rpm, with maximum torque of 7.1 kg/m at 6,350 rpm. Maximum safe revs were reduced to 9,500 rpm. A difference to the 750 Paso was the oil-cooling system, now similar to that of the 750 F1, with a single radiator located in the fairing under the headlight. Final drive was by a 96-link Regina 135-OR 1/4- x 5/8-inch chain, with 15- and 38-tooth sprockets.

Ignition, Electrical System, and Switches

The Kokusan ignition providing 36 degrees of maximum advance was identical to that on the 750 Paso, as were the Champion RA6YC spark plugs. Much of the electrical system also came from the 750 F1, including the white-faced Veglia instruments, foam instrument panel and rectangular CEV headlight. The handlebar switches were the newer-generation Paso-type.

Frame and Cycle Parts

750 Sport frame numbers started at ZDM 750 S 750001, the red-painted frame an adaptation of the 750 F1. To accommodate the large airbox and Weber carburetor, the top frame tubes were much wider, and the side bracing tube now connected the front engine mount with the top frame tube. The battery was also located in a more satisfactory position between the airbox and steering head. Compared with the 750 Paso, the Sport reverted to the more traditional Ducati slower steering geometry, with its 28-degree fork angle and 115mm (4.5 inches) of trail. The motorcycle was significantly longer than the F1, with a 1,450mm (57-inch) wheelbase. The swingarm was a Montjuich-style aluminum Verlicchi unit that soon proved unsuitable for street use. Throughout its production life the 750 Sport suffered swingarm problems, with cracks in the welding of the suspension-unit mounting area. To rectify this, in November 1989, the factory supplied new swingarm kits. This included a new swingarm pivot pin, rear axle, rear fender and chain cover, and replacement was quite an involved process. This was a warranty replacement and all 750 Sports should have been modified.

With its 750 Paso-based air-cooled engine and silencers, 16-inch wheels and traditional Ducati tubular-steel frame, the 750 Sport was a parts-bin special.

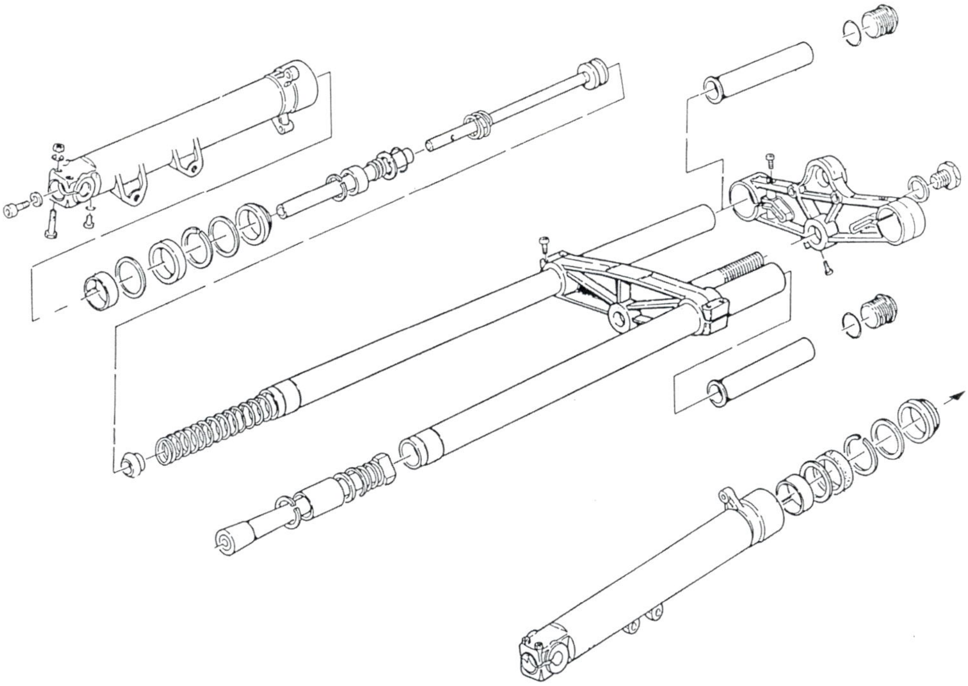

The front forks on both the 750 Sport and 900 Supersport were basic non-adjustable Marzocchi 40mm M1BB.

The Oscam 3.75 x 16-inch front wheel and 280mm Brembo brakes of the 750 Sport.

At the rear was a 5.00 x 16-inch Oscam wheel and a 270mm disc. These, and the aluminum swingarm and plastic tire guard, were similar to that of the 750 Laguna Seca.

Toward the end of 1988, 95 black-and-silver 750 Sports were manufactured, these all having the earlier-specification engine. Like many, this example has aftermarket mufflers.

All the bodywork was new for the 750 Sport, including a steel fuel tank, full fairing and solo seat unit with detachable cover to enable it to become a dual seat. The first Sports were red with blue and white stripes, the 750 Sport also the first Cagiva-Ducati to feature DUCATI decals without elephant logos. The suspension reflected the more basic specification of the Sport compared to the Paso. At the front were non-adjustable 40mm Marzocchi M1BB forks, and at the rear a Marzocchi PBS1R shock absorber, this adjustable for rebound damping and spring preload. Suspension stroke was 140mm (5.5 inches) at the front and 50mm (1.97 inches) at the rear. The 16-inch Oscam wheels and Brembo brakes came directly from the 750 Paso, as did the Pirelli or Michelin radial tires (see Chapter Four). Initial production in May 1988 was 568 European specification in red and blue.

1989 Model Year

First displayed at the end of 1988, there were a number of small modifications to the 750 Sport for 1989, these occurring after frame number 751052. Most notable was a change in colors and graphics. In addition to the earlier red and blue there were also colors of red and silver, with new decals. Some Sports with these revised graphics were black and silver, with a black frame, although only 95 were manufactured and were produced as one batch in September 1988. While the engine was largely unchanged, some 750 Sports now incorporated an air-/oil-cooling system, where jackets around the bore liners allowed additional oil to circulate. While not uniform on 1989 750cc engines, it would feature on all later 750cc engines. The countershaft sprocket retaining system was modified, along with the use of Loctite 242. The air-/oil-cooled engine was fitted to 151 red and blue 750 Sports in 1988 and 34 red and silver models. The black-and-silver version used the earlier engine, and all those manufactured in 1989 (except for Switzerland) featured the air-/oil-cooled engine.

The red-painted frame was modified slightly from March 1989 with the inclusion of an additional brace on each side of the steering head as with the new 900 Supersport, but otherwise the chassis was

Modifications to the 750 Sport And 900 Supersport (1989-90)

Of all the more modern Ducatis, none lend themselves to improvement more than the 750 Sport. In standard form not only was the carburetion poor, but also the handling never matched that of the 750 F1. The combination of slow steering and low-profile 16-inch tires never really worked. As the Weber carburetor exhibited all the problems that were evident on the Paso, a common modification was a Malossi 36mm Dell'Orto carburetor conversion, though 40mm was also possible. The Malossi kit included carburetors, manifolds, cables, and air filters. Both the 750 Sport and 900 Supersport suffered the same problems of excessive fuel pressure that afflicted both the 750 and 906 Paso (see Chapter Four). A replacement two-into-one exhaust system was also available from Verlicchi.

The standard Michelin tires weren't particularly well suited to the Sport, but improvement can come from higher-profile Metzeler Z2 130/70 x 16-inch and Z1 150/80 x 16-inch tires. Suspension also lends itself to upgrading, with lighter (5 weight) fork oil and a replacement shock absorber. However, if charged correctly the standard Marzocchi PBS1R shock absorber still works well enough. To really transform the handling it is possible to graft an entire front end from a Japanese motorcycle. I have seen a 750 Sport with the complete front end from a Suzuki RGV250, including upside-down Kayaba forks, 17-inch wheel, and four-piston Tokico brakes.

Although an improvement on the troubled 750 Sport, the 900 Supersport of 1989 was still a flawed motorcycle. The carburetion was equally poor and this model can also benefit from the replacement of the Weber carburetor with 40mm Dell'Ortos. The handling was superior to the 750, mainly due to the fitting of 17-inch wheels, but the motorcycle was also much taller. This was despite factory claims of a lower seat height. Consequently the 900 Supersport was less agile and more reluctant to turn than the 750 Sport. This can be improved by dropping the forks through the triple clamps to quicken the steering, and installing a slightly longer shock absorber. The engine and exhaust modifications for later 900 Supersports are also applicable to the 1989 900 Supersport (see Chapter Ten). A problem with both the 750 Sport and 900 Supersport is the side stand that was too short.

Most 750 Sports were red and silver with new decals. For 1989 they received a revised oil-cooled engine, but most of the problems with the earlier model remained.

Designed to recapture the sporting spirit of the earlier bevel-drive Super Sport was the 1990 900 Supersport. While an improvement over the 750 Sport, it was still a flawed motorcycle.

unchanged. In response to fuel tanks splitting from vibration, in June 1989 the factory supplied a modified fuel tank fastening system that included seven additional rubber silent-blocks and dampers. Some 750 Sports were also assembled with the incorrect wheel spacer, leading to bearing failure. A factory service bulletin in January 1990 provided information on maintaining an axle-to-bearing clearance of 3mm with the correct spacer. As with the 750 Paso, homologated semi-floating 280mm front discs also became available in January 1990. Though soon to be replaced, production of the 750 Sport during 1989 was similar to that of the previous year, 1,365 being built, with 300 for the U.S. and 100 for California. These U.S. models differed slightly to European specification, mainly in the use of the 906 Marelli Digiplex ignition rather than Kokusan. Along with the U.S. 750 Paso of the same period there was also a different exhaust system and revised carburetor jetting.

900 Supersport (1989-90)

An important development of the large-crankcase 904cc engine occurred in 1989 after the release of the 906 Paso. Following the success of the air-/oil-cooled 904cc Cagiva Elefant Paris-Dakar racer in January 1989, this engine made its way into the production range in the 900 Supersport. As with the earlier 750 Sport, the new model was intentionally titled a 900 Supersport to create a link with a past classic, in this case the 900 bevel-drive Super Sport of 1975-82. Just as with the 750 Sport it was a tenuous link, but the spirit of the new Supersport did indeed recall much that had made the earlier version so appealing. This was a large-capacity air-cooled V-twin engine in a lightweight sporting package. Installed in a 750 Sport frame, with 17-inch 851 Strada wheels and brakes (later shared with the 907 I.E.), the 900 Supersport finally addressed some of the problems of the 750 Sport. However, Ducati still persevered with the Weber carburetor and the handling and balance of the motorcycle was flawed, indicating insufficient development. Apart from water-cooling, the engine was very similar to that of the 906 Paso, extensively detailed in Chapter Four.

Engine and Drivetrain

Engine numbers started at ZDM 904 A 2C 000001, this engine number sequence featuring on

Many of the problems with the 1990 900 Supersport were associated with the Weber carburetor. As with the 750 Sport, the frame was much wider than the 750 F1 to accommodate the large airbox.

The instrument panel of the 1990 900 Supersport with white-faced Veglia instruments was similar to that of the 750 F1 and the 750 Sport.

all 900 Supersports, and used on the 900 Monster through 1999. The letter A indicated air-cooling, and the 2 meant two valves per cylinder. The lower end of the engine was based on the 906, with all the external engine components painted black. Thus it shared the same crankshaft with 130mm con rods, 31-/62-tooth primary drive, six-speed gearbox and hydraulically operated dry clutch with the actuation system on the right side, within the clutch cover. Because of this the 900 Supersport suffered the same problem with the lubrication of the thrust bearing as earlier Pasos and F1s. The cylinder heads were also the same, with tri-spherical combustion chambers and 43 and 38mm valves. Although the camshaft timing was the same as the 906, the valve lift was increased, to 11.76mm on the inlet and 10.56mm on the exhaust. Carburetion too was still the 44DCNF Weber, now a type 118. This didn't solve the carburetion problems and, in addition to the severe flat spot around 4,000 rpm, the 900 Supersport suffered even more than the 906 Paso from carburetor icing as the air ducts were in the front of the fairing. The factory offered a carburetor heating kit in 1992 (see Chapter Four). Also from the 906 came the Marelli Digiplex ignition system, the two Marelli coils located under the battery. The exhaust, although retaining the four-way collector underneath the engine, featured the canister-style aluminum mufflers of the 1989 851 Strada.

It was mainly the cooling system that was different to the 906. Using a development of the air-/oil-cooling system of the 1989 750 Sport, the 900 Supersport featured oil passages between the bore and outer cylinder wall. This circulating oil drained via two external lines

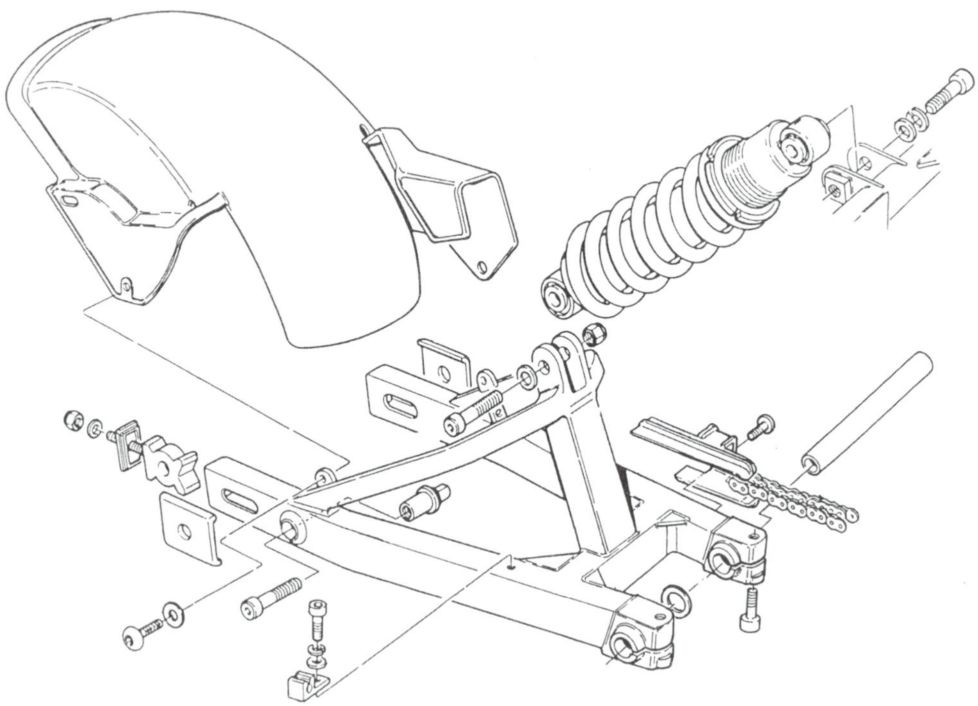

The aluminum cantilever swingarm and Marzocchi PBS1R shock absorber of the 1990 900 Supersport were similar to that on the 750 Sport, but was stronger around the swingarm pivot.

on the left side of the cylinders. All the oil was cooled by a radiator (two rows larger than that on the 750 Sport) fitted underneath the headlight. Still less effective than water-cooling, this saw the claimed power reduced over the 906 Paso to 83 HP at 8,400 rpm. Final drive was by 98-link Regina 135-OR 1/4- x 5/8-inch chain with 15- and 39-tooth sprockets.

Frame and Cycle Parts

Using a similar frame to the 1989 750 Sport, the 900 Supersport had a slightly steeper steering head angle at 27 degrees, achieved by raising the rear with a different swingarm. This was also stronger around the swingarm pivot. Unlike the 750 Sport that retained bronze swingarm bushes, the 900 Supersport swingarm was now in needle bearings inserted in the larger crankcases. These also featured oil seals. Because of the larger front wheel, trail was increased to a long 122mm (4.8 inches). This was even more than that of the original 900 Super Sport, a motorcycle with legendary stability and slow steering. The frame was painted red and frame numbers started at ZDM 900 SC 000001.

The bodywork followed the style set by the 1989 750 Sport, red but with a large white diagonal section running from the seat to the fairing. The suspension was that of the 750 Sport, with 40mm Marzocchi M1BB forks and a PBS1R shock absorber. Early forks had the oil level set at 150mm, this soon changed to

While the Marzocchi suspension was still non-adjustable, the white-painted Brembo 17-inch wheels and four-piston front brake calipers with 300mm stainless steel discs were a significant improvement over the 750 Sport.

160mm to improve damping. Compared to the 750 Sport the shock absorber was re-valved to give 59mm (2.32 inches) of stroke. The biggest change from the 750 Sport was in the wheels, brakes and tires. The white-painted Brembo wheels were shared with the 1989 851 Strada, with more up-to-date sizing than the 750 Sport, utilizing a 3.50 x 17-inch on the front and 5.50 x 17-inch on the rear. Tires were Pirelli MP7S, either a 120/70 ZR17 or 130/60ZR17 on the front, and a 180/55ZR17 or 170/60ZR17 on the rear. The brakes were also upgraded with twin black Brembo P4 32A calipers on the front gripping 300mm stainless steel discs. The master cylinder was a rectangular reservoir Brembo PS 15mm. At the rear was the 245mm disc of the 851, along with the P2 105N Brembo caliper and PS 11mm master cylinder.

Although less problematic than the 750 Sport, one difficulty with the 900 Supersport was the fitting of a Paso sidestand that was too short. Early 900 Supersports also suffered from fuel tanks splitting due to vibration, this soon modified with additional rubber silent-blocks and dampers. Production was 1,471 in 1989, with a further 533 in 1990.

With its 17-inch wheels and 851-style mufflers, the 1990 900 Supersport was a better-proportioned machine than the 750 Sport.

400 Supersport Junior

One of the more unusual Ducatis of this period was the Japanese-market 400 Supersport Junior of 1989. Constructed at the request of the Japanese distributor Murayama, this was very much a parts-bin special, with a few new developments that hadn't appeared on previous Ducatis. Although it is unlikely that anyone outside Japan will encounter these unusual motorcycles, a small number was exported to Australia via Japan in 1991. They deserve documenting because they were still genuine Ducatis. Total production in 1989 and 1990 was 641.

Engine and Drivetrain

Engine numbers started at ZDM 400 L 000001, the black-painted engine being essentially the same six-speed wet-clutch unit of the final 400 F3, but with the now mandatory reversed rear cylinder head. The inlet valve size was 33.5mm, with a 30.5mm exhaust, and the compression ratio from the 70.5mm pistons10.5:1. With a stroke of 51mm, capacity was 398cc. There were also new camshafts with new timing (see Appendix), giving inlet valve lift of 9.35mm and exhaust valve lift of 8.50mm. Along with this was a new primary-drive ratio (34/77), although the six-speed gearbox was as with the 1989 400 F3. The biggest difference between other models and the Supersport however was in the carburetion. Here twin Mikuni CVK-V36 constant-vacuum carburetors replaced the Weber or Dell'Ortos. These were also more efficient than the Dell'Ortos, with a 900 SS exhaust system lifting claimed power to 50 HP at 11,000 rpm. Completing the Japanese influence were NGK BP7HS spark plugs, the only Ducati fitted with NGK as original equipment.

Frame and Cycle Parts

The cycle parts of the 400 SS Junior were an amalgam of various parts from several models. The white-painted frame and aluminum cantilever swingarm were shared with the new 900 Supersport (with the extra brace from the top frame tube to the lower steering head), but with frame numbers beginning at ZDM 400 SS 000001. As with the 900, the steering head angle was 27 degrees, giving quite slow steering characteristics. The front 40mm Marzocchi forks were from the 750 Sport, though the Marzocchi shock absorber was from the 900 Supersport. The wheels and

The 1990 Japanese-market 400 Supersport Junior was an unusual model, with 16-inch Marvic wheels and Mikuni carburetors.

brakes though were left over from the 1988 851 Strada and Santamonica. These were the expensive and light Marvic/Akront composite 16-inch, a 3.5-inch on the front and 5.00-inch on the rear. Tires were Pirelli MP7 Sport. The brakes too were very high specification for a 400. Fully-floating 280mm cast-iron rotors with 08 Brembo calipers were on the front, along with a 260mm fully-floating rear disc and 05 Brembo caliper. All the other equipment was from the 900 Supersport, although the fairing and seat were red, without the central white portion.

CHAPTER SIX

The Cagiva Ducatis: Alazzurra, Indiana, Elefant, Gran Canyon

The initial agreement between Cagiva and Ducati in May 1983 called for Ducati to supply Cagiva with 6,000 V-twin Pantah engines in 1984, with a further 10,000 in 1985. These were initially to be used in a new model called the 350cc and 600cc Cagiva Ala Azzurra (blue wing), the prototype simply being a restyled 350/600 TL. The new Cagiva was displayed at the Milan Show at the end of 1983, along with an even more radical design, the 750cc Elefant trail bike with a reversed rear cylinder head. The 350 Ala Azzurra was red and the 600 white. While still based on the TL all the bodywork was new. Although supplies of engines never met the numbers forecast, from 1985 the Cagiva Ducatis played an integral role in Ducati's lineup, and like the Paso were designed to widen the appeal of Ducatis beyond that of pure sport bikes. As the Cagiva Alazzurra was initially assembled in Bologna they were are very much Ducatis, and the official factory parts list and workshop manual for the Alazzurra actually states the model as a Ducati and not a Cagiva.

650 Alazzurra
1985 Model Year

Delays with negotiations between Ducati and Cagiva saw an inevitable delay in the release of the new Cagiva/Ducati. Although still officially titled the Ala Azzurra, this was simplified to Alazzurra on the side-covers. It wasn't until July 1984 that production was under way, the Alazzurra becoming available in September. By this stage the 600cc Pantah engine had been superseded by the 650, so only 350cc and 650cc Alazzurras were produced. The Alazzurra was also the final Ducati with forward-facing exhausts and rearward carburetors.

When first shown at the Milan Show at the end of 1983 the Ala Azzurra was either a 350 or 600. The 600 here never went into production, being superseded by the 650.

Early production 650 Alazzurras featured polished aluminum engine covers.

Engine and Drivetrain

As the 650cc engine was based on that of the 650 SL, engine numbers continued the same series, beginning at DM 650L 610365. Like the 650 SL, initial engines were unpainted, with polished aluminum engine covers. Although sharing the same bore and stroke (82mm x 61.5mm), and the same valve sizes of 37.5mm and 33.5mm with the 650 SL, the production Alazzurra saw a return to the earlier 500 Pantah five-speed gearbox with the higher (29/27) fifth gear. Pre-production models had featured the normal 650 SL gearbox. From engine number 611077 there was

The production Alazzurra was one of the more attractive sport-touring Ducatis.

By 1985 all Alazzurras had black-painted engines and exhaust systems. Colors were still either red and silver or silver and red like this example.

also a new camshaft. A significant departure from the 650 SL was the clutch and primary drive. All 650 Alazzurras had a new hydraulically operated dry clutch and the higher (36/71) primary drive of the 750 F1. This clutch featured an outer cover similar to that of the 1985 750 F1, although the clutch was a completely new 14-plate combination (see Appendix) with new springs (066716550). Unfortunately it didn't solve the clutch problems, as the springs were still weak and the hydraulic master cylinder required a strong pull on the lever. The engine was painted black from engine number 611554 (frame number 3M000789) and there were several more updates to the engine specification. This included new crankcases, pistons and cylinders, cylinder heads, timing belt covers, engine and valve covers, and a new starter gear assembly. Thirteen screws, with an additional M8mm x 70mm screw near the crankshaft now located the crankcases. This layout would be used on all small-crankcase Pantah engines until 1998. From engine 611591 there were also new timing pulleys.

Carburetion was by the familiar Dell'Orto PHF 36 MD/S carburetors, U.S. versions having locked airscrew adjusters. The usual restrictive Pantah air filter under the tank featured, and removing this and replacing it with pod-type filters yielded a similar benefit as it did on other Pantahs. The choke was rather inconveniently positioned on the left lower frame tube. An odd addition was a CHOKE decal on the frame on U.S. models. Presumably Cagiva felt that U.S. riders needed to be told where the choke was! Only the Silentium exhaust system was fitted to the Alazzurra, this having a bolt-on metal foot shield. Initially chrome-plated, when the engine went black (after frame number 3M000789) the exhaust system became black chrome. U.S. versions also had more restrictive exhaust system. Final drive was by a 100-link 5/8- x 3/8-inch chain with 15- and 41-tooth sprockets. This lower gearing at least represented a realistic approach and was more suited to the power characteristics than the gearing on most Pantahs. Claimed power for the 650 Alazzurra was slightly less than the 650 SL at 56.5 HP at 8,400 rpm, with 40.5 lb./ft. of torque at 5,750 rpm. On all the Cagiva Ducatis torque was quoted in lb./ft., as the U.S. was undoubtedly their main intended market.

The instrument panel for the Alazzurra was completely different to other Ducatis. There was a large tachometer and plastic cover over the handlebars and triple clamp.

Ignition, Electrical System, and Switches

The ignition system on the Alazzurra was shared with the 1985 750 F1 and consisted of the Bosch BTZ ignition pickups and electronic amplifier, with Motoplat coils. The maximum ignition advance was 32 degrees, with Champion L82Y spark plugs specified. There were a number of updates to the electrical system of the Alazzurra compared to other Ducatis. Under the fuel tank was a start checking device that recorded the gearbox position, clutch lever, and sidestand position and cut the ignition out with the sidestand down. The alternator was either a 300-watt Ducati Energia, or an inferior Spanish Saprisa, and the headlight a CEV model 287 rectangular 190mm x 130mm H4 55/60-watt unit. Although the front indicators were incorporated in the sides of the small fairing, the rear indicators and taillight were similar to CEV units on other Ducatis, although none of this equipment was actually shared.

The instrument panel and switches were also new for the Alazzurra. The Veglia instruments consisted of a large left-side tachometer, and a smaller speedometer on the right. Underneath the speedometer was a small quartz analog clock, with a row of eight warning lights under the tachometer. These were for lights on, turn signal indicators, high beam, neutral, fuel, oil pressure, and side stand down. The turn signals also had an annoying beeper, a first for a Ducati. These were all housed in a gray metal dashboard. The ignition was located on the steering stem, the handlebars shrouded under an ugly plastic cover. Other new electrical parts for the Alazzurra were the handlebar switches, and plastic Verlicchi throttle that included a two-into-one cable.

Frame and Cycle Parts

While the black-painted frame was the same Verlicchi item of the Pantah, Cagiva used a new set of frame numbers beginning at 3M000001. Just about all the cycle parts were new for the Alazzurra, very little shared with other Ducatis. From frame number 3M000789 the black 650 engine was fitted, along with black exhausts. With Marzocchi suspension front and rear, the Alazzurra had a slight increase in wheelbase over previous Pantahs to 1,460mm (57.5 inches).

The styling may have been rather bland, but the Alazzurra was an undeniable improvement over its

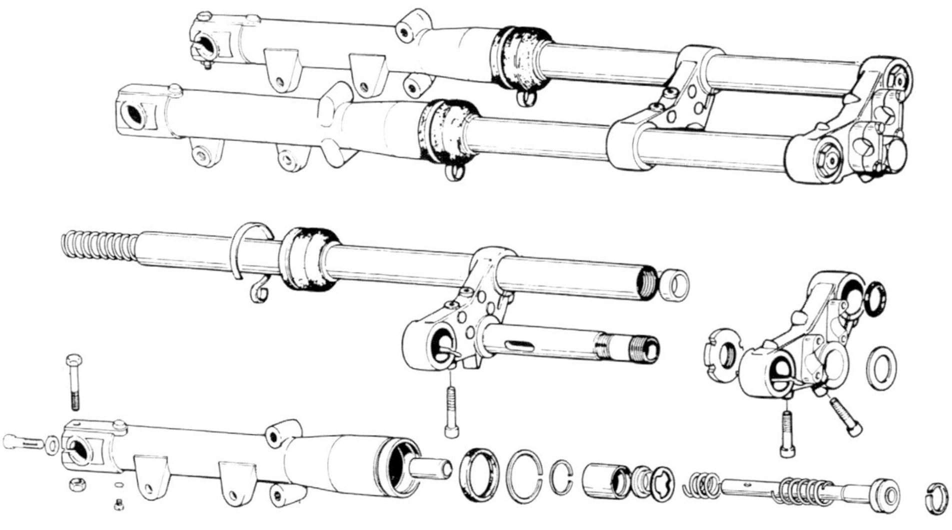

The 35mm forks of the Alazzurra were similar to those on other Pantahs.

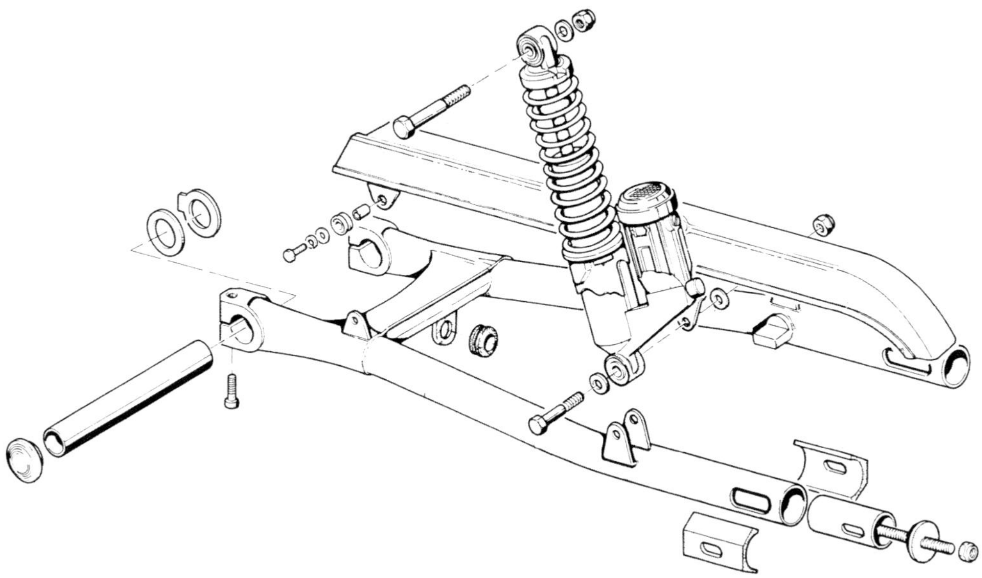

The swingarm and twin Marzocchi shock absorbers of the Alazzurra was similar to the Pantah.

immediate predecessor, the 600 TL. A frame-mounted fairing provided not only increased protection, but also improved the handling by reducing steering inertia. This had a smoked Plexiglas windshield, with U.S. screens lower than European examples. Fenders were plastic, the U.S. versions having a longer rear section. The steel fuel tank was less slab-sided than that of the Pantah, and had large white CAGIVA decals on each side. 650 and Alazzurra decals on the side covers and tailpiece completed the model delineation. A welcome change was the fitting of manual fuel taps, rather surprising considering the other strange electrical features.

Suspension comprised 35mm non-adjustable Marzocchi forks with silver-painted fork legs, U.S. versions featuring a reflector on each fork leg. In line with the intended nature of the machine, these forks had softer springs than the earlier Pantah, and provided increased wheel travel, 140mm (5.5 inches) compared to 120mm (4.7 inches). There were also softer springs on the silver-painted remote-reservoir Marzocchi shock absorbers, these providing 90mm (3.5 inches) of travel. The wheels were 18-inch silver five-spoke Oscams, similar to those on the final 600 and 650 SL. Rim sizes were also identical, at 2.15 x 18-inches and 2.50 x 18-inches, with touring-style Pirelli tires, a 100/90H18 MT59 and 110/90H18 MT58. The brakes were shared with the 600 TL, twin 260mm drilled cast-iron front discs and rear-mounted P2F05N Brembo calipers with Ferit I/D 346 pads. However, as with many other components on the Alazzurra, U.S. models received slightly different brake calipers and master cylinder, and different brake pads. On all models the handlebar Brembo master cylinder and matching clutch master cylinder had round reservoirs. At the rear was another P2F05N caliper, 260mm drilled disc, and a master cylinder with a remote reservoir. None of the levers and footpeg brackets were shared with the 600 TL, although the style was similar. The gearshift rod still featured the strange Pantah combination of a ball joint and sloppy clevis pin, the Cagiva influence slow to filter through to the Alazzurra.

Colors of the Alazzurra were either silver and red, or red and silver. With decent mirrors standard and an upright riding position, the 650 Alazzurra was by far Ducati's best effort at an all-around motorcycle by 1985. Most of the 1985 production of 650s went to the U.S., but unfortunately its qualities were rarely appreciated, and the Alazzurra suffered by not having DUCATI on the tank.

1986 Model Year

While the 650 Alazzurra continued much as before, the GT 650 joined it for 1986. Also known as the SS 650, because of the SS decals on the side covers, this took the sport-touring idea further by incorporating a full fairing. First shown at the Cologne Show at the end of 1984, another version with a larger fairing that merged with the fuel tank and different graphics was displayed at Milan at the end of 1985. This took the form of the eventual production version.

The GT650 Alazzurra on display at the Milan Show at the end of 1985. This was similar to the eventual production version but for 650 SS decals. The luggage never became officially available. The wheels were now Oscam, and along with the full fairing there was a new front fender.

Engine and Drivetrain

There were no engine changes for 1986 except the clutch was standardized to that of the 1986 750 F1, including the clutch cover with HC cast into it. Surprisingly, the same weak 650 clutch springs were retained. From engine number 612550 there were new camshafts with different valve timing (see Appendix). U.S. Alazzurra GTs from 3ME00506 featured black-anodized inlet manifolds, along with black Dell'Orto PHF 36A carburetors.

Frame and Cycle Parts

Frame numbers for the 1986 model 650 Alazzurra commenced at 3M001024, and 3ME000066 for the GT. There were only a few changes for this year. California Alazzurras received different fuel tanks, and U.S. models of the GT got a screw-type filler cap. While the GT featured a full fairing in two parts, there was also a new front fender for this model, patterned on that of the 750 F1 Montjuich. This was two-piece and enclosed the fork legs. All the decals for the GT were new, with 650 SS instead of Alazzurra, and the GT received a new color scheme, dark-blue and silver with red highlighting. This was in addition to the silver and red of before. The only other change to the specification was the wheels, now silver-painted three-spoke Oscams, a 2.50 x 18-inch on the front and 3.00 x 18-inch on the rear. With the wider rear came a 120/80 Pirelli MT58 rear tire. Although intended to compete with the BMW K75S and Moto Guzzi V65 Lario, the Alazzurra 650 GT joined those motorcycles as too expensive for the modest performance offered. Also during 1986, 10 Health Department 650 Alazzurras were built. Production ceased during 1986, with 1,166 650 Alazzurras built.

350/400 Alazzurra

1985 Model Year

Following on from the Ducati 350 TL and 350 XL, the Cagiva Alazzurra 350 was ostensibly the 350 SL engine slotted into the regular Alazzurra chassis. As with other 350s it was also created specifically for the Italian market, although somewhat surprisingly, a U.S. version was listed in the 1985 parts book. While engine numbers were shared with the 350 SL (beginning at DM 350L 032503), there was a new chassis number sequence, starting at 2M000001. Most specifications were as for the 350 SL, including the 66mm x 51mm bore and stroke, valve sizes of 33.5mm and 30.5mm, and 10.3:1 compression ratio. Compared to earlier 350s there were also a number of changes in the specification. This included the 650 Alazzurra camshafts, and the higher fifth gear of that bike and the 1979 500 Pantah. Until frame number 2M001350 the earlier 500 smaller wet clutch was also used, becoming the larger 600 cable-operated wet clutch after 2M001351, along with new clutch springs (065916558) and the clutch plate set of the dry-clutch 650 Alazzurra. These changes coincided with a black engine, and also included new cylinders, crankcases and other external black components. As with the 650 Alazzurra, the 350 crankcases also featured an additional locating screw. Engine number 033806 saw the 11-tooth oil pump driving gear replaced by the 650 item, and from engine 033855 there were new timing pulleys. Carburetion on the 350 was new, now a pair of Dell'Orto PHBH 28 AD/S carburetors, with PHF 30 MD/S for the U.S. Claimed power for the 350 was identical to that of earlier 350s: 40 HP at 9,600 rpm with 22.42 lb./ft. of torque at 8,500 rpm. Final drive was by 14- and 46-tooth sprockets with 96-link 5/8- x 3/8-inch chain. The electrical system was identical to the Ducati 350 but for the 650's 300-watt alternator. The cycle parts and colors were also identical to the 650, except for a slightly different front fender (without a solid front section), and smaller Pirelli MT59/58 tires (90/90 x 18 and 110/80 x 18).

1986 Model Year

For 1986 a 400cc version for the Japanese market joined the 350 Alazzurra. This was identical to the 350 but for crankshaft, cylinder and pistons. Only available in gray (a different shade to the 350), all the 400 bodywork was specifically for that model and it had 400 decals. Frame numbers for 1986 started at 2M002503 and by 1986 production of the 350 Alazzurra had finished. Only 100 400 Alazzurras were produced during 1986.

The engine of the 350 Alazzurra was largely unchanged for 1986, although after engine number 034711 there was a new clutch inner pressure plate, and a change to the driven discs (see Appendix). There was also a slightly lower final drive, with a 47-tooth rear sprocket. Originally it had also been planned to produced a fully faired 350 GT Alazzurra, visually identical to the 650, but this didn't eventuate.

One of the more unusual Cagiva Alazzurras was this 1986 model produced for the Health Department.

Alazzurras have formed the basis of several successful racers. This is Brian Catterson's (former editor of *Motorcyclist*) much modified 1985 650 Alazzurra that he raced after 20,000 miles on the street. Chassis modifications include Yamaha FZR600 forks and wheels and Brembo four piston brake calipers with 320mm discs. The exhaust is a Gianelli two-into-one. *Brian Catterson*

Modifications to the Alazzurra And Indiana

Like all Pantahs, the Alazzurra responded particularly well to alternative air cleaners and exhausts. The stock carburetor jetting was inherited from the 600/650 Pantah, and any alteration to the intake or exhaust will require richening. Suitable engine modifications follow those for the SL and TL Pantah, though the 350 and 400 will always be underpowered. The 650 also lent itself to a simple 750 overbore, though, as with the 1985 750 F1, the small valves will limit ultimate power. A problem with the early Alazzurra was the weak clutch, and although this was improved for 1986 the soft springs were still fitted.

As far as the chassis went, the Alazzurra was similar to other Pantahs. With a 30.5-degree steering head angle the steering was slow but predictable, and frame rigidity questionable. The skinny 35mm Marzocchi forks didn't help either, and were too soft for spirited riding, leading to a high-speed weave. Fork springs from a 600 or 650 SL can improve this. The standard Pirelli MT59/58 tires were also unsuitable. As with all Pantahs it was important to ensure the swingarm pin and crankcase bushes weren't worn. Although theoretically sufficient for the power and weight of the Alazzurra, the Brembo 05 brakes were often weak, with a rather dead feel, but could be improved with softer brake pads and braided steel brake lines. Early Alazzurras often suffered from seized brake calipers, presumably because Cagiva was using old Ducati stock.

In many ways the Indiana was one of the more developed versions of the Pantah. The gearbox ratios were very suitable for this type of motorcycle, and the Bing carburetors on the larger models worked well. The frame was almost over-engineered for the purposes of a cruiser, and the suspension components reasonable. The forks though were typically oversprung and underdamped, as were the shock absorbers, although the braking system was quite adequate. As these motorcycles were hardly sportbikes, most problems with the Indiana centered on the finish and the unusual riding position. The chrome plating was very poor quality and the riding position featured high, sweptback handlebars with fairly rearward footpegs.

While it started life as a 1985 wet-clutch 650, Catterson's Alazzurra was modified by Eraldo Ferracci with a 750cc kit, NCR cams, Barnett clutch and Mikuni 41.5mm flat-slide carburetors to produce 68 HP at 9,250 rpm. This bike was timed at 138 mph at Willow Springs. *Brian Catterson*

Indiana

While they did much to preserve Ducati's heritage and future, Cagiva was also responsible for several dubious marketing moves, none more so than the creation of the Indiana cruiser. Although there was a historical precedent for this type of motorcycle (the bizarre Americano of 1959-1963), the Indiana was undoubtedly the result of misguided market research. Yet there was no denying the Alazzurra was a brave and creditable attempt to broaden the appeal of Ducatis beyond that of the serious enthusiast. This was initially produced as a 650, and displayed at the Milan Show at the end of 1985. As with many prototypes, the show bike differed in a few details from the eventual production version, noticeably in the use of a normal black-painted engine and without 650 decals. In an endeavor to recapture a lost U.S. market, the Indiana was intentionally named after a U.S. state, but someone in Varese forgot that underneath the cruiser exterior was a desmodromic sportbike. Despite this, the Indiana lasted several years, and incorporated some important evolutionary developments.

650

The primary model for the U.S. was the 650 Indiana, released in June 1986. Despite having a normal Ducati twin rear shock absorber setup, the Indiana really shared more with the Paso and Elefant than the Pantah-derived Alazzurra. The Indiana engine featured a reversed rear cylinder head, and the frame was a full-cradle type, constructed of square-section steel tubing, but with a large hollow backbone.

Engine and Drivetrain

Quite a bit of development went into the 650 Alazzurra engine to adapt it to the different requirements of a cruiser. While the cylinder heads were untouched, except for the rear reversed, the camshaft timing was identical to that of the final 650 Alazzurra. During 1986 the valve guides were also changed from cast-iron to bronze. The Indiana received a new five-speed gearbox, the ratios more widely spaced, with a lower first and second gear. The hydraulically activated dry clutch was the same 14-plate unit as 1986 650 Alazzurra and 750 F1. All the external engine covers, including the clutch cover and timing belt covers, were chrome-plated on the production Indiana.

Apart from the reversed rear cylinder head and the chromed engine covers, it was the carburetion that set the Indiana apart from other Ducatis. Unlike the Paso and Elefant, the 650 Indiana featured Bing 64-32/375 36mm constant-vacuum carburetors. With a large cylindrical paper element air filter feeding into the hollow backbone frame, the carburetion was improved

The Indiana wasn't Ducati's first attempt at an American-style cruiser, but it was one of the least successful. This is the prototype with a normal black-painted 650 engine as displayed at the Milan Show of 1985.

over the Paso, however obtaining maximum power was never a serious consideration. The chrome-plated dual exhaust system required the rear cylinder to exit on the right, snaking over the clutch cover. There was large collector box underneath the swingarm, effectively preventing the fitting of a centerstand. Claimed power was 53 HP at 7,00 rpm, with 44.84 lb./ft. of torque at 5,000 rpm. This may have been modest for a 650, but was more than adequate for a cruiser of this type and placed the Indiana at the top of the performance heap for 700cc cruisers. Along with straight-cut 36/71 primary gears, the final drive, through Regina 136 OR 3/8- x 5/8-inch chain, was by 15-/46-tooth sprockets.

By the time the Indiana made it into production it had chromed engine covers. These were particularly poor quality and quickly corroded.

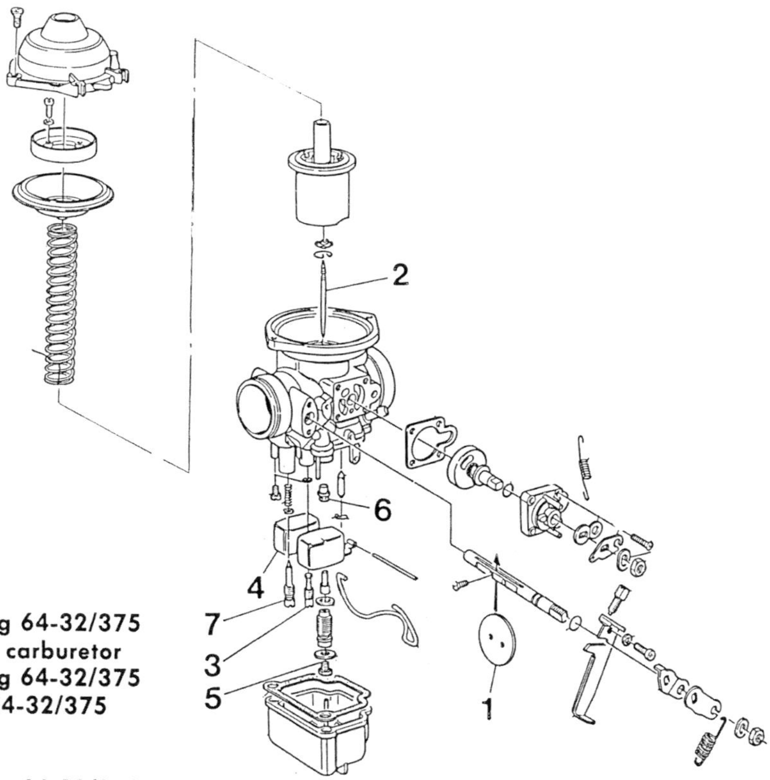

A departure from regular Ducati practice on the Indiana was the use of 32mm Bing constant-vacuum carburetors.

Carburatore Bing 64-32/375
Bing 64-32/375 carburetor
Carburateur Bing 64-32/375
Bing-Vergaser 64-32/375
(INDIANA 650)

Carburatore Bing 64-32/379
Bing 64-32/379 carburetor
Carburateur Bing 64-32/379
Bing-Vergaser 64-32/379
(INDIANA 750)

Ignition, Electrical System, and Switches

Unlike the Alazzurra, the ignition on the Indiana was Kokusan, providing 32 degrees of maximum advance. Spark plugs were Champion L82Y. Most of the electrical equipment was new, including a round 55/60-watt H4 headlight, indicators, handlebar switches, and instrument panel. The choke was also on the left handlebar, an improvement over the Alazzurra. The only part shared with earlier models was the CEV 9350 taillight, which came from the U.S. specification bevel-drive 750 GT of 1972-4, also featuring on a variety of bevel-drive twins until 1983.

Frame and Cycle Parts

When it came to the chassis, the Indiana broke new ground for Ducati. The frame, although obviously inspired by the Elefant, was all-new, with frame numbers beginning at ZDM 650 C 650001. Constructed of black-painted square-section steel tubing, this frame was a full-cradle type that not only supported the engine rigidly at the rear in two positions, but also by two alloy arms to the front mount. An aluminum cross brace connected the front downtubes, the lower-right frame tube unbolting for engine removal. The swingarm was cast-aluminum box-section, pivoting only in the engine cases (unlike the Paso). The most radical departure from earlier Ducatis was the steering geometry, the frame providing 32.8 degrees of rake, with another 7 degrees from the triple clamps. Trail was 132mm (5.2 inches).

There was also new cruiser-style bodywork, notably a small (12-liter, 3.44-gallon) fuel tank with older-style winged DUCATI tank badges. The seat was scalloped to provide a 30-inch seat height, significantly lower than the Alazzurra, but not especially low for a cruiser. Very high and rearward sweeping handlebars, along with forward footpegs, provided a strange riding position. The riding position wasn't really that of a radical cruiser, but was certainly more cruiser-oriented than other all-around Ducatis such as the TL and Alazzurra. While the front 18-inch Oscam alloy wheel was similar to the Alazzurra, the suspension, rear wheel, and brakes were also new. The wheels featured the triangulated six-spoke design of other Ducatis of the period, but were black enameled with polished outer rims. Rim widths were generous, a 2.50 x 18-inch on the front and 3.50 x 15-inch on the rear, the 15-inch wheel standard

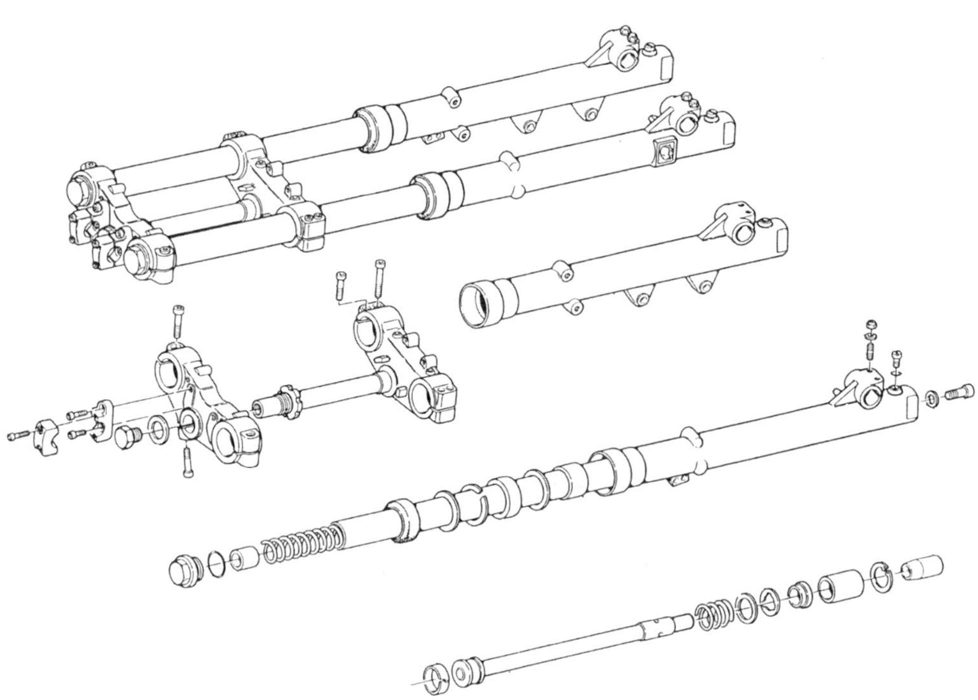

The leading-axle 40mm Marzocchi forks were unique to the Indiana, but were non-adjustable.

cruiser specification. These were fitted with tubeless Pirelli Phantom MT28 tires, a 110/90V18 and 140/90V15. From frame number 650580 there were new wheel spacers for both front and rear wheels, and chain adjustment was by cheap Japanese-style adjusters, rather than the Seeley-type on other Pantahs.

Although the specification of the 40mm Marzocchi P.A. 185/40 leading-axle forks seemed adequate, in reality they offered no adjustment and were too stiff and underdamped. Coupled with the exceptional fork rake they were also not very compliant, although they did offer a generous 160mm (6.3 inches) of front wheel travel. The twin Marzocchi A 84 rear shock absorbers with progressively wound chrome-plated springs provided 90mm (3.5 inches) of wheel travel from their 101.5mm (3.55 inches) of stroke. However, these gave a harsh ride.

Amongst the other evolutionary developments was the use of a single four-piston Brembo PA 32C front brake caliper. This gripped a single 260mm cast-iron disc, on the left side of the wheel, and was operated by a rectangular Brembo master cylinder with a black dogleg lever. A similar leftside handlebar master cylinder controlled the hydraulic clutch. The rear brake was a larger, 280mm, cast-iron disc with a Brembo P2105N caliper. The rear brake master cylinder was also new for the Indiana, and activated by an uncomfortably long foot lever. The Indiana was available in three colors; black, blue, and amaranth. While much was new, completing the specification was a traditional Ducati feature of many separate keys, in this case five: One each for ignition, steering head, seat, fuel cap, and helmet lock. The 650 Indiana continued into 1987, primarily for the U.S., but was produced as a police version until 1990.

350

Produced simultaneously for the Italian market, the 350 Indiana was identical to the 650 except for the engine. This was also the first 350 to receive a reversed rear cylinder head, and included a few updates from the other 350s. The five-speed gearbox was the same as the 650 Indiana, but for a lower fifth gear. The cable-operated wet clutch was the same as final 350 Alazzurra, but unlike the 650 the 31-/69-tooth primary gears were helical. Also different to the 650 were the twin Dell'Orto PHF 30 DD carburetors. Power was 38 HP at 9,250 rpm, with 22.42 lb./ft. of torque at 8,250 rpm. 350 Indiana frame numbers started at ZDM 350 C 350001, but apart from 350 decals on the side covers, all chassis and running gear was shared with the 650. From number 350431 there were new spacers in both wheels. However, unlike the 650 that continued until 1990, the 350 lasted only one year.

In addition to the 350 and 650 Indiana, just over 500 750 Indianas were produced in 1986. These were either silver or black.

750

During 1986 a 750cc version of the Indiana went into production, ostensibly the earlier 650 Indiana with a 750 Paso engine. However, many of the 650 Indiana features were retained, including the same five-speed gearbox and Bing carburetors. Valve sizes were also the smaller 37.5mm inlet and 33.5mm exhaust of the 650 rather than the 750 Paso's larger ones. The clutch and primary drive was also different for the 750 Indiana. Unlike the straight-cut 36/71 primary-gears of the 650, the 750 received a set of helical primary-drive gears, although still with the hydraulically actuated dry clutch. The clutch composition was also slightly different to all other Ducatis of that time, with one less driven plate (066116530). In other respects the 750 was as with the Paso, and featured the stronger crankcases, the same camshafts, and stronger cylinder head studs.

Carburetion for the 750 Indiana was also by Bing, type 64-32/379, with slightly smaller (130) main jets.

As with many models that Ducati found difficult to sell, the Indiana was adapted for police use.

The exhaust system was also new, now a larger diameter, with an expanded and redesigned collector under the engine. Power for the 750 Indiana was only slightly up on the 650, to 53.6 HP at 7,000rpm, although torque was increased to 49.18 lb./ft. at 3,800 rpm. While the ignition was still Kokusan as before, the electrical system was slightly updated with a new regulator, flash relay, and lower-amperage main fuses with two 15-amp instead of the 350/650s 25-amp. The 750 received a new dashboard, headlight and taillight, these not shared with any other model of Ducati. While the Veglia instruments were the same as the 650, the instrument holder was updated.

750 Indiana frame numbers start from ZDM 750 C 750001, but there was little difference to the 650. The same 40mm Marzocchi forks were fitted, these having polished aluminum fork legs rather than being painted silver. Brakes, wheels and rear suspension were unchanged, although the 750 received a new seat. For 1986 the 750 Indiana was available in two colors, black or silver, with only sliver being available for 1987.

Elefant 350/650

Although the dual-purpose Elefant initially seemed an unlikely recipient for the Pantah engine, it was to become one of the longest running of all Cagiva/Ducati models. Over many years it built a loyal following, particularly in Italy and Germany, where large dual-purpose motorcycles have always been very popular, but also in the U.S. The Elefant also had a successful competition life in important desert races such as the Paris-Dakar and Pharaoh rallies. First displayed in 750cc form at the end of 1983, this was the first 750cc version of the Pantah engine in a production motorcycle. However, like the 750 F1 it was some time before the Elefant went into production. This prototype 750 was a high-specification model with gaitered Forcelle Italia forks and a single Grimeca front disc brake. The turn signal indicators were incorporated in the sides of the fuel tank, and the black-painted 750cc engine featured a reversed rear cylinder head, hydraulically actuated wet clutch, and Dell'Orto PHF 36 A carburetors. The red-painted box-section steel frame and Soft Damp rising-rate rear suspension with an aluminum swingarm set the layout for future Elefants. Unveiled at the Cologne Show at the end of 1984 was a further prototype, now 650cc, with Marzocchi forks with exposed fork tubes, and normal indicators on stalks. While some prototypes had a rear drum brake, the show version featured a rear disc brake and De Carbon shock absorber. The first production Elefants, in 350 and 650cc, rolled out of Cagiva's Schiranna plant at Varese in May (650) and June (350) 1985, differing from the prototype in several details. Most notable of these was the addition of a kickstarter. The general layout of the

The prototype Elefant of late 1983 was a 750 and a high-specification motorcycle. The indicators were incorporated in the plastic fuel tank and the suspension was premium quality. There was no kick-start on this prototype. Publicity photo.

During 1984 the Elefant became a 650. This 650 prototype has exposed fork tubes and a rear drum brake.

engine (with a reversed rear cylinder head), frame and suspension would continue through to the Gran Canyon of 1998. It proved to be a successful formula and the Elefant and its derivatives were highly competent dual-purpose motorcycles, with an emphasis more on the street than off-road. However, its off-road capabilities were vindicated when Hubert Auriol rode a works 650 Elf/Ligier Elefant to seventh place overall in the 1985 Paris-Dakar Rally. He followed this with a fourth place in the Pharaohs Rally in October 1985. Auriol almost won the Paris-Dakar event in 1987 on an 860cc prototype but for an accident with only a day to go. The

By the time it was displayed at the Cologne Show in 1984 the 650 Elefant had a rear disc brake.

Modifications to the Elefant

An indication of the excellence of the design of the Elefant was the length of time it continued in production, with the basic design remaining unchanged during that period. They have also developed a reputation for reliability over extremely high mileages. Undoubtedly the Elefant was a Ducati to be ridden rather than put away and cosseted. Pre-900 I.E. models suffered from under-damped front forks, but this was improved after 1990. All models suffer short-lived fork seals if used off-road. The Öhlins rear suspension was excellent, as were the brakes. With the introduction of the Elefant 900 and Elefant 750 with Mikuni carburetors and a catalytic converter, both carburetion and performance suffered slightly. As with other 750 and 900 Ducatis of this period, these models responded to replacement carburetors and exhausts. Although a dual-purpose motorcycle, the Elefant was really more suited to street rather than off-road duties. Later versions (with a 19-inch front wheel) could be fitted with a wide range of more sports-oriented street tires.

Compared with many other Ducatis, the detailing of the Elefant was excellent. The switchgear and instrument panel worked well, although the warning lights were difficult to see in sunlight. The main problem with the Elefant was its size, particularly the seat height. While this was reduced for final models it was still intimidating for those less than 6 feet tall. For the E-900, sold in the U.S. as a Ducati, Corbin offered a replacement color-coordinated saddle to improve comfort and reduce seat height.

A useful modification to the E-900 was a Corbin #DE9 color-coordinated saddle.

92mm x 64mm engine produced 80 HP at 8,500 rpm, enough to propel the Lucky Explorer Cagiva to speeds of more than 180 km/h (112 mph).

Engine and Drivetrain

Early 650s had the cable-operated wet clutch of the 350, this soon becoming the hydraulically actuated 14-plate dry clutch of the 650 Alazzurra (the later type, with HC cast into the cover). In an effort to reduce clutch effort the Elefant featured a rectangular master cylinder with a smaller, 13mm, piston. Unfortunately this also reduced the travel in the clutch slave cylinder, resulting in an abrupt engagement. The engines of both the 350 and 650 Elefant were shared with the respective Indiana, but with black engine cases. This included the Indiana gearbox ratios and primary drive, although the Elefant also had a kickstarter in addition to the normal electric start. The lever was on the right, with the kick-start shaft positioned at the rear of the engine. The 350 used the Dell'Orto PHF 30 DD carburetors of the 350 Indiana, but the 650, rather than featuring Bing carburetors, also had Dell'Ortos. These were PHF 36 MD/Ss. A two-into-one exhaust exited through a large muffler on the right. Power for the 350 was 33 HP at 8,000 rpm, with the 650 producing 52.4 HP at 7,500 rpm. The 650 Elefant also had an oil cooler, mounted on the upper-right frame downtube. Final drive was by a 106-link Regina O-ring chain. For 1986 there were some further developments. In response to complaints of overly strong throttle return springs, the carburetors now featured a push-pull linkage and lighter return springs.

Ignition and Electrical System

Unlike the Indiana with its Kokusan ignition, ignition on the Elefant was the Alazzurra's Bosch BTZ with Motoplat coils. This was a three-step type, providing 5 degrees of advance to 1,700 rpm, 25 degrees to 2,600 rpm, and a maximum advance of 32/33 degrees at 2,900 rpm. Spark plugs were Champion L82Y. In keeping with the trends of the mid-1980s, much of the equipment was square or rectangular. This included all the lights and instruments. These were Veglia, a left-mounted speedometer and right-mounted tachometer,

The first production 650 Elefant appeared during 1985, the black engine similar in specification to the Indiana.

with a set of six warning lights, and the ignition key incorporated on the top handlebar triple clamp. Switches were new, and followed the pattern of other Cagiva Ducatis. During 1986 Elefants received a revised instrument panel, with a more conventional set of warning lights combined with new hexagonal-shaped instruments. The ignition key was now positioned in the usual place between the instruments. Very little of the electrical equipment was the same as the other Ducati twins; even the horn was a Marelli instead of a Bosch.

Frame and Cycle Parts

Frame numbers began at 5N000001 for the 350 Elefant and 1N000001 for the 650. The frames were painted white for the 350 and red for the 650, and the full-cradle frame layout followed that of the Indiana. It was constructed of 30mm x 30mm square-section steel tubing, with a bolt-on right-side lower rail, the paper air filter element under the seat feeding into the rectangular backbone. The steering head angle was 28.5 degrees, giving 114mm (4.5 inches) of trail. Cagiva's own Soft Damp rising-rate suspension system operated a 35mm x 60mm rectangular-section aluminum swingarm. Bodywork followed that expected of dual-purpose motorcycles of that era. This included a high plastic front number plate/headlight shielding the instruments, high plastic front fender, and plastic 17.5-liter (4.63-gallon) fuel tank. The square headlight had a black protective metal grill. Colors for 1985 were red and white for the 650 (with a red seat), and blue and white for the 350 (with a blue seat). White CAGIVA lettering was on each side of the seat. From April 1986 there were new colors and decals, the 650 now black and red, blue and white, or the black and white Explorer. This was the first Elefant in the colors of the Lucky Explorer Paris-Dakar racers. For 1986 there was also a Plexiglas screen instead of the plastic number plate, and plastic hand protectors.

The equipment level of the Elefant was very high, indicating Cagiva's intention to offer a high-quality product. The front forks were specially constructed leading-axle 41.7mm Marzocchi, with CAGIVA cast into the fork legs. These provided 210mm (8.3 inches) of travel, and production versions had protective gaiters. Only the 650 Elefant received air caps in the top of each fork leg. At the rear was an even higher-quality

For 1985 the box-section steel frame was painted red.

Öhlins oleo-pneumatic shock absorber. A unit similar to that of the first 750 Paso, this featured an external hydraulic load adjuster mounted on the left rear frame tube. With a stroke of 63mm (2.5 inches), wheel travel was 195mm (7.68 inches).

The spoked wheels were high quality Akront aluminum, a 1.85 x 21-inch on the front and 2.75 x 17-inch on the rear. The spokes were 4mm, with 36 per wheel, the wheels shod with Metzeler Enduro 545 and 655 or Pirelli MT40 tires. Continuing the high specification was the braking system. At the front was a fully-floating cast-iron Brembo disc with a four-piston Brembo P4 32C caliper. A smaller (240mm) disc was on the rear along with a P2 105N caliper. Although early examples featured a rubber rear brake line, most production versions had a steel brake line on the rear, with a rubber line on the front. The Elefant was not a motorcycle for faint hearted, especially off road. Despite a claimed dry weight of 191kg (420 pounds) for the 650, *Cycle World*, in December 1985 weighed their test bike in at 434 pounds dry and 458 pounds wet. Although a heavy, tall motorcycle, the Elefant proved an immediate success, the 650 soon growing to 750cc. The 350 continued in slightly revised form until 1989.

The 650 Elefant featured a box-section aluminum swingarm with Soft Damp rising-rate rear suspension. There was a 240mm disc on the rear and a 17-inch wheel. Most production versions had a stainless steel brake line.

750 Lucky Explorer

In June 1987, as with other 650 twins, a 750 version replaced the 650 Elefant. The 350 Elefant continued, incorporating the cosmetic changes of the 750, but available in red and black as well as Lucky Explorer colors. The 350 engine was still the same five-speed unit as before. There was significantly more than an increase in capacity with the 750, the entire motorcycle restyled and updated to improve its off-road appeal.

Engine and Drivetrain

The lower end of the 750 Elefant engine was ostensibly the 88mm x 61.5mm unit of the 750 Indiana, without the chromed engine covers. Most of the internal components were identical, including the dry clutch, helical primary drive, and five-speed gearbox (with lower first and second gears). However, the 750 Elefant received lower-compression (9.3:1) pistons, along with the desmodromic cylinder heads of the 750 Paso with larger (41mm and 37mm) valves. Carburetion was also Bing rather than Dell'Orto, the 750 Elefant using the 64/32/375 units of the 650 Indiana. Ignition on the 750 Elefant was now the Kokusan of the 750 Paso, but starting remained either kick or electric. As with the Paso the ignition was a two-stage type, with 6 degrees of advance to 1,700 rpm and 32 degrees from 3,600 rpm. Because of the larger valves than the Indiana, spark plugs were Champion RA6YC. Despite the lower compression, power for the 750 Elefant was up to 60.5 HP at 8,000 rpm.

Frame and Cycle Parts

Although the essential frame and running gear were unchanged from the 650, there were a number of cosmetic updates for the 750. The frame and swingarm

From 1987 Lucky Explorer sponsored the works Cagiva desert racers. By 1990 they were powered by 904cc fuel-injected engines and Edi Orioli won the 12th Paris-Dakar rally in early 1990. The success of these racers led to the production Lucky Explorer.

For 1987, the Elefant gained a 750cc engine and Lucky Explorer colors. Most alloy parts were black, complementing the white bodywork.

were now black, with frame numbers beginning at 6N000001. The 350 continued to use the sequence that began at 5N000001, still with red-painted frames. All 750 Elefants were produced in the black-and-white Lucky Explorer colors and decals of the 1987 works racers. Underneath the new bodywork, though, was an unchanged motorcycle from the final 650. Thus, although just about everything was black, including the anodized wheels and rear sprocket, the brakes and suspension were as before.

The changes with the 750 came with a larger (19-liter; 5.02-gallon) and wider fuel tank, large white

While the 750 replaced the 650 for 1987, the 350 continued, mainly for the domestic market. The colors of this 350 were red and black and the bodywork differed to that of the larger model.

Although the first Lucky Explorer Elefant was the 750 of 1987, most were 900s. 1990 saw the introduction of the 900 I.E., only available in Lucky Explorer colors. The 900 I.E. was larger than earlier Elefants, the engine protected by a drilled alloy guard.

engine-protection plate, and white plastic fork and brake shield that bolted to the wider front fender. The fuel tank now attached to an integral fairing, minus a Plexiglas screen, but with small, round LUCKY EXPLORER decals on the sides of the fuel tank. The seat was black with white CAGIVA lettering. There were also white plastic hand protectors, and the instruments and rectangular headlight were from the final 650 Elefant. For 1989 the 750 Elefant continued basically unchanged but for a new fairing, now with a small Plexiglas screen and substitution of the rectangular headlight by twin round headlights with a protective cover. The rear 05 Brembo brake caliper was upgraded to a 28mm twin-piston type, also requiring a new master cylinder, brake lever, brake line and modified muffler. However, the continual development of the Elefant through racing saw the 750 replaced by the 900 I.E. Lucky Explorer for 1990.

900 I.E. Lucky Explorer

Right from its conception the Elefant had been the basis of a works racing program, and 1987 saw the Elefant's first victory in a major desert race when Ciro De Petri won the Pharaohs Rally. These bikes were powered by 860cc (92mm x 64mm) versions of the five-speed Pantah engine. By 1988 the works Cagiva Lucky Explorer Paris-Dakar racers were using 904cc engines based on the six-speed 851 crankcases, but with a 92mm bore and 68mm stroke. These also featured the air-/oil-cooling system that would later figure prominently on 900cc two-valve Ducatis. The carburetion was by a Weber DCNF 36, and even with a low, 8.2:1 compression ratio, 85 HP was on tap. These 180kg (396-pound) desert racers were capable of over 200 km/h (125 mph), yet reliability problems plagued the Cagivas until 1990. That year Edi Orioli finally won the important Paris-Dakar Rally, the factory Elefant now featuring electronic fuel injection, but otherwise basically unchanged from the previous year. Yet even prior to this victory the 900 I.E. had been displayed at the 1989 Milan Show, and the release of the 900 I.E. in March 1990 was bolstered by this win. Most of the 900 I.E. was new, and as with the 750, it was only available in Lucky Explorer colors.

The engine of the 900 I.E. was based on that of the 900 Supersport, but with a five-speed gearbox. The hydraulic dry clutch was the same with actuation on the right side of the engine. Unlike earlier Elefants there was no longer a kickstarter. The frame was now steel and aluminum with the engine still located by alloy straps.

Engine and Drivetrain

Using the basic air-/oil-cooled 904cc engine of the 900 Supersport, the main update for the 900 I.E. was the replacement of the Weber carburetor by Weber-Marelli electronic fuel injection, along with lower-lift 750 camshafts. Unusually the 900 I.E. also featured a five-speed, rather than the usual 900 six-speed gearbox. Because the 31/62 primary drive was shared with the 900 Supersport, the gearbox ratios were new, and unique to the 1990 model 900 I.E. (see Appendix). The 900 I.E. also received a new 16-plate dry clutch comprising six 1.5mm and two 2mm driven plates, along with seven 2.5mm and one 3.5mm driving plates. Like the gearbox this setup was unique to the 1990 900 I.E. The hydraulic clutch actuation assembly was still incorporated in the right-side clutch cover for the 1990 900 I.E.

While the 9.2:1 pistons, crankshaft with 130mm con rods, and tri-spherical cylinder heads with 43mm and 38mm valves were the same as the 900 Supersport, the 900 I.E. featured the camshafts of the 750 Elefant and Paso. These provided the same valve timing, but less valve lift (9.35mm and 8.50mm). An important difference with the 900 I.E. over other desmodromic 900 Ducatis was the increase in both opening and closing valve clearances. Opening was now 0.15mm for the inlet and 0.2mm for the exhaust, with closing at 0.02mm for both. Cooling was by air and oil, but with twin radiators, one mounted on each side, under the fuel tank.

Oil coolers were mounted on each side of the frame downtubes and the Weber ECU on the left near the steering head.

There was also a new instrument layout for the 900 I.E., with six warning lights and an oil temperature gauge.

Surprisingly, the total oil capacity was reduced to only 2.5 liters. With a new three-chamber stainless steel muffler, power was increased significantly over the 750 Elefant, to 90 HP at 8,500 rpm (at the crankshaft). Unlike the 750, starting was now only electric, and final drive by 108-link Regina 135 OR 5/8- x 3/8-inch chain and 14- and 46-tooth sprockets.

Injection, Ignition, and Electrical System

The 900 I.E. was the first production air-cooled Ducati to feature the Weber I.A.W. electronic ignition system. This was virtually identical to that of the water-cooled 907 I.E. that appeared a few months later, with six sensors and one injector per cylinder. The processor was also a P7, but with a 024 EPROM. Instead of a water temperature sensor, an oil temperature sensor was positioned on the connection between the two oil radiators. Spark plugs were also Champion RA4HC. Unlike the 907, both the fuel pump and fuel filter were positioned outside the fuel tank, with a manual fuel tap.

The handlebar controls, including rectangular clutch and brake master cylinders, were similar to the 750 Elefant, although the switches were shared with the 906 Paso. The revised dashboard included a digital clock, speedometer, tachometer, oil temperature gauge, and six warning lights. Twin round double-filament 35/35-watt headlights were fitted, the electrical system powered by a 300-watt alternator and 12V/16-Ah battery.

Frame and Cycle Parts

Although the general frame layout followed that of the previous Elefant, the 900 I.E. featured a new double-cradle frame constructed of a square-section steel backbone with a detachable cradle of square-section aluminum. The front of the engine was still located by two aluminum straps, this being the weakest section. While it was adequate for the 650 Elefant, the design had its limitations with the larger, heavier, vibratory 900 motor. The 28.5-degree steering head angle was retained, but with an increase in trail to 123mm (4.84 inches). The swingarm was now an 851-style rectangular-section aluminum type, longer than before, and contributing to an increase in wheelbase to 1,570mm (61.8 inches). Frame numbers for the 900 I.E. began at 1B000001.

While the general style of the 900 I.E. followed that of the earlier 750 Lucky Explorer, the 900 was more closely patterned on the Paris-Dakar racers. The overall dimensions were increased, accentuated by the large (24-liter, 6.34-gallon) fuel tank that merged into the fairing. The white Lucky Explorer had larger round, red decals than before, along with red and gold stripes. The seat was black, and the only CAGIVA lettering was on the fuel tank. Besides the new bodywork, that included a larger sump protection plate, there was completely new suspension, wheels, and brakes. At the front was a leading-axle Marzocchi 42mm PA SD Nissin 298 fork, similar to that of the 750 Elefant, but providing 230mm (9.05 inches) of wheel travel. The rear suspension operated through an Öhlins shock absorber and Soft Damp linkage as before. This also provided 230mm of wheel travel. The wheels were now aluminum rims designed for tubeless tires, laced to alloy hubs. Compared to the earlier Elefant, front wheel size was reduced, with a 2.15 x 19-inch rim. The front tire was either 100 x 90 x 19 Pirelli MT60 or Metzeler Enduro 3°. At the rear was

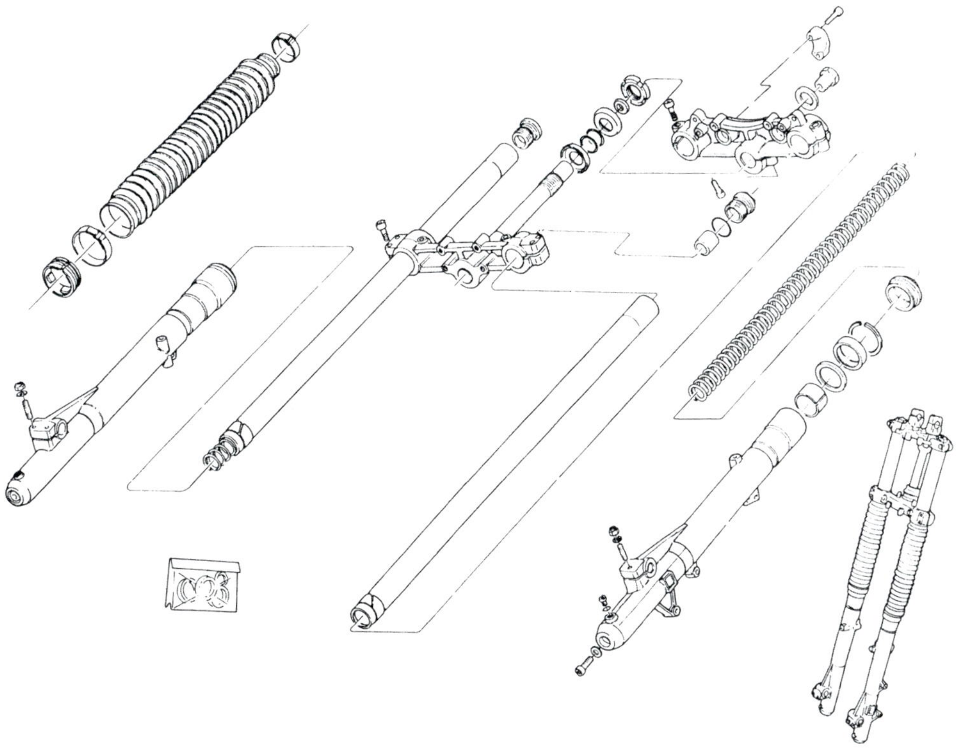

The 900 I.E. had a new front fork. This was a leading-axle Marzocchi 42mm PA SD Nissin 298.

a wider 3.00 x 17-inch aluminum rim, with a Pirelli or Metzeler 140 x 80 x 17 tire. The braking system was new, with Japanese Nissin rather than the usual Brembo components. At the front was a single 296mm stainless steel disc, with a Nissin two-piston floating caliper. A 12mm handlebar master cylinder operated the front brake. The rear brake was similar, but with a 240mm stainless steel disc and 13mm master cylinder.

1991 Model Year

Competition success continued for the works Cagiva in 1991, with ex-250cc motocross World Champion Danny LaPorte taking victory in the Pharaohs Rally. Although the factory bikes were no longer sponsored by Lucky Explorer (now Jean Staleven), the production 900 I.E. Lucky Explorer continued as before with few changes. Still the only 900 Ducati with a five-speed gearbox, the clutch was also unchanged. Final drive was now by a D.I.D. 50V 5/8- x 3/8-inch chain, and from March 1991 the Explorer shared the 350-watt alternator of the 900 I.E. GT. While still using a Marzocchi 42mm fork, wheel travel was increased to 250mm (9.84 inches).

900 I.E.GT

In March 1991 a 900 I.E. GT became available alongside the Lucky Explorer. While the Explorer

The Soft Damp rear suspension was similar to earlier Elefants but for a new aluminum swingarm. There was a wider, 3.00 x 17 inch rear wheel and a 240mm Nissin rear disc brake. The large muffler was a three-chamber stainless steel type.

There was a new 19-inch front wheel for the 900 I.E., plus a single 296mm front disc with twin piston floating Nissin brake caliper.

continued with the five-speed gearbox, the 900 I.E. GT received the six-speed gearbox of other large-crankcase models. As with the 900 SS and 907 I.E., a competition close-ratio six-speed gearbox was also available. The clutch actuation was still incorporated in the right side cover, and the 16-plate composition uniform with other six-speed 900s. The engine was still black with gold valve covers. In other respects the engine was unchanged from the Lucky Explorer, continuing with the 750 camshafts and Weber I.A.W. electronic fuel injection system. The power was now stated at the rear wheel rather the crankshaft, this now 67.7 HP at 8,000 rpm. Torque was 52.1 lb./ft. at 5,000 rpm. In response to problem that had occurred with the earlier model with the battery going flat after prolonged running with the lights on, the alternator was upgraded to 350-watts. This also required a new crankshaft and side cover. Another problem with the Lucky Explorer had been the unshielded muffler, this rectified on the GT by a wire protector. Final drive for the GT was by D.I.D. 50V 5/8- x 3/8-inch chain, with 15- and 48-tooth sprockets.

The 900 I.E. GT had a new frame number sequence, beginning at 1BE001011, and while the frame, swingarm, and most of the cycle parts were shared with the Lucky Explorer, the GT featured a few important updates. These reflected the more street orientation of the GT over the Explorer. The front fork was now a Marzocchi 45mm PA FD 298 Nissin, this providing less travel (210mm; 8.26 inches), and increased trail of 127mm (5 inches). The rear Öhlins shock absorber and Soft Damp linkage provided 190mm (7.48 inches) of wheel travel. The brakes and wheels were unchanged. The 900 I.E. GT continued through 1992, identical but for another small alteration to the clutch layout, bringing it in line with the 900 Supersport (see Appendix). The clutch actuation was moved to the left and both the clutch cover and valve covers were gray. With black bodywork, and large CAGIVA and 900 i.e. decals, with a small powered by DUCATI decal at the rear, the styling of the 900 I.E. GT set the scene for the next series of Elefant.

Elefant 900

For 1992 the works Cagivas were back with Lucky Explorer sponsorship, and success continued with LaPorte's second place in the Paris Le Cap rally. In 1993 Orioli took the works Elefant to victory in the Pharoahs Rally, following this in 1994 with his third win in the Paris-Dakar-Paris rally. Given this result, the final development of the Elefant in early 1993, the Elefant 900, was rather surprising. While much of the Elefant 900 was carried over from the 900 I.E., the Weber I.A.W. injection system was discarded, and replaced by the normal 900 Supersport Mikuni BSDT 38 carburetors. This seemed a retrograde move, but was presumably done to reduce costs. The works racing program continued successfully through 1994, Orioli and Jordi Arcarons dominating the Paris-Dakar-Paris rally with their 80 horsepower Lucky Strike racers. In the 1995 Granada-Dakar rally Arcarons finished second on his Lucky Strike Elefant 900, with Orioli third on a similar Camper Elefant 900.

Engine and Drivetrain

The engine of the Elefant 900 was the six-speed unit of the 900 Supersport, with identical specifications. This

While similar to the 900 I.E. Lucky Explorer, the GT had 45mm Marzocchi forks and a six-speed gearbox. This is the brochure for the 1992 version.

included the primary ratio, clutch, gearbox, crankshaft, pistons and cylinder head. Thus the camshafts were now those of the 900 Supersport (rather than the previous 750), with the same valve timing as before, but with increased valve lift (11.76mm inlet and 10.56mm exhaust). The cooling system now included only one oil radiator. Carburetion was by Mikuni BDST 38 constant-vacuum carburetors (BDST 38 B 135 with different jetting for Switzerland and the U.S. – see Appendix). Ignition was the two-stage Kokusan of the 900 Supersport (with Champion RA6HC spark plugs). One difference from other Ducati models was the inclusion of an open-loop catalytic converter inside the huge muffler. Thus the power was reduced to 68 HP at 6,500 rpm at the crankshaft. Final drive was by 108-link D.I.D. 50V 5/8- x 3/8-inch chain, with 15- and 46-tooth sprockets.

Frame and Cycle Parts

While the steel backbone with detachable aluminum dual-cradle frame was as before (along with the 28.5-degree steering head angle), a new upside-down 45mm Showa fork reduced the trail to 114mm (4.49 inches). There was a new set of frame numbers for the Elefant 900, starting at 5B000001. The Showa forks provided 210mm (8.3 inches) of wheel travel and featured plastic lower fork-leg protectors. The rear Soft Damp suspension unit was no longer an expensive Öhlins, but now a Boge, with a stroke of 190mm (7.48

For 1993 the 900 Elefant was revamped. The fuel injection made way for normal Mikuni 38mm carburetors and there was now a catalytic converter incorporated in the muffler. U.S. versions lost the Cagiva trademark and were known as Ducatis.

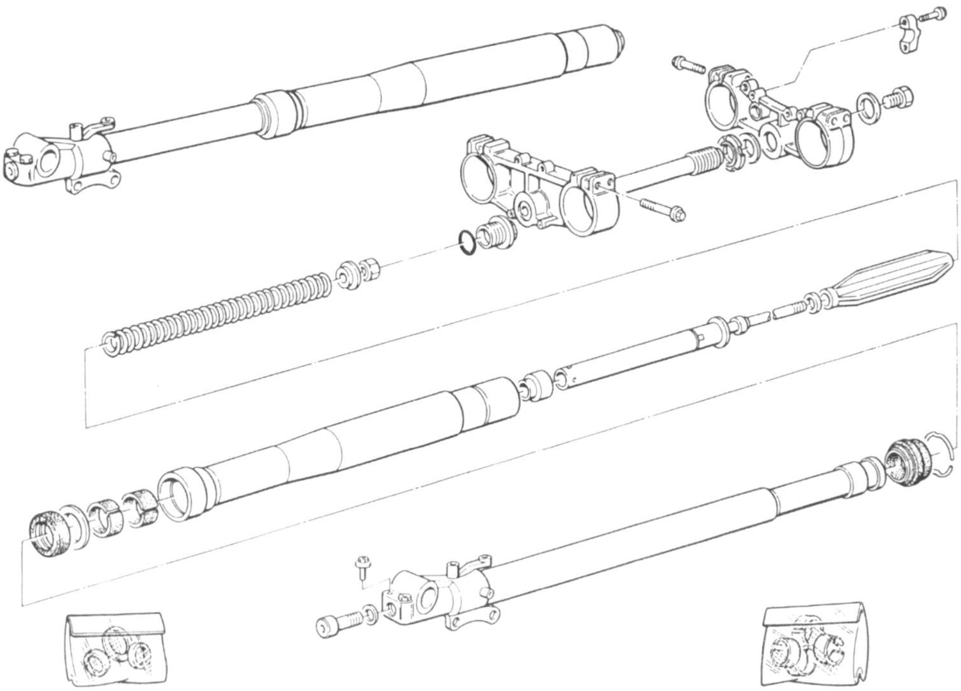

Upside-down 45mm Showa forks were fitted to all 900cc Elefants after 1993.

inches). Along with the new suspension came new brakes, now Brembo. At the front were twin 282mm stainless steel discs, with floating twin-piston Brembo calipers operated by a 15mm master cylinder. The rear disc was a 240mm stainless steel item, also with a twin-piston floating Brembo caliper, but operated by a 13mm master cylinder. The aluminum-rimmed spoked 19- and 17-inch wheels were as before, now also fitted with Dunlop Trailmax tires in addition to the earlier Pirelli or Metzeler. The fuel tank/fairing unit was also unchanged, still with dual headlights, and the same instrument layout was carried over but for the omission of the oil temperature gauge. An important improve-

The instrument panel on the Elefant 900 was similar to that of the 900 I.E. except for the lack of an oil temperature gauge.

From 1994 the Elefant 900 and Elefant 750 were also offered in Lucky Explorer colors. This is a 900 with dual front 282mm Brembo disc brakes.

The final Elefant 900 was an attractive metallic-dark-blue. This is the 1995 version. Although the seat height was lower than earlier versions this was still a very tall motorcycle.

ment was a much lower seat than earlier versions, reducing the seat height to 835mm (32.9 inches). For 1993 the Elefant 900 was painted maroon and gold, with ELEFANT decals on the sides of the fuel tank/fairing. In an effort to associate the Elefant with the better known Ducati brand name, U.S. versions of the Elefant 900 were called the Ducati E-900, and featured DUCATI decals on the sides of the fairing. For 1994 the Elefant 900 was unchanged except for a change in color to dark-blue, with yellow and blue stripes, and a large red E900 decal on the fuel tank/fairing. Lucky Explorer colors were also offered for 1994. U.S. Elefant 900s were still known as the Ducati E 900. There were few updates for 1995. Only Dunlop Trailmax tires were fitted and the colors changed (to metallic-dark-blue), along with new decals and a revised seat. Lucky Explorer versions received DUNLOP decals on the swingarm. Although production was discontinued during 1996, the Elefant 900 was listed again in February 1998.

Elefant 750

Joining the Elefant 900 for 1994 was another 750 Elefant. Reintroduced in November 1993, the Elefant 750 took the basic running gear of the earlier 900 I.E. GT, mated to the five-speed engine of the 750 Supersport. Along with Mikuni BDST 38 B 148 carburetors it featured the hydraulically actuated wet clutch and air-/oil-cooled cylinders, and the external oil cooler of the 750 Supersport. Shared with the Elefant 900 was a catalytic converter, and the power was 60 HP at 6,500 rpm. This reintroduced Elefant 750 received a new set of frame numbers, beginning at 6B000001. While nearly all the chassis components were shared with the larger 900, the 750 still used the earlier 45mm Marzocchi fork and single 296mm Nissin front disc brake. A Nissin was also used at the rear, along with the E900's Boge shock absorber. The Marzocchi fork increased the wheelbase slightly over the 900 (to 1,560mm; 61.4 inches), and, despite only featuring a single front disc brake, the dry weight was increased to 188kg (414 pounds). Colors of the Elefant 750 for 1994 were red and silver, with large E750 decals on the tank. For 1995 the Elefant 750 was in the same colors as the Elefant 900 (with a new seat), and a Lucky Explorer version was also available. There was also a specific Brazilian-market Elefant 750 that had different carburetors and jetting. The Elefant 750 continued through the 1996 season, but, as with other Ducati models, suffered from a lack of supply of various components.

Gran Canyon

As the Elefant was always more suited to the street than off-road, the Gran Canyon represented the most

Joining the Elefant 900 in 1994 was the similarly styled Elefant 750. The five-speed engine was from the 750 Supersport, and this retained the earlier 45mm Marzocchi forks and single 296mm Nissin front disc brake.

practical development of the design. Designed by Pierre Terblanche at the Cagiva Research Center in San Marino. Terblanche took the basic chassis of the Elefant, and created a more street-oriented motorcycle, styled along the lines of the 600cc Cagiva Canyon. The Gran Canyon successfully combined the Ducati 904cc fuel-injected V-twin with a chassis featuring longer-travel suspension and a more upright riding position than other 900 Ducatis. Although displayed at the Cologne Show at the end of 1996, it wasn't until May 1998 that the Gran Canyon made it into production at Varese.

Engine and Drivetrain

No longer purely taking a standard Ducati engine off the production line, Cagiva took a six-speed 1998-spec 900 Monster engine and adapted it to their requirements. Thus all the major components were shared with the Monster, including the gearbox, straight-cut

The 1995 Elefant 750 was painted in the same colors as the Elefant 900 and continued to be available for several years. This example has a non-standard exhaust, replacing the catalytic converter.

The 1995 Elefant 750 was also produced in Lucky Explorer livery.

Representing possibly the ultimate Elefant was Pierre Terblanche's Gran Canyon of 1998. Although still a little heavy and tall, the Gran Canyon was a splendid back-road weapon. This example has Arrow mufflers.

While it looked like a stock 900 Monster or Supersport engine, the Gran Canyon engine was modified by Cagiva. Weber I.A.W. electronic fuel injection replaced the Mikuni carburetors, and camshafts were from the 750. Unfortunately small valves restricted horsepower.

Although the instrument panel was attractive, the Perspex cover created reflections.

31- /62-tooth primary drive, crankshaft, con rods and 9.2:1 Tecnol pistons. For some reason the cylinder head was that of the small-valve (41mm inlet and 35mm exhaust) Monster, but with 750 Supersport camshafts (the same as the earlier Elefant). The cylinders were Asso, with internal oil-return lines, and the engine covers on the Gran Canyon black. The two-into-two exhaust system was high-rise, the large mufflers exiting under the seat. The Gran Canyon also saw a return to the Weber I.A.W. electronic fuel injection, but with the 1.6M CP. Maximum power was 73.4 HP at 8,000 rpm, with 57.5 lb./ft. of torque at 5,500 rpm. Final drive included a D.I.D. 50V 5/8- x 5/16-inch chain, with 15- and 45-tooth sprockets. The electrical system consisted of a 420-watt alternator and 12v18Ah battery.

The Gran Canyon had an all-new front end. This included 45mm leading-axle Marzocchi forks and a 19-inch front wheel. Brakes were Nissin, the twin 296mm discs being gripped by twin-piston floating calipers. Stainless steel brake lines were standard. Falloon

Gran Canyon Modifications

For most street duties it would be difficult to argue against the Gran Canyon being the perfect sporting motorcycle. The combination of a relatively upright riding position, conservative steering geometry and long-travel suspension made it a formidable back-road motorcycle at sub-80-mph speeds. However, lack of power and excessive weight hurt the Gran Canyon, and improvements in these areas pays dividends.

For some reason Cagiva fitted the small-valve 900 Monster engine in the Gran Canyon, along with the low-lift (750) camshafts. Combined with an extremely restrictive (and heavy) exhaust system the Gran Canyon was underpowered in standard form. Unfortunately, increasing the power of the Gran Canyon wasn't an easy proposition. The camshaft could be exchanged for one with a more radical profile (even that of a standard 900 Supersport), but the small valves ultimately limited power. Also, any changes to the inlet and exhaust system required a new EPROM for the 16M I.A.W. ECU. Because of limited demand these are not readily available, as are suitable replacement exhaust systems.

As for the Gran Canyon chassis, only the rear shock absorber needed updating. There were also some dubious plastic styling attachments that were easily removed. The factory addressed some of these problems during 1999 when three additional versions of the Gran Canyon were offered. The first was a supermoto with power boosted by a remapped injection system and freer-flowing carbon-fiber mufflers. Other updates included a black frame, matte black-and-red paintwork, a higher screen and high-performance Metzeler street tires. Joining the super moto was a touring version of the regular Gran Canyon with the higher screen and a hard luggage kit of panniers and rear top box. The final version was a special French tricolor model produced to celebrate the French World Cup soccer victory. Each of the 37 members of the squad was presented with one of the blue, white, and red machines, with a further 200 available in France.

Frame and Cycle Parts

While the Gran Canyon frame was based on that of the Elefant 900, it was now constructed entirely of box-section steel tubing. The engine was also supported more effectively than on the Elefant, the twin aluminum straps replaced by a lower frame loop. Frame numbers started at ZCGM300AAWV000001. All the bodywork was new, the plastic fuel tank merging into the fairing to create enough space for the airbox. The tank featured twin filler caps, and the fairing two 50-watt headlights. There were many cosmetic body parts, including plastic frame covers, sump guard, and rear fender.

The suspension was new, the 45mm non-adjustable leading-axle Marzocchi fork providing 170mm (6.7 inches) of wheel travel. At the rear was a Boge shock operating through the usual Soft Damp linkage, also providing 170mm of wheel travel. Although the black-anodized aluminum-rimmed spoked wheels were similar to the Elefant, the rims were wider. At the front was either a 2.15 or 2.50 x 19-inch rim, with a 4.25 x 17-inch on the rear. The Gran Canyon came shod with any one of Dunlop Trailmax D604, Pirelli MT80RS, Metzeler Enduro 4°, Michelin T66X, or Bridgestone Trail Wing 152 tires.

Braking followed that of the earlier 900 I.E., but with dual 296mm discs on the front, along with Nissin 25.4mm twin-piston floating calipers. After frame number 00911 there were replacement rubber front brake hoses, as the earlier versions were prone to distortion under braking. At the rear was the usual 240mm disc, but with a Nissin 27mm two-piston caliper. Colors for the Gran Canyon were either red and silver or silver and blue. If anything detracted from the excellence of the Gran Canyon as a back-road motorcycle *par excellence* it was the dry weight of 193kg (425.5 pounds). The Gran Canyon was also a large motorcycle, rolling on a long 1,548mm (60.94-inch) wheelbase, with a tall seat height of 825mm (32.5 inches).

CHAPTER SEVEN

The 1990s Supersport

900, 750, 600, 400, 350 Supersport, 900 Superlight, Final Edition

Without doubt, the carbureted Supersport of 1991-98 has become one of the classic modern Ducatis. Until the advent of the 916 in 1994, they were Ducati's mainstay in terms of sales, and remained a competent and desirable sporting machine until they were replaced in 1998. Although still heavily derived from the flawed 1990 version, amazingly the new Supersport looked like a fresh design. It was functionally superior to its predecessor in nearly every respect. Soon after the appearance of the 900 at the Cologne Show at the end of 1990, came a range of smaller Supersports, initially in 750, then 350 and 400, and finally 600. So successful has the model been that total production has exceeded that of any other model, with over 50,000 (including the earlier 750 Sport and 900 Supersport) being produced through until 1997.

900 Supersport
1991 Model Year

Production of the European-specification 900 Supersport commenced in December 1990, and for the U.S. in March 1991.

Engine and Drivetrain

Engine numbers continued the sequence begun with the 1989 900 Supersport (ZDM 904 A2 C 000001), this sequence shared with all air-cooled 904cc two-valve twins until 1999. As with the 907 I.E., 1991 large-crankcase engines were strengthened around the base of the cylinder, although unlike the 907 I.E. the crankcases were now unpainted aluminum. The 900 SS retained the black cylinders and heads. The engine covers were also black, but with silver rocker and clutch

Possibly the classic Supersport, the fully faired 1991 900. Red with a white frame and white wheels, the decals were simple and understated.

Also available with a half fairing, this showed the rather untidy black painted 900cc engine and exposed oil cooler.

covers. Clutch actuation was on the left side for the 1991 900 Supersport. Apart from the ignition and alternator, the only internal modification for 1991 was a new dry clutch, initially carrying part number 19020012A and consisting of seven 2mm driven plates, seven 3mm driving plates, one curved 1.5mm plate, and one inner 3.5mm driving plate. This clutch was superseded in early 1992 by part number 19020013A that could be retrofitted. So problematic was the clutch on early 1991 900 Supersports that the clutch friction material was modified three times during 1991, in January, March and June. Camshafts, valves, pistons, crankshaft, six-speed gearbox and 31/62 straight-cut geared primary drive were all identical to the 1990 900 Supersport. For the 991 Supersport the valve guide seals were Viton instead of silicon rubber. After engine number 001313 the pistons and rings were the modified set as fitted to the 906 Paso. Also unchanged from the 1990 900 SS was the air-/oil-cooling system, although the oil radiator was now located in a far less satisfactory location on the front exhaust valve cover. The oil lines were braided steel, but the oil radiator was especially vulnerable to debris thrown by the front wheel. As with other six-speed Ducatis, a close-ratio competition six-speed gearbox was also available for the 900 Supersport. With a ratio of 2.000 covering all six gears, this was much closer than the standard 2.877 ratio, and considerably closer than the 2.574 of even the 851 SP and 851 Racing.

Finally the troublesome Weber carburetor went, replaced by twin constant-vacuum Mikuni 38 B67 carburetors similar to those successfully fitted to the

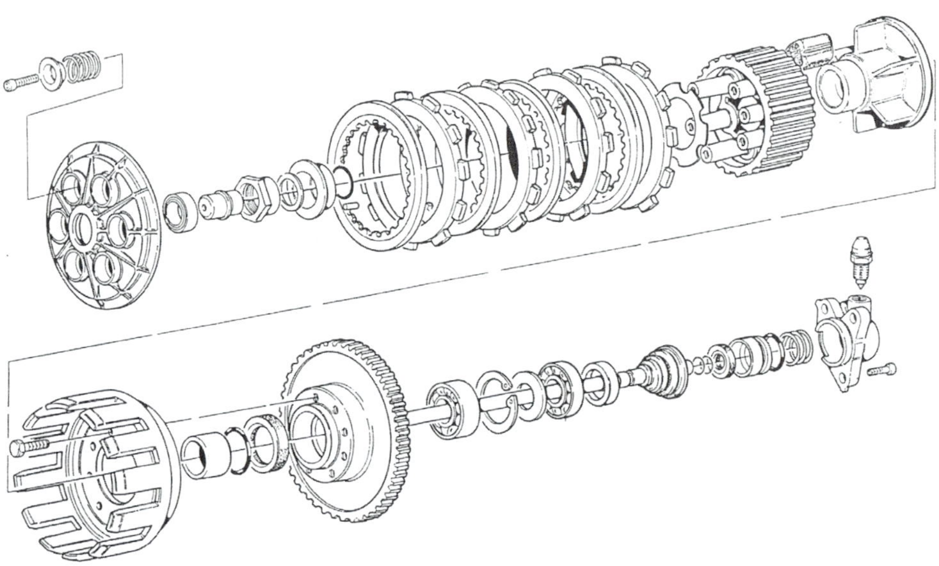

The hydraulic dry clutch of the 1991 900 Supersport. The actuation mechanism was now on the left. Over the next few years there were a number of changes to the clutch plate composition.

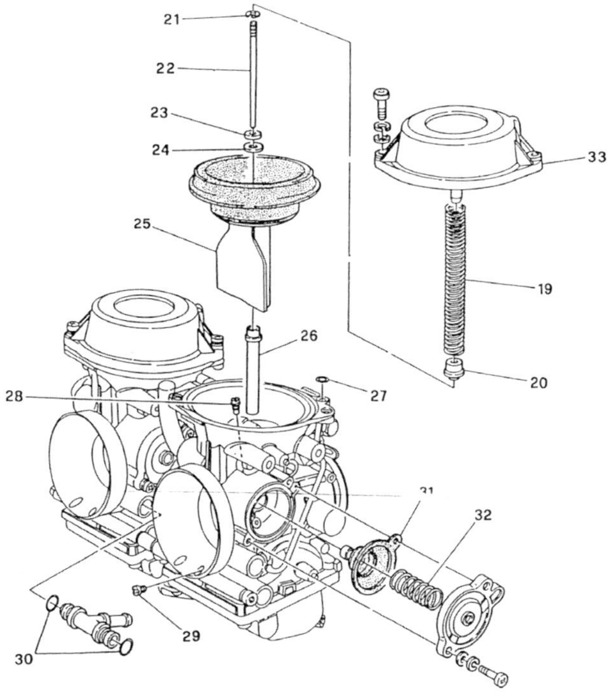

Following the success of the Mikuni constant-vacuum carburetors on the Japanese-market 400 Supersport Junior of 1989 and 1990, they found their way onto the 900 Supersport for 1991. Although still not perfect, these were an improvement on the previous Weber.

Japanese-market 400 Supersport Junior of 1989 and 1990. While not perfect, they were much better than the Weber, hampered largely by the very long inlet tracts that led to poor carburetion when cold, and carburetor icing in severe conditions. U.S. and Swiss versions featured BDST 38 B73s and B97s with leaner jetting (see Appendix). There was also trouble with dirt from the front wheel entering the mixture adjustment screw, these fitted with small covers from June 1991. Despite the long equal-length inlet manifolds there was still room for a large-capacity air filter under the reshaped fuel tank. The exhaust system was similar to the 1990 900 Supersport, with a two-into-two system and aluminum mufflers. The final drive was by 98-link D.I.D. 520 VL2 1/4 x 5/8-inch chain, with 15- and 38- tooth sprockets. Power for 1991 was quoted at the rear wheel, this being 73 HP at 7,000 rpm.

Ignition, Electrical System, and Switches

After a brief flirtation with the Marelli Digiplex on the 1990 900 SS, ignition returned to the electronic inductive Kokusan. Advance was 6 degrees up to 1700 rpm, and progressively to 32 degrees from 1700-2600 rpm. Spark plugs were Champion RA6YC. With the change of ignition there was also a return to the 300-watt alternator. Other electrical equipment consisted of a 12V/16-Ah battery, a fuel pump inside the fuel tank, and a rectangular 55/60-watt headlight. The switches and instrument panel were largely unchanged.

Frame and Cycle Parts

Most of the changes for 1991 were to the chassis, and here they were significant. Frame numbers began at ZDM 900 SC 2 000001. The white-painted chrome-molybdenum steel frame was similar to before, but with a number of changes to the layout of the tubing, as well as a different rear subframe. One of the weaknesses of the new frame in relation to the earlier version was the small front bracing tube now connected the top of the steering head to the lower tube rather than the other way round, but generally the 1991 model frame was an improvement. The steering head angle was steeper at 26 degrees 15 minutes, and trail was down to 103mm (4.05 inch), with 25 degrees of steering lock on either side. Not only did the 1991 Supersport steer more quickly, but also a new aluminum swingarm helped reduce the wheelbase to 1410mm (56.5 inch). The swingarm pivoted on needle bearings, and featured a new chain adjustment system with the axle located by rather weak M6mm x 70mm bolts. The footpeg and muffler brackets were bolt-on aluminum pieces, rather than being incorporated in the subframe. Front and rear suspension too was an improvement on the earlier Marzocchis. Shorter inverted 41mm Showa GD 011 forks provided adjustment for spring preload (10mm-25mm), as well as 14 positions for compression and rebound damping. Front wheel travel was 120mm (4.7 inches). At the rear there was still the cantilever rear suspension with a single shock absorber, also now a Showa, a GD 022-007-OX with a remote reservoir, yellow-painted spring, and a stroke of 65mm (2.56 inches). The 12mm-longer (0.5 inch) shock also contributed to a raised rear end, and effective rake was 25 degrees.

None of the bodywork was shared with the earlier Supersport, and the new model was not only a styling triumph, but also much easier to service. Simply by releasing a clip on the front of the tank it could be pivoted to allow easy access to the battery, airbox and fuel pipes. Only a dual seat was provided, and there were two versions, full or half fairing, both red. Ducati North America specified a paint code of #7530 with paint available from Color Rite in California (800-736-7980). Decals on the 1991 Supersports were very understated, with

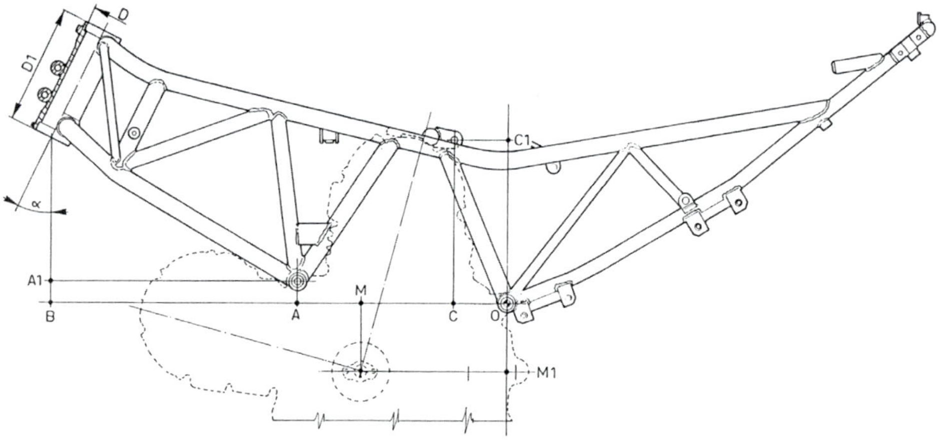

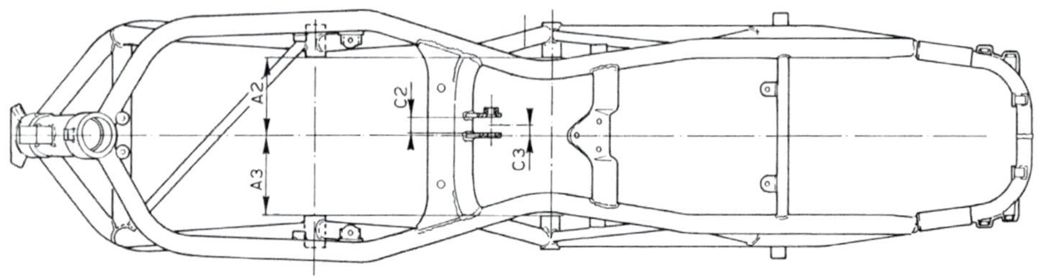

Although the 1991 900 Supersport frame was similar to that of the 1990 model, it had a steeper steering head angle and revised steering head support tubes. The frame was unchanged throughout its model life and cracks around the steering head were not unknown.

A practical feature of the 900 Supersport was the hinged fuel tank.

white and black DUCATI on the tank and full fairing. These were complemented by small 900 SS decals on the tail section, DESMO on the sides of the fairing, and a small DUCATI above the headlight. All 1991 Supersports suffered a problem with interference between the seat and base, rectified from 1992 by higher rubber seat supports. Red mirrors attached to the top fairing mount were standard, and continued to be an inferior fitment throughout the Supersport's production life. While the white-painted 17-inch Brembo wheels were carried over from before, the brakes were now standardized with the 851. These consisted of twin 320mm x 5mm stainless steel front discs with Brembo P4 32d calipers on the front. After frame number 001601 the braking system was updated to newer P4 30/34 Gold-series Brembo calipers with 34mm and 30mm pistons. The front master cylinder was the rectangular PS15 of before, and at the rear was a 245mm x 6.4mm disc with a Brembo P2105N caliper and PS 11mm master cylinder. Standard brake pads were FREN-DO 965 on the front and FREN-DO FD 72GG on the rear. After frame number 002306 there was a revised rear brake pedal switch, now mounted on the back of the footpeg bracket rather than incorporated with the banjo bolt. Tires were Michelin A/M59, these not the most suitable, although the higher-profile (120/70 x 17) front tire provided much improved steering characteristics over the earlier model. Where the Supersport really scored was not so much in the power but the weight, which at a

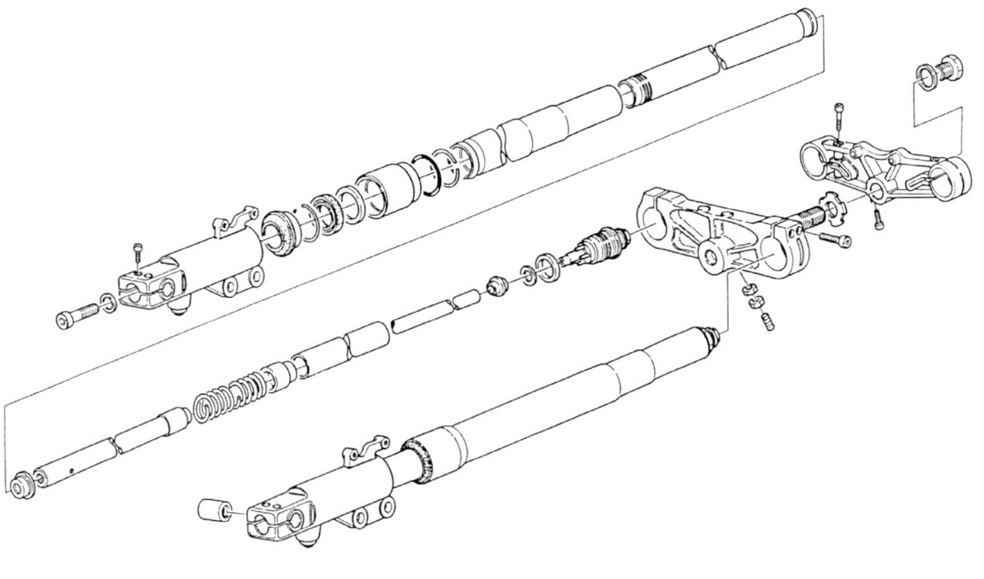

New for the 1991 900 Supersport were fully adjustable inverted 41mm Showa GD 011 forks.

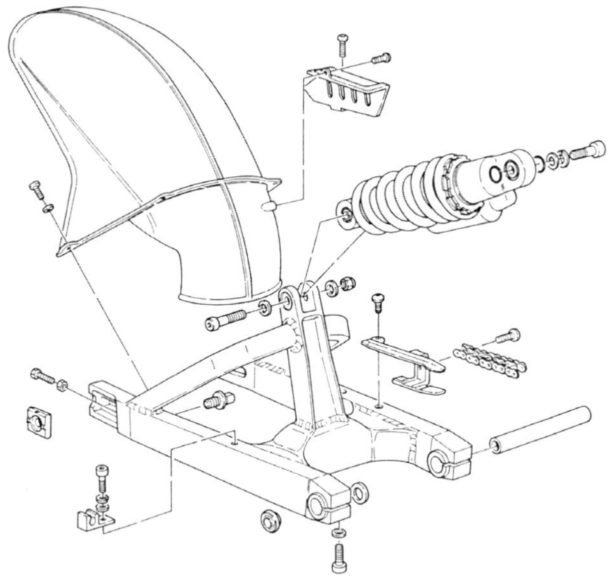

The aluminum cantilever swingarm was also new for 1991, with a less satisfactory chain-adjustment system. The shock absorber was a Showa GD 022-007-OX with a remote reservoir.

measured 440.5 pounds (200kg) wet by *Cycle* magazine in September 1991 gave the 900 Supersport an enviable power to weight ratio.

The riding position was also completely updated, the higher-rise clip-on handlebars and lower footpegs giving a unique sport-touring riding position. When initially released this new Supersport was an instant success, with 2,308 1991 versions built, of which 255 came to the U.S. Still, this production represented a large increase on previous years, indicating the growth of Ducati as a niche market manufacturer.

1992 Model Year

For 1992 there were only a few changes to the specification of the 900 Supersport, these mainly cosmetic. Although the engine was essentially as before, an important update was to the clutch. To improve the action from standstill, a 2mm steel plate splined to the clutch drum (1901 0011A) replaced the 3.5mm plate splined to the clutch housing. The complete 16-plate set carried the part number 19020013A and now consisted of two 2mm driven plates, one 3mm driving plate, one 1.5mm convex spring plate, and six driving plates alternated with six driven plates. After several years of clutch experimentation on 900 engines this clutch set would continue through until the advent of the fuel-injected model of 1998. The flywheel-to-flange fastening was also improved, with seven (rather than five) screws, these also stronger (7714 0011A). From January 1992 the valve guides were changed from cast-iron to aluminum-bronze, all cylinder heads featuring these new valve guides being identified by a V1 marking on the timing cover side. Carburetor icing was still a problem, and in November 1992 a Mikuni carburetor heating kit became available for the 900. This ran two pipes from the oil radiator to the carburetor float bowls.

For 1992 the 900 Supersport was again offered in fully faired and half-faired versions, but with a black option alongside the red. The frame was still painted white and there was a removable solo seat cowling. The black and white decals were much as before, though now there was only SUPERSPORT on the tailpiece, and red, white, and black flashes with the DESMO

Changes for 1992 were mainly cosmetic. There was a rear seat cowling, new decals, gold brake calipers and black wheels.

on the fairing. Half-faired versions didn't receive these decals, only the DESMO. Mirrors on the half-faired models came in black. From April 1992 there were new seat-to-frame buffers fitted to alleviate interference between the seat padding and the fairing side panels. After problems with the weak chain-adjustment bolts, these were increased in size to M8mm x70mm from frame number 003306. For the U.S. these were from 002474-2505 and 002596-2605, with California 900 Supersports from 002578-2595. All 1992 900 Supersports featured the Gold series Brembo P4 30/34 front brake calipers. While the 17-inch Brembo wheels were as before, these were now painted black on red models, the black Supersport retaining white wheels. The front fork travel was also reduced to 103mm (4 inches) for 1992. Production for the 1992 model year

Also available for 1992 was a black 900 Supersport, this continuing with white wheels.

For 1993 there were more cosmetic changes. Although the wheels were still black, the frame was bronze and there were new decals. The red color for 1993 was slightly lighter than before.

commenced in September 1991, with total production being 3,482. Most of these were full-fairing and red, the black being less popular.

1993 Model Year

Cosmetic changes again predominated for 1993. There were new graphics, all decals now being silver with gold borders. On the fairing were now SUPERSPORT DESMODUE decals, and the frame was a new bronze color. The wheels were still painted black, and only red 900 Supersports were available, the black of 1992 not being successful. The red was slightly lighter, with a code of #7530 and this would continue through until 1997. Within the engine the only change was a larger, 350-watt, alternator, and a new oil pressure switch (5394 0081C). Spark plugs were now Champion RA6HC. An important development during the year was the increasing of the diameter of the cylinder head studs to 8.0mm (766 1 001 2C), up from 7.6mm. These were fitted from engine number 013833. This was in response to the problem of cylinder head studs breaking, but still wasn't a totally satisfactory modification. There was an M stamped on the cylinder head to identify the new bolts, earlier engines being distinguished by an O.

There were some small alterations to the front suspension and brake specification. While the Showa front forks were still 41mm upside-down, the travel was increased to 120mm (4.72 inches) and the front master cylinder now a Brembo PS 16mm (up from 15mm) to improve braking feel. From July 1993 there were also new front brake calipers, still Brembo P4 30/34C, but modified to reduce the handlebar master cylinder stroke. These revised calipers were identified by a blue paint mark. All 1993 models received a new horn (5164 0011A). As before both full- and half-fairing versions were available. Production for the 1993 model year was 4,767, with most still being fully faired. Of these 850 made their way to the U.S.

1994 Model Year

With the 888 fading, and the 916 not yet in production, by 1994 the 900 Supersport was the leading sporting model in Ducati's lineup. For this year there were many more changes than before, with the Supersport inheriting many of the components from the Superlight. Although the engine specifications were largely unchanged, the engine covers were now painted silver, but still with black timing belt covers. As the engine was shared with the 900 Monster, the cylinders and heads were now also silver, but with black rocker covers. Although the camshafts were unaltered, these now had timing figures quoted at 0.2mm measurement clearance (see Appendix). Also taking some time to come were offset camshaft keys, now available to fine-tune the valve timing if required. Five keys now provided advance or retard in a range from 2 degrees to 10 degrees. Power for 1994 was quoted at the crankshaft, 80 HP at 7,000 rpm. The alternator cover bearing was now lubricated, the blind cap on the crankshaft replaced by a cap with a 0.5mm hole to allow oil to lubricate the bearing. To improve battery charging the alternator cable was increased in section to 2.5mm^2 and was now PVC. The voltage regulator was updated in May with the same Ducati Energia unit as fitted to the 916 (54040081A). This was stamped with identifying numbers 343637. To aid voltage regulator cooling, the regulator was now mounted on metal bushes rather than plastic.

Cosmetically the 900 Supersport looked much as before, except for frame-matching bronze wheels and headlight support, along with black footpeg supports and foot levers. The big change came with the swingarm and suspension. These were from the 1993 900 Superlight, the 41mm forks being upgraded Showa GD 021 with bronze fork legs, providing 120mm (4.72 inches) of travel. While the fork was of higher specification, it provided less range of adjustment for both compression and rebound damping, four for compression and six for rebound. With the new forks came a larger (20mm) axle, though the 17mm rear axle was unchanged. The rear suspension unit was the Showa GD 022 of before, but operating the stronger 1993 900 Superlight aluminum swingarm. The tires were now Michelin A/M89 and the rear chain a D.I.D. 520 VL4 5/8- x 1/4-inch. Also from the Superlight were remote fluid reservoirs for the clutch and front brake master cylinders (this was contrary to the official workshop manual which showed the 900 sharing its brakes with the 750 for 1994). The front brake discs were also slightly thinner (to 4mm), not the most practical modification considering the problems with discs warping under severe use, and there were new brake pads, FREN-DO 222 front and rear. There was also a new sidestand for 1994, along with revised seat and helmet locks. This year the 900 SS was still available in full- and half-faired versions, but only in red. Production of the 1994 model year 900 Supersport was only 1,877, excluding the slightly different 900 CRs and SPs for the U.S. (see accompanying sidebar).

1995 Model Year

Rather than alter the basic design, the 900 Supersport continued with minor developments for 1995. From engine number 023160 (frame number 016373) there was a new alternator (26440122A), still 350 watts, both the stator and rotor being distinguished by a blue paint mark. As before, the main changes were cosmetic, the engine timing belt covers and rear sprocket cover gray. After two years of bronze the frame was now the gold of the 916, and the sidestand gray rather than black. There were more significant changes to the instrument panel and braking system. Above the speedometer was now an oil temperature gauge. The rear P2 105N brake caliper was positioned under the swingarm, as with the 900 Monster. With the new rear brake came a revised

There were more changes for 1995. The rear brake caliper was underslung and the frame 916-gold. This half-faired example has Termignoni mufflers.

A 1996 half-faired 900 Supersport, much the same as for 1995 but for new engine castings and a sound-absorbing clutch cover.

rear master cylinder, lever, fluid reservoir location, and brake pads retained by a spring rather than split pins. Completing the revisions were a new windshield, black rearview mirrors, and Dunlop Sportmax tires. Still popular, production of the 900 Supersport for the 1995 model year was increased to 2,850, again most being fully faired. As in the previous year the U.S. received specific CRs and SPs.

1996 Model Year

By 1996 there was talk of replacing the Supersport, but serious financial and production problems at Ducati meant this would be delayed for some time. Thus there were few changes to the 900 Supersport, these including the incorporation of sound-absorbing panels in the full fairing, and a sound-absorbing clutch cover. As before the cover was steel and prone to corrosion. The crankcases for 1996 were new castings, finally without the boss originally intended for the kickstarter. These also featured a stronger screw arrangement, with four M8mm x 90mm screws at the cylinder base, and an additional M6mm x 75mm screw near the starter motor. Beginning at frame number 021039 a protective washer was inserted under the lower steering head bearing. The colors and decals were as before, and some 900 Supersports were fitted with Pirelli MTR03 tires. There was also a change in brake pad material for 1996, with Ferodo Ferit I/D 450 FF pads front and rear. Production levels were significantly down on the previous year, with only 900 1996 model year 900 Supersports built. A limited number of CRs and SPs also went to the U.S. However, most of the reduction in numbers was due to production difficulties rather than lack of demand.

1997 Model Year

Although a new company, Ducati Motor S.p.A., was formed in September 1996 between the Texas Pacific Group and Cagiva, a replacement Supersport was still a year away. In the meantime the 900 Supersport was slightly updated and produced for one more year.

From 1995 there was a revised instrument panel with the inclusion of an oil temperature gauge. While remote-reservoir master cylinders had featured from 1994, this 1997 model had adjustable levers.

The 1997 900 Supersport had new decals and revised fairing air intakes. Much was shared with the previous Superlight. The rear brake was now fully-floating and there were revisions to the front brakes. Under the full fairing was a relocated oil cooler.

Essentially the engine was as before, but with bimetallic inlet and exhaust valves. This was to provide an improved compatibility with unleaded fuel and more stable valve clearances. Initially the valve seats were to be sintered steel, but this didn't eventuate on production examples. There was also a change to the quoted valve timing (see Appendix), although the power remained at 80 HP at 7,000 rpm at the crankshaft. Another modification was to the Mikuni carburetors, with the carburetor heating kit that had been an option since 1992 now standard. A two-way valve directed engine oil from the oil cooler to the carburetor float bowls. The oil cooler was finally mounted in a more sensible position, under the lower triple clamp as with the Monster, and for 1997 the clutch cover was gray. The ignition and electrical system was as before, but from May there were new Shindengen regulators, with kits offered for retrofitting to earlier models.

There were many more changes to the chassis and cycle parts, with a general overall increase in specification as the Supersport reached the end of its production life. The frame continued unchanged, except for a slight increase in steering lock (28 degrees), but there was a new fairing and revised seat padding. The footpeg brackets were silver instead of black. Integral sound-absorbing panels were still incorporated in the full fairing, and also the half-faired version. In the full fairing there were now also additional vents to the rear cylinder to improve cooling, but the most noticeable change was to the graphics. Large DUCATI decals featured on the sides of the fairing, and colors were either red or yellow. Other changes in specification included a carbon-fiber front fender, and several improvements to the braking system. While still retaining the 320mm stainless steel front discs, these were initially to be 5mm, but ended up being the 4mm of before. From frame number 025450, however, brake discs with a revised floating system to smooth the brake operation were fitted, and from frame number 025220 new front brake calipers. Although looking identical externally, they were a new generation internally with more fluid volume. Both the clutch and all brake lines were now braided steel (though the U.S. and Australia still received rubber lines), and the rear brake was the Superlight fully-floating setup. While the front brake and clutch master cylinders again featured remote reservoirs, these also had adjustable levers. Completing the upgraded specification were more sporting tires, Michelin HiSport or Pirelli Dragon, still in the same sizes as before. Undoubtedly the 900 Supersport for 1997 was the most developed of the entire seven-year series, but production levels were still down. Only 1,621 1997 model year 900 Supersports were produced, most red with a full fairing. Yellow half-faired examples were quite rare. Once again the U.S. received the CR and SP, but the design was definitely showing its age and in need of updating. The carburetion in particular had always been less than satisfactory and the complicated heating kit was obviously only a short-term solution. In October 1998 there was also a safety recall for all 1997 900 Supersports (from frame number 024037 to 026295) to fit a longer screw to the rear brake rod engine mount.

This was how the first prototype 900 Superlight looked when released at the end of 1991. But for the Marvic wheels, solo seat and upswept mufflers it was very much a hastily modified 900 Supersport.

900 Superlight
1992 Model Year

First displayed at the end of 1991, the prototype Superlight was conceived out of a regular 1992 900 Supersport, the only differences being the 17-inch Akront/Marvic composite wheels, solo seat, and upswept exhaust with specially fabricated aluminum brackets. This prototype was without a white number plate on the seat, although one appeared when it was used for the early publicity brochure. By now it had a neater exhaust bracket, but still neither a vented clutch nor cast-iron front disc rotors. When it went into production the Superlight had both an aluminum vented clutch cover, and 320mm x 4.5mm floating cast-iron front disc rotors, adding to its appeal. These brake rotors were significantly superior to the stainless steel items of the regular Supersport. The mufflers (from the 888 SP4) were a larger diameter, and stepped down to fit

The 1992 900 Superlight was one of the most desirable Supersports. When it finally made it into production there were fully-floating cast-iron front brake discs and a white patch on the seat.

Bimota DB2

Following the success of the 750 F1-engine DB1 of 1985-89, Bimota reached an agreement with Ducati for them to supply 900 Supersport engines for the second Ducati-Bimota, the DB2, during 1993. Designed by Pierluigi Marconi, and first displayed at the Cologne Show at the end of 1992, the DB2 used a red-painted steel trellis frame with cantilever swingarm, and pioneered the twin exhaust exiting underneath the seat. Unlike the DB1 the bodywork wasn't full-coverage, and two versions of the red-and-white machine were available, one with a full fairing and another with a half fairing and belly pan. While the engine was a stock 900 Supersport, a different air filter for the Mikuni carburetors and a new exhaust system saw the power increase slightly to 75 HP at 7,000 rpm. However, compared to the DB1 the DB2 lacked many of the finely crafted individual components and shared many more with the stock Ducati.

The DB2 was superior to the 900 SS in the suspension department. The front forks were 43mm Paioli; while not being upside-down, they were high-quality and provided compression and rebound damping adjustment. At the rear a single Öhlins shock absorber controlled the cantilever rear suspension, offset to the right to allow for the routing of the exhaust system. The white-painted wheels were 17-inch, shod with Michelin 120/70 ZR17 TX11 and 180/55 ZR17 TX 23 tires. Front brakes were 320mm fully-floating cast-iron discs with the usual street specification gold P4 30/34 Brembo calipers. At the rear was a 230mm disc and Brembo 05 caliper. Surprisingly the brake and clutch master cylinders were the standard Ducati budget items. Dry weight was a claimed 168kg (370 pounds), and the wheelbase only 1,370mm (54 inches). The steering was quicker than a Superlight, too, with a 23.5-degree steering head angle with 3.8 inches (96.5mm) of trail. A six-speed 49 HP 400cc DB2J (Junior) was also produced, this identical to the larger version but for a single front disc brake and narrower (4.5 inch) rear wheel, but it wasn't successful. Production of the DB2 between 1993 and 1995 was 408 units.

In 1994 a fuel-injected DB2 SR became available, offering an increase in horsepower to 89.4 HP at 7,500 rpm. As Ducati wasn't yet offering an electronic fuel injection system for the two-valve air-cooled engine, Bimota used the TDD system, developed in-house. The colors of the DB2 SR were more radical than the DB2, with purple, red and white bodywork, or red, white and green. Both the wheels and frame were now black. A wide range of optional accessories was available for the DB2 SR. These included an engine tuning kit, suspension modification kit including spacer and springs, and carbon-fiber mufflers. 157 DB2 SRs were produced between 1994 and 1996. The final series of DB2 was the EF (*Edizione Finale)* of 1997-98. Painted black and silver with a red frame, this also had the fuel-injected engine and polished Marvic aluminum wheels. Only 100 were produced, presumably to use up surplus parts, and each carried a numbered plaque.

Bimota's version of the Superlight was the DB2 of 1993. Unlike the similar Ducati, the DB2 featured a tubular-steel swingarm. Though this example has a full fairing, the DB2 was also available with a smaller fairing and belly pan.

For 1994 Bimota produced the fuel-injected DB2SR. The colors of purple, red and white were more radical and the engine produced more power.

the standard 900 SS collector. Of all the Superlights, the 1992 version epitomized the concept of minimum weight the most effectively, later versions compromised by the use of standard wheels.

Setting the Superlight apart from the 900 Supersport was a numbered plaque on the top triple clamp. Apart from the Marvic wheels (in the same 3.50 x 17 and 5.50 x 17-inch sizes) the chassis was unchanged. This included the white-painted frame and Showa suspension. There were some troubles with the wheels on several 1992 Superlights. From frame numbers 004456-004750 and 004951-005306 the rear wheel

Also featured on the 1992 Superlight was a vented clutch cover.

Although the publicity material showed the 1993 Superlight II with fully-floating brake discs, these were not fitted to production examples.

hub retaining screws were prone to loosening, and a factory modification provided six replacement screws (771 512 92B). Tires for 1992 were Michelin A/M89X. The first series of Superlights wasn't that much of a limited edition, with a total of 952 built, production commencing in March 1992. There were 652 in red for Europe and Australia, with 300 in yellow for the United States. This was the first time yellow was used by Ducati on recent models, and Ducati NA specified a paint code of #7505.

1993 Superlight II

As with many earlier limited edition Ducatis, the Superlight's specification was downgraded following the success of the 1992 version. Regular production items replaced some of the more expensive components, this also leading to an increase in weight. Although the publicity brochures indicated the Superlight would have the fully-floating cast-iron front disc rotors, all production versions came with regular stainless steel Supersport items. These, along with normal Brembo wheels, did little to differentiate the Superlight from the Supersport. While the Supersport had black wheels for 1993, the Superlight shared its bronze wheels and Michelin TX11/23 tires with the 888 SP5, along with a fully-floating rear brake linkage. Like the limited-production SP5 this was initially via a carbon-fiber rod, soon changed to aluminum after initial failures. Also replaced for 1993 was the vented clutch cover, although the carbon-fiber front fender was retained. The Superlight still received the rectangular numbered plaque on the top triple clamp, now with a Superlight II designation.

Small styling changes appeared on the Superlight II. In line with other 1993 bikes the frames were painted bronze, with new gold and silver decals. The Superlight now had a large 1 in the white plate on the seat, and this would continue until the Superlight V. Despite seemingly offering little over a 900 Supersport, 755 Superlight IIs were manufactured, none going to the U.S.

1994 Superlight III

Some amends for the disappointing specification of the Superlight II were made for the Superlight III of 1994. The regular 900 Supersport received an upgrade in suspension, this also being shared with the Superlight III. This included upgraded Showa GD 021 forks, similar to those that had featured on the 888 SP5, along with the stronger aluminum swingarm. Other changes shared between the 1994 900 SS and SL were the gray engine covers, new sidestand, black footpeg brackets and levers, larger-diameter front axle, Michelin A/M89X tires, new seat and helmet locking system, and remote reservoirs for the brake and clutch master cylinders. The brake pads were the FREN-DO 222 shared with other Supersports that year. While it was undeniably an improvement over 1993, all that

900 Supersport Sport Production

After the yellow Superlight of 1992, there were no more Superlights for the U.S., although this model was sold through 1993. The year 1994 saw the introduction of two specific U.S. market 900 Supersports; the more basic 900 CR (Café Racer) and the higher-specification 900 SS SP (Sport Production). The 900 SS SP was an amalgam of the Supersport and the Superlight, and basically a fully faired Superlight with a dual seat and lower exhaust pipes. However, the Sport Production wasn't a real SP in the true sense, as it offered no performance increase over a standard Supersport. Sport Production Ducatis had originated in 1989 as special performance racing versions of the 851 for the Italian Sport Production racing series. Colors and decals mirrored the Supersport, but like the Superlight they carried numbered plaques on the top triple clamp, with Supersport SP, and a new sequence. Apart from the dual seat and lower mufflers, Supersport SPs shared all the refinements of the Superlight III. This included the carbon-fiber clutch cover and front and rear fenders, fully-floating rear disc brake, and floating 280mm x 4.5mm cast-iron front disc rotors. Carburetion was slightly different for these U.S. models (see Appendix), California models also receiving a recycling filter canister. SP numbers were similar to that of the U.S. 1992 Superlight. There were 125 (plus 40 California) 1994 model year SPs built in 1993, with a further 390 (plus 160 California) in 1994.

So successful was the 900 SS SP in the U.S. that it was offered again in 1995, with a new number sequence. Basically this was identical to the earlier version, but for the usual changes that appeared on the Supersport and Superlight IV that year. The 900 SS SP continued virtually unchanged for 1996, but for Dunlop Sportmax tires, and sound deadening incorporated in the fairing. There was still a numbered plaque, now using a letter and two digits. 340 (plus 60 California) were built for the 1995 model year. The 900 SS SP continued for 1996 with all the changes applying to the regular 900 Supersport that year. Production was 520, with an additional 160 for California. As with the 900 Supersport, the 900 SS SP continued for a final series in 1997. Changes included the relocation of the oil cooler and carburetor heating kit. With the European-specification 900 Supersport encompassing most of the previous Superlight features, the SS and U.S. SP were now very similar. Distinguished only by the numbered plaque, floating cast-iron discs, and carbon-fiber rear fender and clutch cover, the SP also didn't receive braided steel brake and clutch lines. Colors were now red or yellow, with the revised 1997 graphics. Only 80 were available in the U.S., though for California there were an additional 40 red and 180 yellow code-named the H.T.

As with the Superlight, 900 SS Sport Productions received a numbered plaque on the top triple clamp. For 1996 and 1997 there was a letter and two numbers.

differentiated the Superlight III from the Supersport was a solo seat and upswept exhausts, carbon-fiber clutch cover and fenders, a fully-floating rear disc, and a return to the fully-floating cast-iron front discs. There was also a numbered plaque on the top triple clamp, and production was down slightly from the previous year, with 756 built. Most were now in the yellow (498) that had appeared on the first U.S. Superlight of 1992, although red was still available.

1995 Superlight IV

There were only a few cosmetic alterations to the Superlight IV for 1995, these also shared with the 900 Supersport. This included a gray sidestand, timing belt covers and rear sprocket cover, the frame painted in 916 gold, and a new windshield. Superlight IVs received a revised seating support, with two new brackets and rubber pads. Except for the oil temperature gauge on the dashboard, the Superlight IV was almost

After the disappointing Superlight II of 1993, 1994 saw the Superlight III with a stronger swingarm, improved forks and a return to fully-floating cast-iron brake discs. Most were also in yellow rather than red.

indistinguishable from the Superlight III. There was the usual numbered plaque, now with Superlight IV. Unlike the previous year, most of the 850 Superlight IVs were in red (490).

1996 Superlight V

Although the Superlight was selling slowly, with fewer produced each successive year, the Superlight V was offered for 1996. Only 309 were manufactured, and they were visually very similar to the Superlight IV. Apart from 11 examples all Superlight IVs were in red. Along with the 900 Supersport was the incorporation of sound-absorbing panels in the full fairing, a sound-absorbing clutch cover, revised crankcases and Ferodo brake pads. The plaque on the top triple clamp carried a Superlight V designation. In October 1998 there was also a safety recall for all Superlights from 1992-96 (from frame number 004456 to 023636) to fit a longer screw to the rear brake rod engine mount.

1997-98 Final Edition

In September 1997 and January 1998 the final Superlight series was produced. Harking back to the days of the silver-and-blue 900 Super Sports, the 900 FE (Final Edition) had silver bodywork with the new-for-1998 graphics, accentuated by black wheels. As on other 1998 model year Ducatis there were no tank decals, only two DUCATI decals on the fairing, with two small DUCATI SUPERSPORT 900 FINAL EDITION

The Superlight V of 1996 was the final Superlight and produced in the fewest numbers. Unlike earlier examples most were produced in red, with only a few yellow available. Still a handsome and purposeful machine.

From 1993 until 1996 (Superlight II to V) there was this large 1 on the seat of the Superlight. This 1996 Superlight V has Termignoni mufflers.

The aluminum swingarm and rear brake setup of the Superlight was identical to that of the 1997 900 Supersport. From the Superlight came the upswept mufflers, though the FE had black wheels. This European specification FE has a carbon-fiber clutch cover, U.S. versions received a normal sound deadening steel item. On this 1997 specification engine were silver rather than gray engine side covers. A feature of all '91-'97 Supersports was the lower engine mount that could be used to support a workshop stand.

decals on the tailpiece. Two 900 FE versions were built, one for Europe and one for the U.S. The 500 European FEs used 1997-specification engines with silver engine covers and external cylinder oil lines. They also had a carbon-fiber clutch cover and braided steel clutch and brake lines. The 300 U.S. 900 FEs were produced in January 1998 using 1998-specification engines (similar to the Monster 900 S) with gray engine covers and clutch cover. The new Tecnol cylinders were neater looking as the oil lines were now incorporated internally. The power of the 900 SS FE was 75 HP at 7,000 rpm with 7.8 kg/m of torque at 6,500 rpm. One improvement of

The Final Edition of 1998. Produced in silver to replicate the first 900 Super Sport of 1975, the Final Edition was basically a Superlight V with a few extra carbon-fiber parts.

Bimota DB4

For 1999 Bimota released their fourth series with a Ducati engine, the DB4. Also a Supersport model like the DB2, this used the light (11-pound) oval-tube aluminum trellis frame from the DB3 Mantra rather than the tubular-steel frame of the DB2. The swingarm was also oval-tube aluminum, with cantilever rear suspension. No longer with fuel injection, the DB4 featured a stock 1999-specification 900 S Monster engine, complete with twin Mikuni 38mm carburetors, but with a distinctive right-side twin muffler giving a claimed 80 HP. An extremely light and compact machine, the weight was only 165kg (363 pounds), and the wheelbase 1,370mm (53.9 inches). Steering was also quicker than the stock Ducati, with a 23-degree steering head angle and 91mm (3.5-inches) of trail.

Other specifications were similar to the Mantra or DB2 EF. 3.50 x 17 and 5.50 x 17-inch Antera wheels, 43mm Paioli forks and Öhlins remote-reservoir rear shock absorber. On the DB4 the forks offered preload and rebound damping adjustment and provided 120mm (4.72 inches) of front wheel travel. The rear suspension gave 102mm (4 inches) of wheel travel. Tires were Michelin, 120/70ZR17 TX15 on the front and 180/55ZR17 TX25 on the rear. The front brakes were 320mm fully-floating stainless steel Brembo at the front with the usual P4 30/34 calipers and braided steel brake lines. At the rear was a 230mm disc with Brembo 05 caliper. As with other Bimotas, all the major components bolted to the engine, including the airbox, electrics, and 20-liter (5.3-gallon) nylon fuel tank. These were all hidden under a one-piece body unit. The electrical system differed to the parent Ducati by using two 12V/13Ah batteries. Unlike the DB3 Mantra, the instruments came off a contemporary Ducati, in this case the 900 Supersport. Only available with a solo seat, the DB4 also came with carbon-fiber front and rear fenders. Colors of the DB4 intentionally emulated the red, white and green of the original, and now legendary, DB1.

The Bimota DB4 of 1999 created a sportbike out of the radical DB3 Mantra. While the general layout was similar to that of the DB2, the DB4 was slightly lighter and produced more power from its carbureted 904cc engine. As with all Bimotas the detailing was superb, right down to the beautiful Antera wheels.

Although it looked like the 900 Supersport, the 1991 750 Supersport was really a development of the earlier 750 Sport. The black-painted five-speed engine was similar, as was the dry clutch. 1991 models came with white-painted wheels and this has the optional oil cooler fitted.

the FE over earlier 900 Supersports was the change in primary-drive ratio to 32/59 (1.84:1), also shared with the 1998 900 Supersport. This did, however, increase the overall gearing slightly. As usual for the U.S., the 300 FEs had rubber brake and clutch lines (as did those for Australia). Much of the rest of the FE specification was as for the earlier Superlight. There was a solo seat with upswept Termignoni exhausts, cast-iron fully-floating front brake discs, and carbon-fiber fenders. Carbon fiber extended to the chainguard and simplified dashboard (without a battery warning light). The full fairing was that of the 1997 900 Supersport with additional air intakes. All 800 900 SS FEs carried a numbered plaque, there being separate number sequences for the U.S. and elsewhere. Tires were Dunlop Sportmax II D 207F.

750 Supersport
1991 Model Year

In May 1991, shortly after the release of the 900 Supersport, Ducati presented the 750 Supersport. This was ostensibly the engine of the earlier 750 Sport, along with Mikuni constant-vacuum carburetors, installed in a chassis similar to that of its larger brother. Engine numbers began at ZDM 750 A 2C 000001. The 9:1 compression ratio was lower than the earlier 750 Sport, but the valve sizes, camshaft, and 36/71 primary gears were as before. The claimed power was 60 HP at 8,500 rpm, but the new Supersport was not as powerful as earlier 750s. Carburetion was by Mikuni BDST 38, Europe receiving the B70, the U.S. B76s with leaner jetting, and Switzerland B94s. The five-speed engine was painted black (including the crankcases) and shared its hydraulically operated dry clutch of the 750 Sport. As with earlier 750s, 13 screws held the crankcases together, although these were now five M8mm x 75mm, one M8mm x 70mm, one M8mm x 90mm, five M6mm x 35mm, and one M6mm x 50mm. The 14-plate clutch was of two possible types. If a 3.5mm outer plate was used all the other plates were 2.5mm, and with a 2.75mm outer plate the other discs were 2.6mm. From September 1991 a 900-style oil-cooler kit also became available for the 750 Supersport (6992.0301A). Ignition was also by Kokusan, but with different Champion RA6HC spark plugs. Final drive was the same as for the 900 Supersport.

Frame numbers for the white-painted frame began at ZDM 750 SC 000001. While this was ostensibly identical to that of the 900, the 750 received more basic front forks, and a different aluminum swingarm. The 41mm Showa GD 031 upside-down forks offered no provision for any damping adjustment. There was only a single 320mm stainless steel front disc brake with a gold P4 30/34 Brembo brake caliper and PS13mm master cylinder. The rear brake was as with the 900, as was the Showa shock absorber. After frame number 001364 there was the revised rear brake pressure switch. Although the white-painted Brembo front wheel was shared with the 900, the 750 received a narrower 4.50

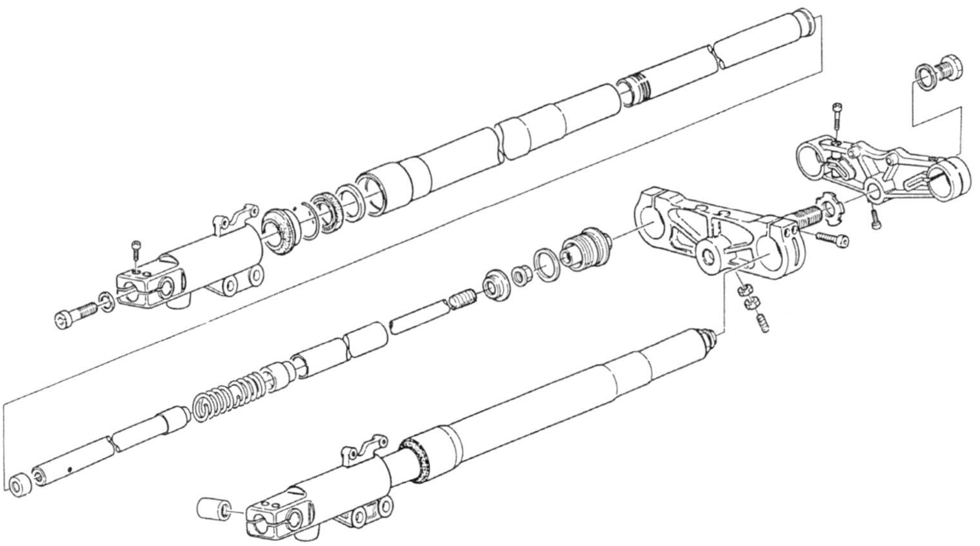

The 750 Supersport had more basic suspension than the 900, the Showa GD 031 forks being non-adjustable.

x 17-inch Brembo rear wheel along with a smaller 160/60 x 17 Michelin M59X. A lower-profile 120/60 x 17 Michelin A59X was on the front. Only available in red, 1,156 1991 model year 750 Supersports were produced. While most of these were supplied with a half fairing, those for Germany had a full fairing.

1992 Model Year

There were only a few alterations to the 750 Supersport for 1992 (from engine number 001275). Within the black-painted engine there was now a hydraulically operated wet clutch with a new 17-plate arrangement. Carrying part number 19020051A this consisted of eight 1.5mm driven plates, eight 2.5mm driving plates, and one outer 3.5mm driving plate. Complementing the new clutch were 31/62 straight-cut primary gears, now giving the same ratio as the 900. The oil cooler that had become an option late in 1991 was now a standard fitting. As with the 900, 1992 engines (from January) received aluminum-bronze valve guides instead of cast-iron. Although the primary gearing was higher, the final drive remained the same.

In line with the 900, 750 Supersports from frame number 001210, were fitted with the stronger chain-adjusters (M8mm x 70mm bolts). Also for 1992, the 750 Supersport had black-painted wheels, and Dunlop

For 1992 the cosmetic changes of the 750 Supersport mirrored those for the 900. The oil cooler was now standard, and while most were produced with a full fairing, all U.S. 750 Supersports had a half fairing.

Although the 1993 750 Supersport had a new frame color, the wheels were still black.

Sportmax tires. In April 1992 raised seat buffers were fitted to prevent interference and chafing with the bodywork. Fully faired 750s were also available in addition to half-faired, with the option of black (with black wheels rather than the white of the 900) as an alternative to red. As the single front disc was marginal on the 750, a twin-disc kit was offered as a factory option in June 1992, but still wouldn't appear as standard for more than a year. Production of the 750 for the 1992 model year was increased over that of 1991, to 1,890. While most were produced with a full fairing, the U.S. received only half-faired versions. These numbered 140 plus 60 for California.

1993 Model Year

While the only change to the 750 Supersport engine for 1993 was a new oil pressure switch and silver crankcases (still with black engine covers, cylinders and heads), there were a number of cosmetic alterations. In line with other models the frame was painted bronze, and the silver and gold decals were new, as was the horn. The wheels were black as before, and there was no

There were a number of changes to the 750 Supersport for 1994. The wheels were color-matched to the bronze frame and there were color changes to the footpeg brackets and engine side covers. The main update was a twin-disc front end and steel swingarm.

The 1995 750 Supersport had another new frame color, this time 916-gold.

rear seat cowling. 1993 models still used a single front disc brake, and were fitted with either a full or half fairing. Production was significantly increased for the 1993 model year, with 2,752 750 Supersports built. Again only half-faired versions went to the U.S., these being 210 plus 120 for California.

1994 Model Year

With the introduction of the 600 Supersport in 1994, the 750 was upgraded slightly to place it apart from the newer model. Along with slight modifications to the Mikuni carburetor jetting, there was a new voltage regulator, and the 750 received all the 1994 changes to engine colors and footpegs (black). The power was now quoted at 66 HP at 8,500 rpm at the crankshaft. However, the most significant alteration was the fitting of a standard front 320mm dual disc brake that had previously been an option. This also saw an increase in the front master cylinder piston to 16mm, and in line with the 900 there was a change in brake pad material. The 750 Supersport continued with non-adjustable Showa front forks during 1994, but now with the larger, 20mm, front axle. The wheels were painted bronze, along with the instrument panel support. An important change update was to the swingarm, the steel item of the 400 Supersport replacing the previous aluminum. This also included a revised chain adjustment system. No longer being available in the U.S., production of the 750 Supersport for the 1994 model year was only 1,700 units.

1995 Model Year

Color changes for 1995 mirrored those of the 900 Supersport, and included a 916-style gold frame, black horn, and grey timing belt covers, rear sprocket cover, and sidestand. From frame number 007707 Marzocchi 40mm forks replaced the 41mm Showa used previously, still with the double front disc setup. While the 900 CR now used a Sachs Boge rear shock absorber, the 750 still used the Showa GD 022. Production for the 1995 model year was 1,750.

1996 Model Year

Apart from the incorporation of sound-deadening panels in the fairing, and Ferodo brake pads, there were no changes to the 750 Supersport for 1996. From frame number 008201 to 008900 there was a safety recall to rectify possible interference between the alternator rotor and stator. This was caused by deformation of the stator due to interference with the bushes. Beginning at frame number 009401 a protective washer was also inserted under the lower steering head bearing. 1996 was a difficult year for the factory, and only 60 750 Supersports were produced. As with the 900, most updates would be saved for the 1997 model year.

1997 Model Year

In a choice of red or yellow, and full- or half-faired, Ducati was aiming to get the most out of the 750 Supersport as it neared the end of its production run. As with the 900, there was a new fairing with an air

900 Supersport CR

After the failure of the 750 Supersport in the U.S., Ducati replaced it with the 900 CR for 1994. The 900 CR was 900 Supersport engine mated to the more basic 750 Supersport chassis. Originally titled the 900 Supersport Economy, this was only available with a half fairing. This Ducati for the budget conscious still used a non-adjustable 41mm GD 031 Showa front fork, 4.5 x 17-inch rear wheel, Dunlop Sportmax tires (120/60ZR17 and 160/60ZR17), and a steel swingarm. This swingarm was a unit specific to the 900 CR to fit the 900 crankcases. The rear shock was the Showa GD 022 of the 750 and 900 Supersport. In 1995 900 CRs received the even more basic 40mm USD/E non-adjustable Marzocchi fork of the 750 Supersport, and Sachs-Boge shock absorber of the 600 Supersport. Yearly changes to colors and specification were shared with the 900 Supersport SP. They were produced in relatively large numbers, 1,315 for the 1994-95 model years and a further 590 for the 1996 model year.

The final Ducatis with the older Cagiva-style graphics were 50 red and 250 yellow 900 CRs for the U.S. built late in 1997. These had 1998-specification U.S. 900 Supersport Final Edition engines (new pistons and cylinders), but with the oil cooler mounted underneath the front cylinder on a bracket from the lower rocker cover. Unlike earlier versions, the final 900 CRs also featured a rear seat cowling.

The 900 CR was an economy Supersport specifically for the U.S. Mating a 900 Supersport engine in a 750 Supersport chassis, this 1994-95 model has non-adjustable Showa GD 031 front forks.

A final yellow 900 CR at the factory awaiting shipment to the U.S. in January 1998. This still featured the old-style Ducati graphics under the tank cover. Other interesting aspects are the use of the latest specification (1998) engine with gray engine side covers and clutch cover, and the low mounting of the oil cooler.

Only a few 750 Supersports were built in 1996.

750 Supersports for 1997 were either red or yellow like this example. The decals mirrored those of the 900 Supersport and there was a rear seat cover.

1997 750 Supersports had the oil cooler mounted above the front cylinder.

intake, new graphics, bimetallic inlet and exhaust valves, 28-degree steering angle, carburetor heating kit, and anodized aluminum footpeg brackets. The oil cooler on the 750 Supersport was now mounted above the front cylinder. During 1997 a Shindengen regulator replaced the Ducati Energia, with kits offered for retrofitting. There were also new brake calipers and front brake discs with a different spring loading system.

The earlier instrument panel that had started life with the 750 F1 of 1986 continued through until 1997 on the 750 (and 600) Supersports. 750s also featured rectangular master cylinders until 1997.

The revised calipers were from frame number 010113 and new discs from 010189. With the company's production difficulties behind them following the TPG buyout of September 1996, 1,206 750s were built for the 1997 model year. Just about all of these were fully faired, most also red. There was then some time before the replacement fuel-injected 750 Supersport appeared for the 1999 model year.

600 Supersport
1994 Model Year

Developed from the 400 Supersport, the 600 relived the days of the 600 SL Pantah. However, while the crankcases, five-speed gearbox and cylinders were similar, the 600 Supersport used 400 cylinder heads with 33.5mm and 30.5mm valves. As with the 600 SL the bore and stroke was 80mm x 58mm and engine numbers began at ZDM 600 A 2C 000001. The camshafts were those of the 750 Supersport and carburetion by Mikuni BDST 38-B156 carburetors. An optional Mikuni carburetor heating kit became available in June. Unlike the 900 and 750 the cylinders didn't receive additional oil cooling and there was no oil cooler. The hydraulically actuated wet clutch was that of the 750 Supersport, the plate set 19020051A. With a 10.7:1 compression ratio, there were two versions of the 600 Supersport, both with a two-into-one exhaust and 110mm (4.33-inch) muffler: a 33 HP at 7,500 rpm version specifically for European insurance

The first 600 Supersport of 1994. Forks are Showa GD O31 with provision for a second front brake caliper. Although visually similar to the larger Supersports, the engine had its roots back in the 600 SL Pantah.

classification, and the regular 53 HP at 8,250 rpm version. Production commenced in March 1994 and early examples used a 32/73 primary drive, with 15/36 final drive. The chain was a 96-link D.I.D. 520 VL2 5/8- x 1/4-inch. From frame number 001853 the primary drive was altered to be consistent with the 750 and 900 at 31/62, and final drive altered to 15/41 with a 98-link chain. There was a new voltage regulator for the 600 and the ignition was the usual Kokusan, but with Champion RA4HC spark plugs.

Frame numbers for the 600 Supersport began at ZDM 600 S 000001, the bronze-painted frame and steel swingarm shared with the 1994 750 Supersport. This gave a 23 degree steering head angle, providing 103mm (4.05 inches) of trail. Also shared were the new sidestand, seat retaining system, and wiring harness. The first 600 Supersports were fitted with the 41mm Showa GD O31 forks and Showa GD022-007-OX rear shock absorber of the 400 Supersport, but these were soon changed to 40mm Marzocchi USD/E along with a Sachs Boge shock absorber. As with the Showa forks the Marzocchi also allowed for an additional front disc caliper on the right side, but had the larger, 20mm front axle. Both provided 120mm (4.72 inches) of front and 125mm (4.92 inches) of rear wheel travel. The 600 came only with a single 320mm front disc brake with FREN-DO 222 pads. Available in red only and in either full- or half-faired versions, production for the 1994 model year was 1,852, most fully faired.

1995 Model Year

With the success of the 600 during 1994, the Supersport lineup was rationalized for 1995. With only 100 400 Supersports built for Japan, the 600 remained the smallest model. Apart from gray timing belt covers and sprocket cover there were no changes to the engine specification. From engine number 05025, and frame number 002287, there was a modified vertical cylinder and piston assembly to overcome reliability problems. With the front forks standardized to 40mm Marzocchi, these differed in that the right fork leg was now without a brake caliper attachment. The frame was now painted 916-gold, there was a gray sidestand, and a black horn. 600 Supersport production was down considerably on the previous year, to 1,000 for the 1995 model year.

1996 Model Year

For 1996 the 600 Supersport continued with very few changes. There were sound-deadening panels in the fairing, new brake pads, and a stainless steel exhaust system. In October 1995, from frame number 002853 a washer was inserted beneath the lower steering head bearing. From frame number 002601 to 002900 there was a safety recall on the 600 Supersport to rectify possible interference between the alternator rotor and stator. This was caused by deformation of the stator due to interference with the bushes. In August 1996 a twin front disc kit became available. Production

By 1996 the 600 Supersport had 40mm Marzocchi forks without provision for an additional brake caliper. Only fully faired versions were produced this year.

was down yet again for the 1996 model year, to 699. All these were fully faired.

1997 Model Year

With the revised 750 and 900 Supersports for 1997 the 600 followed suit. Now available in red or yellow, full- or half-faired, the 600 had the new graphics and colors of the larger models, along with their small engine-revisions. From May there were new rectifiers by Shindengen, with kits offered for retrofitting. Although still featured, the red battery charge light on the dashboard was no longer operational. There were new brake calipers from frame number 003598, and new discs with a different spring system from frame number 003754. There was yet another change to the pistons and cylinders for the 600 Supersport. New piston assemblies featured on 600 Supersports from chassis number 003752 (engine number 012938). 739 600 Supersports were built for the 1997 model year, most being red with a full fairing.

350/400 Supersport

1991 Model Year

Complementing the 750 Supersport in 1991 was a Japanese-market-only 400 Supersport Junior. The black-painted engine was similar to that of the earlier 400 F3, also sharing the same six-speed gearbox and 34/77 primary gears. With its 70.5mm x 51mm bore and stroke and 10:1 compression ratio, the 400 Supersport produced 42 HP at 10,000 rpm. Valve sizes were 33.5 and 30.5mm, and the camshafts the same as the 750. There was a two-into-one exhaust system with a muffler diameter of 110mm, this located on the right. For 1991 the smaller dry clutch was initially carried over from the 750 Sport (seven driving and seven driven plates) and was of two possible types. If a 3.5mm outer plate was used all the other plates were 2.5mm, and with a 2.75mm outer plate the other discs were 2.6mm. Carburetion for the Japanese 400 Supersport was Mikuni BDST 38-B79s. Ignition was the usual Kokusan, with Champion L82Y spark plugs.

The white-painted frame differed to the 750 Supersport, providing less trail (88.5mm, 3.48 inches), but used the same aluminum swingarm. The forks were 41mm non-adjustable Showa GD031, but provided less wheel travel at 103mm (4.05 inches). Rear suspension was by a Marzocchi PBS1R shock absorber, this having a red spring and a stroke of 60mm (2.36 inches). The 320mm single front disc, Brembo P4 30/34 caliper and PS13 master cylinder was the same as the 750, as was the rear 245mm disc brake with P2105N caliper and PS11 master cylinder. The white-painted wheels were also the same as the 750 Supersport, and the 400 Supersport Junior was fitted with Michelin A/M59X tires. All 1991 400 Supersports were red and came with the option of either a full or half fairing. Production for the Japanese market was 494 for 1991.

The 1992 350 Supersport Junior was produced primarily for the Italian market. This took the idea of a small engine in a larger-sized motorcycle to the limit.

1992 Model Year

For the 1992 model year a 350 Supersport for the Italian market joined the 400 Supersport. Most 1992 Supersport Juniors were the 350, only six 400s built as 1992 models. The 350 had a bore and stroke of 66mm x 51mm with a compression ratio of 10.7:1 and produced 36 HP at 10,500 rpm. The engines for both the 350 and 400 were as for 1991, but from January 1992 the valve guides were changed from cast-iron to aluminum-bronze. From engine number 000202 (350) and 000008 (400) the wet clutch became uniform with that of the 750 Supersport (19020051A). Carburetion was different between the 350 and 400. The 350 used Mikuni BDST 38-B100 carburetors, and the European specification 400 got Mikuni BDST 38-B91 (the Japanese 400 still used BDST 38-B79s). From engine number 000503 to 000802 there were alterations to the jetting (see Appendix). While the exhaust system with right- side muffler was also as before, the 350 used a slightly smaller-diameter muffler (100mm).

Unlike the 750 and 900 Supersports that received black wheels for 1992, the smaller versions still used white-painted wheels, both the 350 and 400 now featuring Dunlop Sportmax tires. Rather than the 400's Marzocchi, the 350 shared the Showa GD022-007-OX shock absorber with the larger 750 and 900 Supersport. This had a yellow spring and more stroke at 65mm (2.55 inches). Both the 350 and 400 were visually identical, though all 502 350 Supersports came with a half fairing.

1993 Model Year

Both the 350 and 400 continued for 1993, largely unchanged. The 350 was only available in Italy (with a half fairing), but the 400 was now more widely available. This also only had a half fairing except for 220 fully faired examples for Japan. The frame was now painted bronze, the swingarm steel, and the wheels painted black. The silver and gold decals were as with other Ducatis of 1993, with SUPERSPORT DESMODUE appearing on the fairing. While the engine side covers were still black, the crankcases were silver in line with the 750 Supersport. Production for the 1993 model year was 350 350 Supersports and 500 400 Supersports.

1994 Model Year

Only the 400 was available for 1994, in two versions; a 27 HP European 400 Supersport, and a 42 HP for Japan. There were also a number of changes to the specification. Within the engine there were new primary-drive gears (32-/73-tooth), with a different final drive of 14- and 43-tooth sprockets. The engine sidecovers were now silver, along with the cylinders and heads. There was a new optimized ignition advance and different, Champion RL82Y, spark plugs. The changes

Similar to the 350, the 400 was produced for the Japanese market until 1998. This is the 1994 version, still with Showa front forks. Publicity photo.

continued through the chassis that was now shared with the 600 Supersport. While the frame was similar, it provided 103mm (4.05 inches) of trail. The Showa GD 031 forks too were from the early 600 Supersport, with the 20mm axle and providing 120mm (4.72 inches) of wheel travel. Changes for 1994 extended through to the black foot controls and footrests, new sidestand and bronze wheels. Still only generally available with a half fairing (except for Japan) 650 400 Supersports were built for the 1994 model year.

1995-98

Although no longer officially listed after 1994, the 400 Supersport continued to be built for the Japanese market through until 1998. For the 1995 model year 270 were built, in both fully faired and half-faired forms. From 1996 the 400 Supersport was essentially a 600 Supersport with a smaller engine and a five-speed gearbox. Also shared with the 600 was the Marzocchi fork, Sachs Boge shock absorber, gold frame and wheels, and the other alterations that typified these years. In line with other Supersports new discs were fitted from frame number 001956. From 1998 yellow became available and production from 1996 until 1998 totaled 400.

Modifications to Supersports

Because the Supersport was in production for such a long period, constant development meant that by 1997 there were few problems. Apart from Mikuni carburetion glitches that have plagued the model since it's release, the Supersport was well sorted. However, there were some problems specific to the Supersport series. Early models could suffer oil leaks from the vertical cylinder that could be rectified by assembling the cylinder head studs with Loctite 242. Engines with cast-iron valve guides were known to suffer premature valve guide wear, and broken cylinder head studs were a common problem on earlier 900s. This can also be a problem with later engines. Some pre-1993 900 Supersports have suffered cracked aluminum swingarms at the pivot point, and all models can have trouble with both the clutch slave cylinders and pushrod seals leaking. Alternator nuts on '91-'97 Supersports need tightening after 10,000 kilometers (6,000 miles), taking care to watch the location of the washer behind the flywheel that can get trapped between the inner ring and gear. Some problems with Hitachi starter solenoid switches were generally due to incorrect installation. A common

A common stage-one modification to the Supersport is the removal of the top of the airbox. While noise levels are increased, so is the airflow.

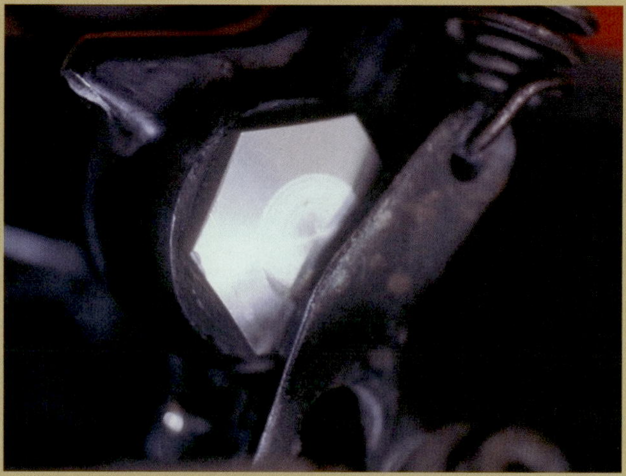

All pre-2000 Ducatis should have the automatically retracting sidestand disengaged. One alternative is a replacement bolt like this, another is to use a genuine Ducati part.

assembly problem at the factory was insufficient grease on the steering head bearings. The swingarm retaining screws could also loosen, requiring thread lubrication with Molykote G-Rapid Plus grease. In November 1997 there were new fuel level sensors that could be fitted to all models of Supersport (592.1.005.1A).

Common modifications to Supersports include the opening of the airbox, disengaging the self-retracting sidestand, and lowering the overall gearing by fitting either a 38- or 39-tooth rear sprocket, or 14-tooth front sprocket. The reduction in gearing is one of the most beneficial modifications, greatly improving the engine's responsiveness, and can be done without replacing the final-drive chain. A Corbin Gunfighter seat, either single or dual, can improve comfort substantially. Corbin also offered a Superlight solo seat, overcoming one of the Superlight's deficiencies. One of the Supersport's least satisfactory components, the poor rearview mirrors, can be replaced by bar-end mirrors such as Napoleon AP-104 or similar. The problem with replacing the mirrors is that the stock items also locate the fairing, requiring the fabrication of a retaining plate. Another solution is replacement mirrors and extensions moving the mirrors further out visibility. While originally designed for automotive applications, Vitaloni Baby Turbo mirrors and mirror extensions fit the Supersport nicely. Replacement of the rear shock absorber can also be beneficial, as the stock Showa has been known to

These Vitaloni Baby Turbo automotive mirrors and extenders solve the problem of poor rear vision as well as maintaining the stock fairing mounts.

lose damping after as little as 5,000 miles (8,000 kilometers). Other cosmetic and weight-saving modifications can include billet aluminum footpegs, and carbon-fiber fuel tank, fairing, seat, fenders, chain guard and sprocket cover. Superlight-style solo seats are also available. Most reports have found the Supersport from 1991-97 generally reliable, most problems electrical and more prevalent in 1993 models. Although there have been some problems with Supersport frames cracking around the steering head, contrary to reports indicating that a factory solution occurred during 1997, there is no official documentation to substantiate this.

CHAPTER EIGHT

600, 750, 900 Monster

First displayed at the Cologne Show in October 1992, the M900, nicknamed *Il Mostro* (the Monster), was the product of Varese-based Argentinean designer Miguel Angel Galluzzi. Galluzzi was born in the U.S.A. and studied at the Pasadena Design Center in California. The term Monster was derived from the Latin word monstrum, referring to a divine sign, a prodigy, or something exceptional. Out of a combination of existing components Galluzzi cleverly created a naked and minimalist street bike, with all the eminent sporting credentials expected of a Ducati. The Monster has since become one of the most popular Ducatis in the past 20 years. Although it was originally intended for the 1993 model year, production was delayed until May 1993 because of component supply problems.

900 Monster
1993 Model Year

Engine numbers were shared with the 900 Supersport, and while the engine was the same 73 HP unit, there were slightly different Mikuni BDST 38 B129 carburetors. U.S. Monsters were fitted with B132s, with leaner jetting. The engine was painted silver, with a silver clutch cover, although the rocker covers and belt covers were black. Different Champion RA6HC spark plugs were also used on 900 engines from 1993. An important difference to the Supersport was the positioning of the oil radiator above the front cylinder and away from the front wheel. The Monster also received a different twin exhaust system, which offered less ground clearance, and there was no tachometer drive. Apart from a lower final

Released during 1993, the 900 Monster was a completely new concept of motorcycle. Although it looked like a street cruiser, it was a very competent sportbike.

drive, 15- and 39-tooth sprockets with a 98-link D.I.D. 520 VL 4 1/4- x 5/8-inch chain, the drive-train was shared with the Supersport. M900s for Germany used the higher, 37-tooth, rear sprocket of the Supersport.

There were many more changes to the frame. While the basic layout was similar to that of the 888, the bronze-painted frame was allnew for the Monster. Frame numbers began at ZDM 900 M 000001 and with a 24 degree steering head angle, trail was 104mm (4.09 inches). An aluminum swingarm operated an 888-style rising-rate system through a yellow-painted linkage. The forks were non-adjustable Showa GD 041, similar to those fitted to the 750 Supersport. These provided 120mm (4.72 inches) of wheel travel. In order to improve fork action the fork oil quantity was increased by 30cc August 1993, with only Showa N.8 or AGIP Rotra ATF stipulated. At the rear was now a Boge shock absorber, with a stroke of 65mm (2.56 inches) providing 110mm (4.33 inches) of wheel travel. The 17-inch black-painted Brembo wheels were from the Supersport, as were the Michelin A/M89X tires. The brakes too were shared with the Supersport, and consisted of twin P4 30/34 Brembo front calipers with a PS 16 master cylinder. Different front brake pads to the 900 Supersport were used on the Monster, these being FREN-DO 965. The rear brake was the usual 245mm disc, with a Brembo P2 105N caliper and PS 11 master cylinder. The rear brake pads were FREN-DO FD 72 GG.

The prototype M900 bristled with carbon fiber, not only the small side panels, but also the instrument surround, front fender supports, rear guard, clutch cover and muffler heat shields. By the time it made it into production the only carbon fiber was the side panels and the exhaust heat shields. Although the handlebar switches were shared with the Supersport, the instruments and bodywork were new. The instrument panel was noted by the absence of a tachometer, and there

Dimensioni generali mm
Overall dimensions mm (in.)
Dimensions générales mm
Allgemeine Dimensionen mm
Dimensiones generales mm

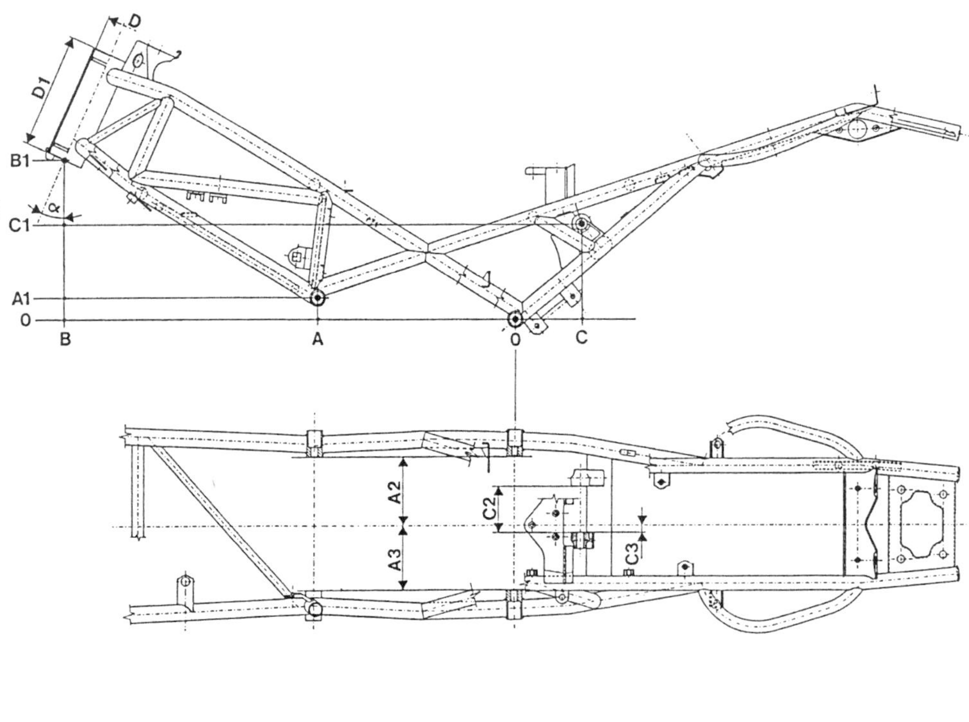

A	= 315 (12.401)	A1	= 32 (1.259)	A2	= 105,2÷105,45 (4.142÷4.151)	A3	= 100,2÷100,45 (3.945÷3.954)
B	= 707,5 (27.854)	B1	= 239.5 (9.429)				
C	= 102 (4.015)	C1	= 144 (5.669)	C2	= 70÷70,2 (2.756÷2.763)	C3	= 11 (0.433)
D	= Ø 51,966÷51,961 (2.0459÷2.0457)	D1	= 175 (6.889)				
α	= 24°±15'						

The frame for the Monster was new, and based on that of the 888 rather than the 900 Supersport.

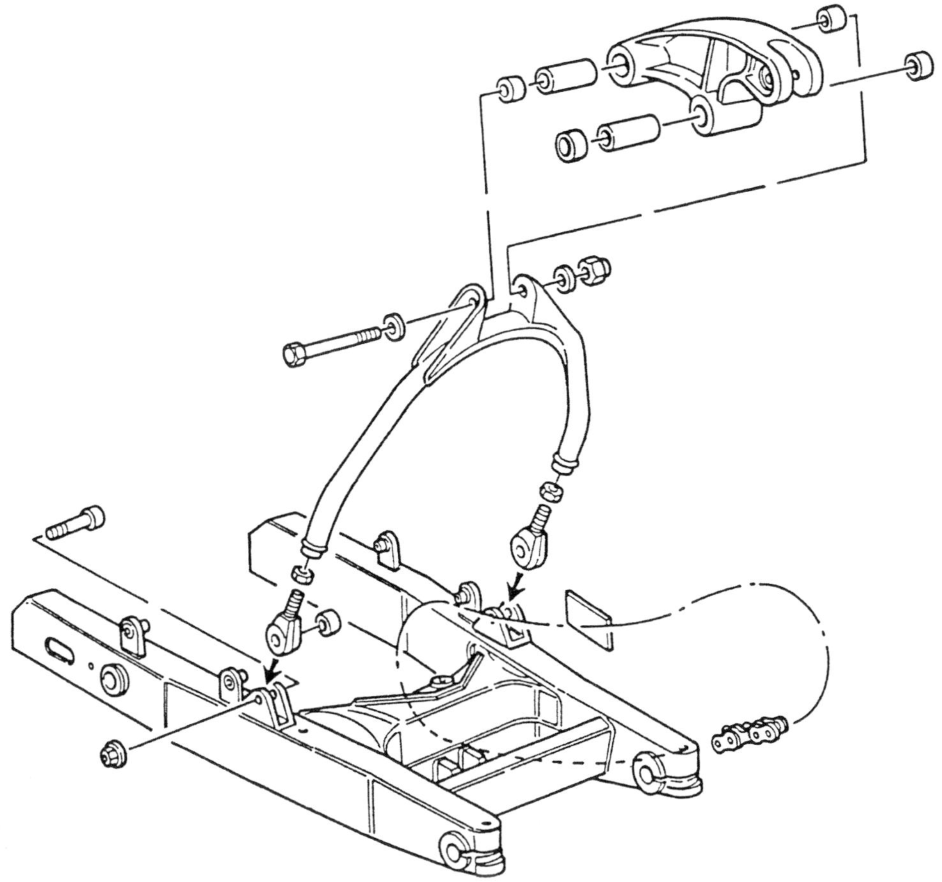

The aluminum swingarm of the Monster with its rising-rate suspension also owed more to the 888 than the Supersport.

was also a return to a classical round headlight. The first Monster was only offered in red, the lighter red of the 1993 Supersport (paint code #7525), with silver and gold DUCATI decals on the fuel tank and silver M 900 decals on the side covers. Production versions also had a black MONSTER decal on the fuel tank, though this was absent on the prototype. Although production was delayed, 2,162 were produced for the 1993 model year, including 190 for the U.S. plus 120 for California.

One item that has been continually replaced by owners was the basic Monster instrument panel without a tachometer. Finally for the 2000 model year the Monster received a tachometer.

1994 Model Year

As production had only begun a few months before the commencement of the 1994 model year, there were few updates to the basic specification of the M900. Thus, although the Supersport series received bronze wheels and a larger-diameter front axle for 1994, the Monster continued with black wheels and the smaller front axle. The only change was an optional black color scheme (paint code #7510), and although the frame was new with a reduced steering head angle (23 degrees), the trail remained the same as before. Black Monsters had red MONSTER decals on the fuel tank. As with all 900 engines, from engine number 014364 there were stronger, 8mm cylinder head studs. There was an M stamped on the cylinder head to identify the new bolts. From April 1994 there was an optional carburetor heating kit available, and from May the Ducati Energia regulators were standardized with those of the 916. The brake pads for 1994 were also FREN-DO 222.

New colors and chamfered mufflers distinguished the 1995 900 Monster.

Also available during 1994 was a Police 900 Monster, generally available in white, but with a black frame and wheels. The frame had side rails to allow for the mounting of sirens, there was an integral solo seat and pannier unit, and a small fairing that would be standard fitment on the 900 Monster for 1997. However, despite special brochures being printed the Police version was a failure. Only four examples were produced.

1995 Model Year

There were only a few changes to the M900 for 1995, affecting mainly the color of various components. The frame was now 916-gold, with matching wheels, and there were gray timing belt covers and sprocket cover. This was matched by a gray sidestand and carburetor air chambers, along with a black horn (instead of silver) and silver clutch cover. The clutch was now standardized and supplied as a set of plates (19020013A). The rear suspension U-bolt too was now painted to match the frame. The fuel tank now only held 16.5 liters (4.359 gallons). From engine number 023160 (frame number 006465), there was a new alternator (26440122A), both the stator and rotor being distinguished by a blue paint mark. There were also revised Showa forks (fitted from frame number 005327), the earlier type no longer being supplied, and a new rear fender. To improve the marginal ground clearance, the mufflers were now chamfered underneath. In addition to the red and black of before yellow was also available, but only for the U.S. By now the Monster was well established and in demand worldwide. Production for both the 1994 and 1995 model years was 7,744. Of this 790 were for the U.S. plus 285 for California.

1996 Model Year

The basic specifications for the M900 continued as for the previous year, but as with the Supersport, there was a sound-absorbing clutch cover. The engine crankcases were new, sharing the revised fastening of the 1996 900 Supersport, and the choke lever was now mounted on the handlebar. There was also a new frame for 1996, with the same dimensions as before but with altered fuel line and clamp brackets to accommodate a vacuum fuel tap. The footpegs were now made of rubber, and beginning at frame number 009281 a protective washer was inserted under the lower steering head bearing.

The biggest change for 1996 was the adoption of the Marzocchi 40 USD/REG fork. Unlike the Marzocchi forks of the 750 Supersport and M 600, this was fully adjustable (seven compression and seven rebound settings) and fitted from the beginning of the 1996 model year (frame number 009915). These forks also included an increase in the front axle diameter to 20mm (0.78 inches). From frame number 009915 to 011629 there was a recall to replace the line connecting the fuel cock with the fuel filter. The only other change was a different specification brake pad, now Ferodo Ferit I/D 450FF. Now with yellow more generally available in addition

The 1996 900 Monster was very similar to that of 1995 but for new adjustable Marzocchi front forks.

to red and black, general production problems during 1996 saw only 2,428 900 Monsters manufactured. The U.S. received 560 M900s for 1996, now no distinction between California and the rest of the country. All U.S. 900 Monsters from 1996 were California specification.

An interesting variation on the regular M900 that would have ramifications in the future was the M900 Club Italia. This limited-edition Monster was essentially standard, but with some factory customizing. While the forks were the adjustable Marzocchi 40mm USD of other 1996 model year 900 Monsters, the rear suspension was by Öhlins. The brakes were fully-floating cast-iron 320mm Brembo front discs with remote-reservoir master cylinders, and there was a fully-floating rear caliper. The specification was completed with Pirelli Dragon tires, carbon-fiber fenders and clutch cover, and a Connolly tan leather solo seat. While only 39 were produced at the request of the Castiglioni brothers for an elite club of Italian automotive dignitaries, the Club Italia was the basis for the later M900S.

Although the 1996 brochure indicated a production version of the Club Italia M900 would be available as the Special Edition Monster 900, or Special, this didn't eventuate and only three examples ended up being produced. As with the Club Italia, the Special had a Connolly leather seat, braided steel brake and clutch lines, fully-floating cast-iron front discs, floating rear caliper, and remote-reservoir handlebar master cylinders. Additionally, each Special featured a small fairing from the Police Monster, and in the manner of the Superlight, a numbered plaque, paddock stand and bike cover. Undoubtedly the production problems of 1996 were the reason this model didn't make the production line. However, it remains one of the rarest of all Monsters, and one with some of the nicest standard features.

1997 Model Year

Although all the improvements incorporated in the Supersport (such as bimetallic valves and a carburetor heating kit) were also included in the Monster, the biggest change for 1997 was the detuning of the 900 engine. In an endeavor to improve torque at low rpm, the valve sizes were reduced to that of the 750 (41mm inlet and 35mm exhaust), and the camshafts also new. These retained the 11.76mm and 10.56mm valve lift of the 900 Supersport, but shared timing figures with the 600 and 750 Monster. Carburetion was now by Mikuni BDST 38 B222 carburetors, with the U.S. 900 Monster receiving the 38 Bs of the U.S.-specification Elefant 900. With a revised ignition advance curve from the Kokusan ignition, the claimed power was reduced to 66.6 HP at 7,000 rpm. 1997 engines were also distinguished by a gray clutch cover to match the timing belt covers, and began at engine number 037728.

While there was now a single handlebar fixing plate, the 1997 Monster was differentiated from earlier versions by a standard handlebar fairing. Initially

The Limited Edition Monster was intended for the 1996 model year, but only a few were built.

it was also intended to offer an M900 Solo, a limited-edition version similar to the Club Italia of 1995 and Special Edition of 1996. Along with the incorporation of a solo seat with in-built panniers (from the Police Monster), many of the Club Italia features were retained. These included braided steel brake and clutch lines, fully-floating cast-iron discs, remote-reservoir master cylinders with adjustable levers, and a floating rear brake caliper. The Solo was also fitted with a centerstand, and like the 1996 Special it was also featured in brochures but didn't become generally available. Only three were built. There was also a Police Monster for 1997, now with the frame and wheels painted the usual colors, but only one was produced. If there was one area that Ducati has failed over the years it has been in capturing the police market.

The 1997 900 Monster received a detuned engine and the small handlebar fairing of the 900 Limited. The clutch cover was gray to match the timing covers.

Detail improvements to the M900 continued through the year. From May there were new rectifiers by Shindengen, with kits offered for retrofitting. As with other models the alternator nuts needed checking at 10,000-kilometer intervals. From frame number 013875 new front brake calipers were fitted (610.4.010.4A/610.4.009.4A), and from frame number 014103 there was a new vacuum fuel tap (58840141B). From frame number 014273 there were revised 320mm brake discs (8A0062587), still stainless steel but with a different spring loading system. Later there was a safety recall (for all 1997 900 Monsters between frame numbers 015352 to 015458) to install new handlebars (36010122C). Production was up to 2,922 units for the 1997 model year, with only 301 coming to the U.S.

1998 Model Year

Although 1998 saw the return of the larger-valve engine in the M900S, the regular M900 continued with a lower-output engine (71 HP at 7,000 rpm). Engine changes for 1998 (shared with both 900 Monsters and the 900 Supersport) were new cylinders (Tecnol), pistons (Asso), and piston rings (NPR) in place of the previous Mondial items. The redesigned cylinders incorporated the oil return internally, making external oil lines unnecessary. New piston rings (121.2.014.1A) were available for earlier 92mm pistons to reduce excessive oil consumption. From February 1998 the crankcase sealing compound TB1215 replaced the Loxeal 59-10, this also applying to the new 900 Supersport. As on the 1998 900 Supersport there was a new triphase 520-watt alternator, and the engine side covers were the gray of the timing belt covers and clutch cover. Other updates included a new sprocket cover.

An important improvement for 1998 was the fitting of the 41mm adjustable Showa fork of the 900 Supersport FE to all 900 Monsters. The brake and clutch lines were now braided steel (except for the U.S. and Australia), and while they appeared on the brochures and in publicity material, the production 900 Monster (including the S) didn't come with remote-reservoir master cylinders. The normal M900 saw a reduction in features, specifically the elimination of the handlebar fairing and exhaust heat shields, and also plastic side panels. While there was a mount for a lower rear fender, this too was absent. All the decals for 1998 were the new Massimo Vignelli type, these appearing on the fuel tank in silver, without adornment. From frame number 015459 to 018555 there was a recall to install new handlebars and also a safety recall on Monster 900s for California and Australia to check the front rubber brake line. This affected the M900 California from frame number 015464 to 015563 and Australia from 015714 to 015717.

Monster 900 S

In response to complaints about the reduced engine performance of the 1997 M900, the M900S

For 1998 there was a wider range of 900 Monsters available. Top of the line was the 900S, with the 74 HP Supersport engine, cast-iron front discs and carbon-fiber fenders.

The M900S had a revised engine with gray side covers and a fully-floating rear brake.

was released for 1998. This featured the 900 Supersport engine, although it differed in that the 31/62 primary-drive ratio of the regular M900 was retained and carburetion was still by Mikuni B38 carburetors rather than EFI. The power was 74 HP at 7,000 rpm, and as with the 900 Supersport the alternator was a 520-watt. As a higher-specification Monster, the M900S had its roots back in the Club Italia of 1995. The color was black, and this included the tank, frame, wheels, small fairing and seat cover. The front discs were 320mm fully-floating cast-iron, and there was a floating rear brake caliper. Carbon fiber extended to the front and rear fenders,

The 900 engine for 1998 had new cylinders with the oil return lines incorporated internally. There was also a new gray alternator and ignition cover.

The Monster 900S had fully-floating front disc rotors.

side panels and exhaust heat shields, and higher-performance (Michelin Hi-Sport TX15/25) tires fitted. The M900S also came with a lower rear fender.

Monster 900 Cromo

Another variation of the M900 offered for 1998 was the Cromo. This was a standard 71 HP M900 with some cosmetic alteration, notably a chrome-plated fuel tank, black frame and wheels, and carbon-fiber fenders, side panels, and seat cover.

1999 Model Year

As the only carburetor-equipped model in Ducati's lineup for 1999, the Monster range was widened to include Dark, City, City Dark, and California variants, alongside the regular M900, M900S, and Cromo of before. Three versions used the 74 HP engine, the M 900 S, California, and unlike the previous year, the Cromo. The other four variants were fitted with the 71 HP engine. The only change to the basic M900 was a new regulator, titled Average. Both the Cromo and M900S were similar to the previous year, although the M900S now featured a steering damper and an Öhlins rear shock absorber. The handlebar master cylinders had remote fluid reservoirs. The California version also featured remote-reservoir master cylinders, along with braided steel brake and clutch lines.

Monster 900 City/Dark/City Dark

Based on the M900, the City was a further attempt to broaden the appeal of the Monster concept. With a new seat specifically designed to carry two people, windshield, Mandarina Duck bags and higher handlebars (1,025mm instead of 955mm), the City was targeted at a new buyer, with an emphasis on around town use. Following the success, particularly in Italy, of the basic 600 Dark during 1998, the 900 Dark also offered a no-frills Monster as a platform for customization with Ducati Performance accessories. With its black frame and wheels, matte-black tank and fenders without any clear lacquer, no seat cover or rubber foot-

The expansion of the Monster range was evidenced by the Cromo, with a chrome-plated fuel tank. This was introduced in 1998 but not generally available until 1999.

1999 saw the 900 City and City Dark with windshield and luggage. These not only expanded the Monster concept, but were practical alternatives. Publicity photo.

pegs, the 900 Dark was the budget 900 Monster in the lineup. By combining the features of the 900 City and 900 Dark, a budget 900 City was created, the 900 City Dark. This was essentially a 900 City with the higher handlebars, windshield, and bags, but with the Dark black frame and wheels, matte-black tank and guards, and lack of rubber footpegs. The City models were also slightly heavier at 187 kg (412 pounds).

2000 Model Year
Monster 900 i.e.

For the 2000 Model Year the Monster received its first stylistic revisions since its inception. As the range comprised 43 percent of Ducati sales these were significant alterations, and chief designer Pierre Terblanche set about tidying up the styling. This involved a new rear license plate, taillight assembly and front fender. The Cromo was no longer available, but instead there was now a Monster Metallic. Derived from the Dark and inspired by the metalflake fashion of the 1960s and 1970s as evidenced by the desmo silver shotgun and Imola racers, these had metalflake black, blue, red, silver or fuchsia fuel tanks.

Engine and Drivetrain

All 900 Monsters for 2000 used an engine based on that of the post-1998 900 Supersport. The camshafts were the same, with 11.8mm of inlet and 11.4mm of exhaust valve lift. Unlike the Supersport the cooling system was now entirely by air, with no oil circulation of the cylinders. This was claimed to result in lower operating temperatures with improved oil circulation in the cylinder heads. Jets directed oil underneath the piston crowns, and a larger oil cooler was installed to cope with the increased temperatures. The electronic fuel injection system was the same Marelli 1.5 CPU as the 900 Supersport, with 45mm throttle bodies and new single injectors operating at a pressure of 3 bar. Shared with the Supersport was the 32-/59-tooth primary drive. The six-speed gearbox, however, was different, this being the close-ratio unit from the 748 Superbike. New, larger silencers saw the power slightly reduced from the Supersport at 78 HP at 8,250 rpm. The silencers were quieter than before by 1.5 dB.

Frame and Cycle Parts

While the basic frame was unchanged, 43mm Showa upside-down front forks replaced the earlier 41mm units. However, these were now the non-adjustable units similar to those of the 750 Supersport. There was, however, a larger-diameter axle (25mm) contributing to increased front end rigidity. The Sachs Boge rear unit of before featured on all 900 Monsters except the 900 S. There was also a steel swingarm on all 900s

For the 2000 model year the Monster received the first redesign in eight years. While the general style was unchanged, Pierre Terblanche improved many details, and the 900 was now fuel injected. This is the top-of-the-range Monster 900 Special.

except the 900S. In line with the rest of the range the front discs were now 320mm x 4mm with aluminum carriers, and the P4 30-34 Brembo brake calipers with wider bolt-spacing. The front brake master cylinder was the new PSC 16 and the clutch master cylinder a smaller PSC 12mm giving an increased hydraulic ratio. The master cylinders also had remote reservoirs and the brake lines were braided steel. Along with the new forks and swingarm came Brembo 17-inch wheels similar to the ST2. These were 400 grams lighter than before, as well as being stronger.

Terblanche's redesign of the bodywork was notable for the emphasis on ergonomics, long a Terblanche strong point. To enable a more comfortable riding position the fuel tank was narrowed and reshaped where it met the more thickly padded seat. This saw a slight reduction in the capacity to 16 liters (4.23 gallons). The handlebars too were raised 10mm. Cosmetic restyling included a small fairing that incorporated a complete instrument panel. Finally the most popular aftermarket addition, the tachometer, was fitted standard. The restyling continued to the rear number plate and taillight assembly, another popular aftermarket replacement on earlier versions. Terblanche completed the 2000 Monster with a new front fender that was closer

One of the improvements for the 2000 model year was full instrumentation, including a tachometer. On the M900 Special these were incorporated in a small handlebar fairing.

Pierre Terblanche also created a new tailpiece incorporating the turn signal indicators for the 2000 Monster.

fitting. Also, at long last and in line with other 2000 models, came a sidestand that wasn't automatically retractable. Electronic sensors prevented the engine starting with the sidestand down. It had taken a few years, but the 2000 Monster 900 was undoubtedly the best yet and also the most coherent in terms of styling uniformity. With more power and the same weight as before (187kg, 412 pounds) improved performance in standard form was also promised.

Monster 900 Special

Sensing the market for modified and custom Monsters expanding, Ducati released their version of the ultimate Monster for 2000, the M900S. Although sharing its 78 HP engine with the regular 900 Monster, the M900S had considerably upgraded suspension. The 43mm Showa forks featured adjustable compression and rebound damping as well as spring preload. Completing the superior specification was an aluminum swingarm and Öhlins shock absorber. The M900S also featured a small handlebar fairing, integrated instruments that now included a tachometer, and carbon-fiber fenders, heat guards and side panels. As on the other range leaders, the M900S was also distinguished by the gunmetal wheels and frame complementing the red, yellow, or black fuel tank. The specified tires were Michelin Hi-Sport.

A new Monster for the year 2000 was the Metallic. Inspired by the fashions of the '60s and '70s, these came in a variety of colors. The 900 Monster also received a tachometer and fuel injection.

Bimota DB3 Mantra

Designed by Frenchman Sasha Lakic, the Mantra was one of the more unusually styled motorcycles of the mid to late 1990s. Using a standard 904cc M900 engine with a special four-muffler exhaust system the power was 85.7 HP at 7,000 rpm. Every other component was different to the M900, and the Mantra was lighter and more compact. The trellis frame was constructed of oval-section aluminum tubes, with a cantilever aluminum swingarm and single Öhlins rear shock absorber. This gave a wheelbase of 1,370mm (53.9 inches). Front forks were 43mm Paioli, these providing rebound adjustment. The wheels were black-painted 17-inch Marchesinis fitted with Michelin 120/70ZR17 TX11 and 180/55ZR17 TX23 tires. Although fully-floating cast-iron 320mm Brembo front discs were featured on publicity machines, the front brakes were standard Ducati 320mm stainless steel discs with the usual Brembo P4 30/34 calipers. At the rear was a 230mm rear disc with a Brembo 05 Gold series caliper.

Sasha Lakic's DB3 Mantra was possibly too radical for the conservative motorcycle buyer. However, as with all Bimotas the quality of many of the individual components was superb and the Mantra a highly competent machine.

It was Lakic's yellow-and-black bodywork that was the most controversial. From the front fender to the belly pan, every part represented a new styling experiment. The smoked black windscreen was designed to be easily removable, and a small baggage compartment under the fuel tank cover housed a rainproof suit and gloves. The 16-liter fuel tank itself was a twin saddle-style to give optimum weight distribution. Most of the ancillary components were also specifically designed and built for the Mantra. This included the chromed mirrors, white-faced instruments, CEV headlight and taillight, and wide adjustable alloy handlebars. Standard features also included a burglar alarm.

In 1997 the Mantra's front and rear sections were restyled, and the colors changed to black and red. Two kits were available to bring earlier models up to the 1997 specification. There were also new handlebars, windshield, headlamp cover, rear fender and uprated Michelin TX15 and 25 tires. The new styling also saw an increase in the capacity of the twin saddle fuel tanks to 24 liters. Other changes were to the front brakes (now regular stainless steel 320mm discs) and silver wheels. As with the DB2, there was a wide range of optional equipment available for the Mantra. Some of these were a taller windscreen, engine uprating kit and front fork kit. More sophisticated fork action was provided through titanium fork tubes, along with spring preload and compression damping adjustment. Production of the Mantra commenced in September 1995, the total production being 454 through until 1998. The final 50 were constructed in November of that year. Not particularly successful, even with the restyling, the basic Mantra frame and running gear was then used for the DB4 of 1999.

The front end of the Mantra generally consisted of excellent components such as Marchesini wheels and Paioli forks. Unlike the publicity versions the production Mantra had poor-quality standard Ducati stainless steel discs.

Another significant improvement for the Year 2000 was the non-self-retracting sidestand.

2001 Model Year

As the 2000 model year Monster represented the most significant development since its inception, there were few updates to most models for 2001. Most interest centered on the expansion of the traditional two-valve Monster range to include the Desmoquattro 916-powered S4. This represented a considerable break from the initial Monster philosophy that emphasized minimalism and eschewed complexity. The water-cooled S4 also challenged the aesthetic purity of the Monster layout. Another important update to all models was the universal use of braided steel brake lines.

Monster 900 Dark/Metallic/Cromo/Special

The 900 continued with electronic injection as in 2000 and four versions of the Monster 900 i.e. were offered for 2001. The Dark; Metallic, basically a variant of the Dark metallic paint; the Cromo, and Special. To minimize camshaft timing variations new toothed timing-belt rollers were introduced. The hub of the rollers could now be removed from the rim to facilitate timing and improve accuracy, allowing the timing tolerance to be reduced to only 2 degrees. Accompanying the belt rollers were new N35 type timing belts, with a junction at the tooth head. These featured elastomeric toothing and a crossed-strand band for greater stiffness and geometrical stability. Other updates included a more reliable neutral switch and the lociting of the alternator nut to prevent premature removal, a perennial problem with earlier engines. Although redesigned for 2000, the clutch slave cylinder continued to be problematic, and was the subject of a recall early in 2001. A new KTM oil cooler was fitted to the 900, and to improve starting in colder conditions the starter motor gear ratio was lowered. Simplified wiring and a more compact sealed for life battery shaved 1kg off the weight. Engine color was metallic silver gray this year.

Chassis updates included larger-diameter (12mm) engine fasteners to the frame and the repositioning of the rear brake caliper above the swingarm. The engine bolts now also threaded at both ends, the double nut design intended to overcome problems of bolt breakage on some earlier models. Apart from Metallic and Darks, the frame color for 2001 was gunmetal gray, as on the Ducati Corse Superbikes. 900s received a 260 km/h speedometer and both the standard 900 and 900S now shared an aluminum swingarm (derived from the earlier 888 Superbike) and adjustable Sachs rear shock absorber. All versions featured an improved Brembo clutch master cylinder and stainless steel exhaust pipe heat guards (carbon-fiber on the 900S and Cromo).

2002 Model Year

By 2002 total Monster production had reached over 100,000, ensuring this range was the most successful in Ducati's history. In nearly a decade the Monster had become established as a lifestyle motorcycle, accumulating a cult following. There were five different-displacement Monsters available for 2002, the previous

The 900 i.e. Cromo remained a popular option in 2001.

The 900 i.e. received a fairing and aluminum swingarm for 2002, all Monsters also sharing the S4-type frame.

600 continuing as the 600 Dark, the new 620 i.e., 750 i.e., 900 i.e., and the S4. Apart from the 600 Dark all models now featured electronic fuel injection.

Monster 900 i.e./Dark

The 900cc air-cooled Monster engine incorporated many of the updates of the 620 introduced in 2000. This included the Marelli 5.9 electronic fuel injection, new timing belt covers and rocker arms, oil jet for the vertical piston, and oil temperature sensor. The exhaust system was also new. As the new 1000cc dual-spark engine was already in production (in the Multistrada), 2002 was to be the final year for the 900 Monster. The 900S was discontinued, the 900 i.e. now featuring an aluminum swingarm with provision for ride height adjustment independent of spring preload, and a fully adjustable Showa fork. The 900 Dark continued with the non-adjustable fork and steel swingarm. The 900 i.e. also had a headlight fairing this year. All 900s had an aluminum clutch housing with aluminum discs, and a small switch on the clutch to manage the sidestand safety device. The lighter aluminum clutch allowed

2002 was the final year for the Monster 900.

The frame tubing was increased in diameter to 28mm.

The Magneti Marelli dash panel was new for 2002, with the speedometer on the left and an updated warning light display.

The front fork included a larger-diameter axle.

the engine to be quicker revving, but the price was increased wear.

The 900 Monsters received the S4-derived frame, new electronic instrument panel (with electronic speedometer and rear wheel sensor), S4-type airbox, immobilizer, new rear suspension layout and Sachs shock absorber, updated rear axle adjustment, new front fork with 40mm axle, and the new Asahi Denso handlebar switches.

750 Monster

The expansion of the Monster range was completed with the 750 Monster for 1996, the only new model for that year. Essentially this was derived from the 600 Monster, with an engine similar to the 750 Supersport.

1996 Model Year

The engine number sequence for the 750 Monster continued that of the 750 Supersport (from ZDM 750 A 2C 000001). The engine specifications were shared between the two 750s, though, but with Mikuni BDST 38 B216A carburetors. Thus the 750 Monster still had the relatively low 9:1 compression ratio, 41mm and 35mm valves, and the same camshafts with 9.35mm and 8.50mm of inlet and exhaust valve lift. The primary drive was by 31-/62-tooth straight-cut gears to the usual wet multi-plate clutch and five-speed gearbox. Because of the slightly different intake system and airbox, the power for the 750 Monster was slightly less than the 750 Supersport, at 64 HP at 8,000 rpm. Unlike the M600 the M750 received an oil cooler, and there was also a different final-drive ratio, with 15- and 38-tooth sprockets. The electrical system was shared with the 600, including the 300-watt alternator and Kokusan ignition, though the 750 used the 900's Champion RA5HC spark plugs. The ignition consisted of two right-angle electromagnetic pickups energized by four notches on the flywheel on the left side of the crankshaft.

There was new set of frame numbers for the 750 Monster, beginning at ZDM 750 M 000001. The basic specification followed that of the 600, with non-adjustable Marzocchi 40USD/E forks, a Sachs Boge rear shock absorber, and a steel swingarm. Only a single 320mm disc was fitted, with a Brembo P4.30-34 caliper and PS 13 master cylinder, there being a caliper mount on the right fork leg. In August 1996 a twin front disc kit became available, but this required a replacement right fork leg. The wheels and tires were also as with the 600, the rear rim being an MT 4.50 x 17-inch, and the tires smaller than the 900 (120/60VR17 and 160/60VR17). From frame number 000001 to 000356 there was a recall to replace the line connecting the fuel cock with the fuel filter. The 750 Monster was also available in different colors to the 900, silver along with red and a solitary yellow example. As with the 600 the side panels were a plastic titled Xenoy, and there were no exhaust heat shields. A 750 Police version with windshield, two-tone sirens, antenna and front and rear flashing blue strobe lights was also available but not produced. Only 356 750 Monsters were produced for the 1996 model year, most being silver.

1997 Model Year

For 1997 there were few changes to the 750 Monster. The engine incorporated bimetallic inlet and exhaust valves, and the carburetor heating kit became standard. From May there were new rectifiers by Shindengen, with kits offered for retrofitting. A new front brake caliper, disc and vacuum fuel tap were fitted from frame number 001567, and between frame numbers 002947 to 003316 there was a recall to install new handlebars (36010132B). Many more 750 Monsters were produced for the 1997 model year. In black, red, silver, and yellow, 2,828 were manufactured. The 750 Monster was also available in the U.S. and California for the first time. There were 100 U.S. 750 Ms plus 400 for California, all in silver.

1998 Model Year

There were many more changes to the 750 Monster for 1998. The engine was redesigned, with new crankcases now featuring a smoother finish with less external finning. There was also a new wet clutch, with the actuation moved to the left as with the 900. The camshaft drive belt covers were now the 900-style as well allowing the checking of belt tension without removing the entire cover. While 13 screws were still used to hold the crankcases together there were now seven M8mm x 25 screws (including one drilled screw), one M6mm x 75mm and five M6mm x 35mm screws. The right-side engine cover now featured a relocated oil pressure switch (like the 900), and there was a new alternator cover and 520-watt alternator. The engine side covers now also matched the gray

The 750 Monster was to become one of the most successful of the genre. Offering similar performance to the 900 at a budget price, most were in silver like this 1997 model.

For 1996 and 1997 the 750 Monster engine was identical to that of the 750 Supersport. The wet clutch actuation was still incorporated in the right cover.

timing belt covers. Despite the new clutch, there was a clutch recall for 1998 models from frame number 003317 to 003718. This was due to problems with the clutch pressure plate and required the substitution of the ten 3mm lined plates with nine 3.5mm lined plates (191.1.021.2B). Along with the new clutch came revised primary gears, now 33/61 (1.85:1), with 15- and 41-tooth sprockets and a 100-link D.I.D. 520 VL 2 5/8- x 1/4-inch chain. The quoted power was slightly less for the new engine, at 62 HP at 7,500 rpm at the crankshaft.

While the chassis specifications were much as before, the Marzocchi top outer fork tubes were now silver rather than gold, and, except for the U.S., the 750 received twin 320mm front disc brakes. Twin-disc versions had a PS 16mm master cylinder, with the usual rectangular master cylinders. From frame number 003317 to 004119 new handlebars were fitted. Colors were still red, yellow, silver, and black, and the tank decals were the new Vignelli type.

1999 Model Year

As with other Monsters for 1999, the model range was expanded to include the City, Dark, and City Dark. Apart from also being available in black, the adoption of the new regulator and a braided steel clutch line, this was identical to the previous year. The color range was expanded to include dark blue.

750 City/Dark/City Dark

Although based on the 750 Monster, the City incorporated all the features of the 900 City. This included a windshield, more comfortable seat, pulled-back and higher handlebars, and Mandarina Duck bags. Similar to the 600 and 900 Dark was the 750 Dark with a black frame and wheels, along with matte-black tank and fenders without lacquer. This also had footpegs without rubber inserts, and only a single front disc brake. The 750 City Dark was a combination of the two, being a City with the Dark features of black frame, wheels, tank and fenders. Both 750 City models weighed 180kg (396 pounds).

2000 Model Year

As before the 750 Monster was available in standard, Dark, and City varieties, with the addition of the Metallic for 2000. General styling revisions were shared with the 900 Monster, these the first since its inception. The 62 HP engine was unchanged and unlike the 750 Supersport still retained the Mikuni BSDT38 carburetors. These now featured electrical heaters in the float bowls that were automatically activated at temperatures lower than 3 degrees Celsius. The front fork was the same as the regular 900 Monster, these non-adjustable 43mm Showa. Braking was still by twin discs, with revised brake calipers and 320mm discs with aluminum carriers and a new PSC 16 master cylinder. Braided

The 750 Dark was new for 1999.

steel brake lines completed the upgraded specification. Wheels too were the new, lighter three-spoke Brembo, the rear still being a 4.50 x 17. Colors were red, yellow, silver, and blue/black for the 750 Monster, the Dark being black or yellow with a black frame and wheels. As with the 900 Monster, the Metallic was a Dark (black wheels and frame) with a metalflake fuel tank. The City was black or yellow. Despite the small changes in specification the weight and performance was unchanged.

2001 Model Year

There were three versions of the 750 Monster this year, all still including carburetors. The 750 engine now featured fully air-cooled cylinders, first introduced on the M900 in 2000, as well as a more efficient oil pump. As on the 900 a new KTM oil cooler was fitted this year and to improve starting in colder conditions the starter motor gear ratio was lowered. Simplified wiring and a more compact sealed for life battery shaved 1kg off the

The 750 Monster still retained carburetors for 2000.

The 2002 750 Monster, now with electronic fuel injection and a 900 chassis.

weight. Engine color was metallic silver gray. The 750 Monster also included the M900 instrument layout.

2002 Model Year
750 i.e./S

The 750 received electronic fuel injection this year and for the U.S. a 750S was available. This was ostensibly a 750 i.e. engine in a 620S i.e. chassis. Like the 900, the 750 received the S4-derived frame, new electronic instrument panel (with electronic speedometer and rear wheel sensor), S4-type airbox, immobilizer, new rear suspension layout and Sachs shock absorber, updated rear axle adjustment, new front fork with 40mm axle, and the new Asahi Denso handlebar switches. 2002 was the final year for the 750, the updated 800cc engine replacing it for 2003.

600 Monster
1994 Model Year

A lightweight Monster, the 600, became available during 1994, going into production in March. This featured the wet clutch five-speed engine from the newly introduced 600 Supersport, and was also available in two versions, 33 HP and 53 HP. This engine is covered in detail in Chapter Seven. Until frame number 002961 the primary drive was 32-/73-tooth gears, with a 15/38 final drive and 98-link D.I.D. 520 VL 2 chain. From frame number 002962 this became the 31/62 primary drive of the 900, now with a 15/43 final drive, with a 100-link chain. Carburetion was by the usual Mikuni BDST 38mm constant-vacuum carburetors, the variant for the 600 Monster being B159s. A Mikuni carburetor heating kit became available in June. Ignition was by the same Kokusan system as on the 600 Supersport, with identical Champion RA4HC spark plugs.

Frame numbers began at ZDM 600 M 000001, and for 1994 the fork rake was 24 degrees. The swingarm was steel, and the front suspension non-adjustable Marzocchi USD/E40 forks. For 1994 these had provision for a right-side brake caliper, this being enclosed by a plastic cover. At the rear was the usual Monster Sachs Boge unit with a yellow spring. Unlike the M900 the M600 suspension rocker arm was painted bronze to match the frame. As on the 600 Supersport there was only a single 320mm front disc (with Brembo PS 13 mm master cylinder), and a smaller rear wheel (4.50 x 17-inch). On early 1994 600 Monsters the wheels were black, and later the usual bronze. The 600 Monster was available in yellow and red, with black plastic Xenoy side panels. Unlike the M900 there were no exhaust heat shields. Production for the 1994 model year was primarily for Europe only, and 2,495 were built.

Undoubtedly the Monster lends itself more to modification and customization than other models. This is partly due to the naked concept that emphasized the individual elements of the design without them being covered by acres of fiberglass. While obviously at ease in city traffic, the Monster was also an agile and competent handling motorcycle, aided by a strong chassis and low weight. Most modifications to the Monster are to increase power, improve the handling, reduce weight or individually customize the cosmetics. There were few complaints about the standard Monster frame, after all this was close to that of the World Superbike 888s from 1988-93 and was capable of handling up to 150 HP. However, in the interest of keeping costs low most Monsters were fitted with poor suspension. The non-adjustable Showa forks on earlier models were over-sprung, with too much compression damping. This can be improved by the substitution of lighter fork oil (7 weight instead of 10 weight). A better solution would be to replace the fork legs with the Showa GD 021 from the 900 Supersport. Later 900 Monsters with adjustable Marzocchi forks and the larger, 20mm axle can be made to perform better. Benefit can also be obtained by replacing the Sach Boge shock absorber.

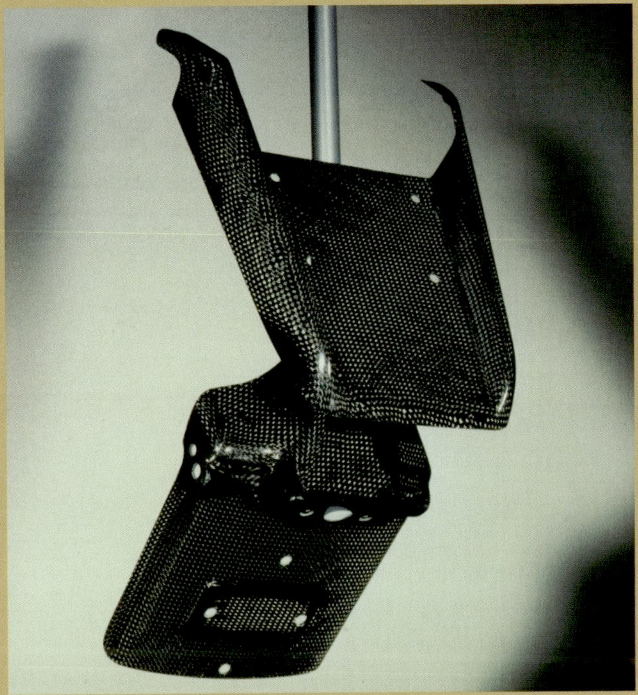

Amongst the first items to be replaced on the Monster is the license plate bracket.

Most owner modifications to the Monster are cosmetic. Many of the body parts (taillight, license plate bracket and footpegs brackets for instance) were unnecessarily large and heavy. Particularly popular are replacement license plate brackets, billet footpeg brackets, and instrument panels that incorporate a tachometer. Also popular are carbon-fiber body parts, aftermarket seats, tank bras, and custom paintwork. All pre-2000 Monsters should have the automatically retracting sidestand deactivated by replacing the protruding bolt with a flat type.

With the 2000 model year Monster many of the earlier styling compromises were overcome, but there are still considerable weight and power gains to be had through substitution of the standard exhaust system. However, replacement of this brings the same problem with re-mapping the Marelli 1.5 CPU that occurred with the 900 Supersport. Although the 43mm Showa fork was non-adjustable (except for the M900 Special), this was a stronger assembly than before, the larger, 25mm axle contributing to this. The 2000 Monster also had an improved braking system with braided steel brake lines as standard. There was also now no need to replace the sidestand retaining bolt.

Color-coordinated aftermarket saddles are also popular for the Monster.

Most 1994 600 Monsters were yellow. As an entry-level Monster they were very successful, lasting through until 1998 with only detail changes.

1995 Model Year

Although the engine specifications were unchanged for the 600 Monster for 1995 (still in 33 HP and 53 HP versions), from engine number 05025 (frame number 003204) there was a new vertical cylinder and piston assembly. The engines also received gray timing belt covers and sprocket cover, and the lower part of the mufflers were chamfered for increased ground clearance. The frame was now painted 916-gold, and provided a 23-degree steering head angle. Color changes extended to the horn that was now black rather than silver, and the sidestand and carburetor air chambers that were gray. For 1995 the wheels were also painted to match the frame. While the Marzocchi USD/E40

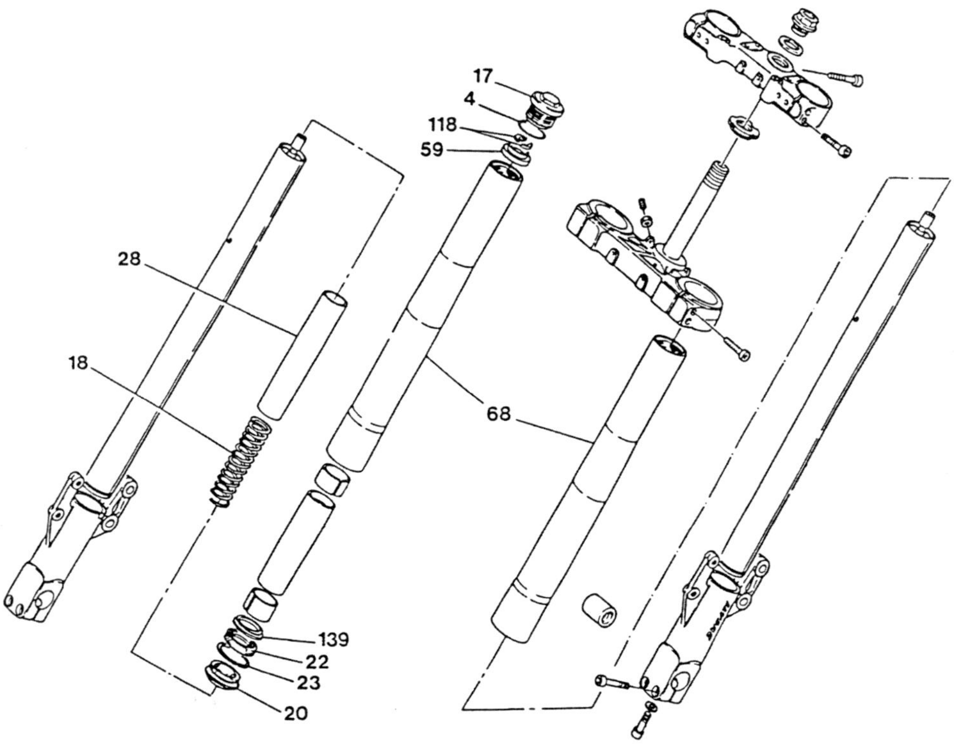

The 600 Monster was the first Ducati to feature non-adjustable Marzocchi USD/E40 forks.

forks were retained, these no longer featured a right-side brake caliper attachment. Colors for 1995 were still red or yellow and 3,295 55 HP versions were produced only with 572 33 HP versions.

1996 Model Year

Only detail changes affected the 600 Monster for 1996, these including the positioning of the choke on the handlebar, a vacuum-operated fuel tap, rubber inserts in the footpegs, sound-deadening panels, and a change in brake pad material to Ferodo Ferit I/D 450 FF. The engine was unchanged (still in 33 HP and 53 HP versions), and from engine number 012190 (frame number 008993) there were new piston and cylinder assemblies (120.2.033.2A/120.2.034.2A). From frame number 004800 to 005800 there was a safety recall to rectify possible interference between the alternator rotor and stator. There was another recall from frame number 006839 to 008076 to replace the line connecting the fuel cock with the fuel filter.

Beginning at frame number 006781 a protective washer was inserted under the lower steering head bearing. A new front brake caliper was fitted from frame number 009711, and from number 009797 a new 320mm front disc. In August 1996 a twin front disc kit became available, this requiring a replacement right fork leg with caliper attachment for post-1994 models. Also from number 009797 was a new vacuum fuel tap. Production for the 1996 model year was 1,492 55 HP models and 79 33 HP. 36 were also produced for the Bologna municipal police.

1997 Model Year

The only alterations to the specification for 1997 were bimetallic inlet and exhaust valves, and the standard fitting of the carburetor heating kit. From May there were new rectifiers by Shindengen, with kits offered for retrofitting. There was also a safety recall from frame number 010567 to 011516 to install new handlebars (36010132B). As with all models production was increased for 1997. There were 2,541 55 HP 600 Ms and 389 33 HP versions.

1998 Model Year

After several years virtually unchanged, more developments were in store for the 600 Monster for 1998. Most of these centered on the engine, which was now generally available with 51 HP at 8,000 rpm, although a few lower-horsepower Darks were produced. While the general specifications remained as before, there were new crankcases (with less external finning), a revised primary-drive ratio (33/61), and a new clutch and engine and timing belt covers. As with the 750, there was a clutch recall on 1998 600 Monsters from frame number 0011517 to 013107 that included replacing the previous clutch plate pack. Also like the 750 Monster the hydraulic clutch actuation was moved to the left, and there was a new (520-watt) alternator and cover. The final drive was now by 102 link D.I.D. 520 VL 2 chain with 15- and 46-tooth sprockets (although Swiss versions used the higher M750 gearing). The Marzocchi forks were now also shared with the 750, having a right-side brake caliper mount. From

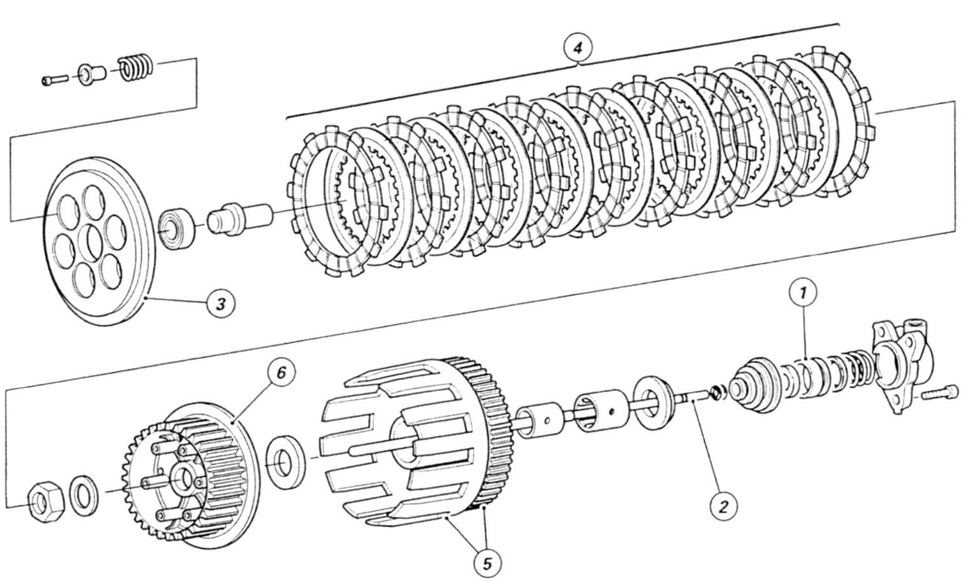

1998 saw the first redesign of the 600 and 750 Pantah engine since the 750 F1 of 1986. Amongst other improvements was a new wet clutch with actuation on the left as with the 900.

One of the most successful Monsters in recent years has been the Dark. This is the 600 of 1998, with a matte-black frame and fuel tank. Other versions had a bronze frame.

frame number 011517 to 015932 there was a recall to install new handlebars.

600 Dark

One of the most significant new models for 1998 was the release of a budget 600 Monster, the Dark. Primarily intended for the domestic market the Dark was promoted as an entry-level Ducati, *La Tua Prima Ducati* (Your first Ducati). It was extremely successful in its first year, easily being Ducati's best-selling model in Italy. The Dark came with a plain painted fuel tank with no lacquer, unpainted front fender, no seat cover, and no footpeg rubbers. The 600 Dark was available in three color combinations, all with the matte-black fuel tank: bronze frame and rear shock absorber U-bolt with black wheels, black frame, U-bolt, and wheels, yellow frame, U-bolt, and wheels. Most were produced with the black frame.

1999 Model Year 600 Monster/Dark/City/City Dark

Apart from the new Average regulator and braided steel clutch cable there were no changes to the 600 Monster and 600 Dark for 1999. There was however an expansion of the range of colors available for the normal 600 Monster. Along with red and yellow this now included black, silver, and dark blue. The 600 Monster model range was also expanded to include the City and City Dark. Both the 600 City and City Dark featured the same specifications as the 750 City and City Dark

New for 2001 was the 600 Monster USA, with a lower seat.

but for the single front disc brake. The dry weight was to 176kg (388 pounds).

2000 Model Year

The general updates to the 600 Monster for the 2000 model year followed those of the 750 and 900 Monster. Even the 600, sold as the most basic Ducati, received the 43mm Showa forks and new Brembo wheels. The braking system was also upgraded, though the 600 still only featured a single 320mm disc with an aluminum carrier. The Mikuni-carbureted 51 HP engine was identical to the 1999 version but for automatic electric carburetor float bowl heaters and lighter clutch springs to aid city use. Still offered as the Dark and City, these were also joined by the Metallic. The 600 Dark and City were available in more colors than other Monsters, bronze and silver in addition to black and yellow. The weight for the 600 Monster was unchanged at 174kg (383 pounds).

2001 Model Year

Three models of 600 Monster were offered for 2001, the 600, 600 Dark, and 600 USA. Engine specifications were unchanged, and as on the 750, the 600 included fully air-cooled cylinders, as well as a more efficient oil pump. A new KTM oil cooler was installed, and to improve starting in colder conditions the starter motor gear ratio was lowered. Simplified wiring and a more compact sealed for life battery shaved 1kg off the weight. Engine color was metallic silver-gray. The 600 also featured the M900 instrument layout, while the U.S. received a specific 600 model. This was identical to the regular 600 Monster but for a 35mm-lower seat height. Other updates saw the 600 Dark with a new molded polyamide fuel tank that provided improved durability and saved 1kg in weight, while the Monster 600 USA was fitted with a new AV fiber rear fender.

The 400 Monster was only available in Japan. This is the 1995 version.

2002 Model Year

As the smaller 600 Monster still represented the bulk of sales, most development was centered on this model for 2002, the 600 growing to 620 and gaining electronic fuel injection. As this engine incorporated many updates it can be considered the beginning of a new generation and the cut-off for this book. The 600 did continue for one more year as the 600 Dark. This was unchanged from 2001 and was basically stock left over from the previous year

400 Monster

Only Saudi Arabia had shown any interest in specific police models, and the first series of 400 Monster was 300 for the Saudi Arabian police built during 1994. In 1995 the 400 Monster became available for Japan, in red and yellow. These were essentially a 400 Supersport engine in a 600 Monster chassis. Production continued through until 1998 with the addition of a small number of black (16) and silver (36) examples. From 1996 the engine was the five-speed 400 Supersport unit. For 1997 and 1998 this was unchanged, the engine still featuring one-piece timing belt covers and hydraulic clutch actuation on the right side of the engine. The primary-drive ratio was 32/73 (2.28:1). The camshafts were shared with the 600, as were the 33.5 and 30.5mm valves. Carburetion was by twin Mikuni BDST 38 B190 carburetors and the crankshaft power 43 HP at 10,500 rpm. While the 600 received a 520-watt alternator for 1998, the 400 continued with the 300-watt version of before. The entire chassis was also from the 600, although the 400 didn't receive a rear seat cover. From frame number 000843 there was a new front brake disc. Also from this number was a new vacuum fuel tap (58840141B).

No 400 Monsters were built in 1999, but from 2000 it again became a regular export to Japan. The specification mirrored the 600, and for 2001 the 400 engines now included fully air-cooled cylinders, first introduced on the M900 in 2000, as well as a more

As the Monster lends itself to customization more than any other Ducati, several companies exist with a wide range of aftermarket components. Roadracing of Varese offer a complete range of custom chassis parts for the Monster. This is an M900 fitted with their Special Collection Limited Series. Most components are polished alloy, and special parts include spoked wheels, Forcelle Italia forks, and stainless steel exhaust exiting under the swingarm.

Another no-expense-spared modified 900 Monster. This is a more individual customization. The engine is a full Vee Two 944cc unit with 41mm FCR Keihin carburetors and a Skorpion exhaust system. Chassis modifications include Marchesini wheels, Öhlins shock absorber, adjustable Showa forks and fully-floating front brake discs.

efficient oil pump. Simplified wiring and a more compact sealed for life battery shaved 1kg off the weight. Although the engine specifications were unchanged, the Japanese-market 400 Monster was now available with a Ducati performance kit that raised the power from 43 HP to 55 HP. As on the larger models engine color was metallic silver-gray this year. The 400 also included the M900 instrument layout. For 2002 the 400 (still Japan-only) was basically stock left over from the year before. This year there was a Monster 400 and 400 Dark, both with a lower seat and carbon-fiber rear fender.

CHAPTER NINE

900, 750 Supersport 1998-2002

Although a replacement for the classic post-1991 Supersport had been considered for some time, it wasn't until December 1996 that this got under way. Prior to this Ducati had suffered a crisis in supply of components, significantly curtailing production. However, the buyout of the company by the Texas Pacific Group in September 1996 meant that delayed projects could proceed. With a new Supersport at the top of the agenda, Pierre Terblanche was engaged to create the successor, under the code of Project 9701. Terblanche's brief was quite specific, with immediate implementation an important element. To reduce tooling costs he was required to carry over the basic frame and the bottom of the steel fuel tank. Other parts, such as the taillight, instruments, footpegs, brakes and front suspension would be shared with existing models. As the Supersport customer was considered a traditionalist, the concept had to remain much as before. While initially it was envisaged to maintain a similar semi-sports riding position, Terblanche decided that as they now had the ST2 they could go for a slightly more sporting riding position. Working from clay mock-ups and some mathematical surfaces at Futura Design, near Birmingham, England, Terblanche produced the Supersport very quickly, and from the first drawings until production was only 15 months.

900 Supersport 1998-1999

Engine and Drivetrain

Although there were a number of significant alterations to the engine, notably the use of Weber Marelli electronic fuel injection, engine numbers for the new Supersport continued the previous ZDM 904 A 2 sequence. To complement the injection there are new camshafts (with new valve timing—see Appendix), these also providing more valve lift than before, 11.8mm for the 43mm inlet valve and 11.4mm for the 38mm exhaust valve. The capacity remained at 904cc

Pierre Terblanche's 900 Supersport of 1998 was a radical development of the classic air-cooled 900 Supersport that had first appeared in 1989. Colors were either red or yellow like this example.

Much of the shape of the fuel tank and seat drew on his earlier Supermono. The headlight was intentionally designed to place the Supersport apart from the higher-performance 916.

and the compression ratio 9.2:1. The main reason the factory didn't increase the capacity or the compression ratio was due to the heat of the rear cylinder, particularly on the fully faired version. However, the engine still made more power than before, 80 BHP at 7,500 rpm, with 8.1 kg/m of torque at 7,000 rpm. The new camshafts and injection system meant that there was no need for a high-inertia flywheel and a lighter flywheel was now fitted. Other engine changes for 1998 were new cylinders (Tecnol), pistons (Asso) and piston rings

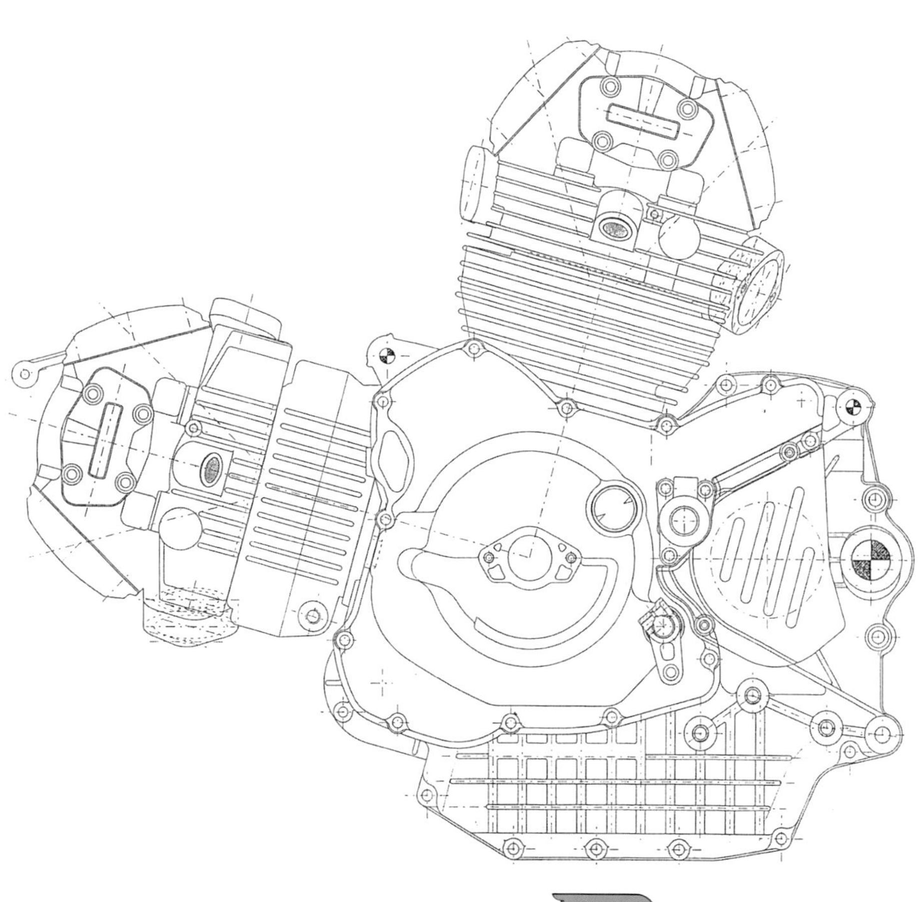

While the 904cc 90-degree air-cooled engine was much as before, developments saw the power increase 80 HP.

Over the years the Weber-Marelli CPU has become much smaller. Here are three generations. On the left is the 1.5 of the 1998 900 Supersport, in the center the 1.6 of the ST2, and on the right the P7 of the 907 I.E.

(NPR) in place of the previous Mondial items. The redesigned cylinders also incorporated the oil return internally, making external oil lines unnecessary. The 31-/62-tooth primary drive became the 32/59 (1.84:1) of the ST2 (also shared with the 900 SS FE), although the final-drive gearing was more realistic with 15- and 40-tooth sprockets along with the usual D.I.D. 520 VL 4 chain (102 links). The clutch was unchanged, still the 19020013A set of plates. This consisted of two driven plates 2mm thick, one 3mm driving plate, one 1.5mm convex plate, then six 2mm drive plates alternated with six 3mm driving plates. Although the basic exhaust system was carried over, the new Supersport received much larger, quieter, mufflers. While the new 900 Supersport didn't make significantly more horsepower than before, the injection completely transformed the motorcycle. The engine started immediately and idled and ran from cold perfectly. All the cold running problems of the Mikuni carburetors were completely eradicated.

Ignition, Injection, and Electrics

The Weber Marelli fuel injection ECU, code-named the 1.5, was the third generation used by Ducati. With a single injector and incorporating the absolute air pressure sensor inside the ECU, it promised better reliability. The injection system used five sensors, including an oil temperature sensor incorporated in the front inlet rocker cover and included a larger, 10-liter, airbox and new intake manifolds. A complete diagnostic system was also incorporated in the ECU and a tri-phase 520-watt alternator improved the electrical system.

Frame and Cycle Parts

For the new Supersport there was also a new set of frame numbers, these beginning at ZDM U1 00AA 8 B 000001. While the frame and aluminum cantilever swingarm was essentially carried over from before, the rear section was new. The cross brace now went from the right to the left, some frame tubes narrowed, and the steering head angle reduced to 26 degrees. The frame tubing was 25mm x 2mm. By using a longer shock absorber the actual fork rake was steepened 1 degree to 24 degrees, with front fork offset of 30mm. Trail was 100mm (3.94 inches). The forks were similar to those of the ST2, 43mm Showa GD 131 providing 120mm (4.72 inches) of travel. These were a new generation of fork featuring an improved oil stop system to prevent bottoming. At the rear was a Showa GD 132-007-00 shock absorber with a stroke of 71mm (2.79 inches) providing 135mm (5.31 inches) of wheel travel. Both the fork and shock absorber were fully adjustable for spring preload, and compression and rebound damping. With Brembo wheels (3.50 x 17 and 5.50 x 17-inch) from the 916 and ST2, and larger-diameter (25mm) axles, the steering and suspension was considerably improved over the earlier version. Constructed of a new alloy with more silicon (GA/Si7), the wheels were also lighter than before by 225 grams (0.5 pound) on the front and 800 grams (1.75 pounds) on the rear. This improved suspension action by reducing unsprung weight. Tires were either Metzeler TL MEZ4F or Michelin Macadam, in sizes of 120/70-ZR17 and 170/60-ZR17. With improved weight distribution (49 percent on the

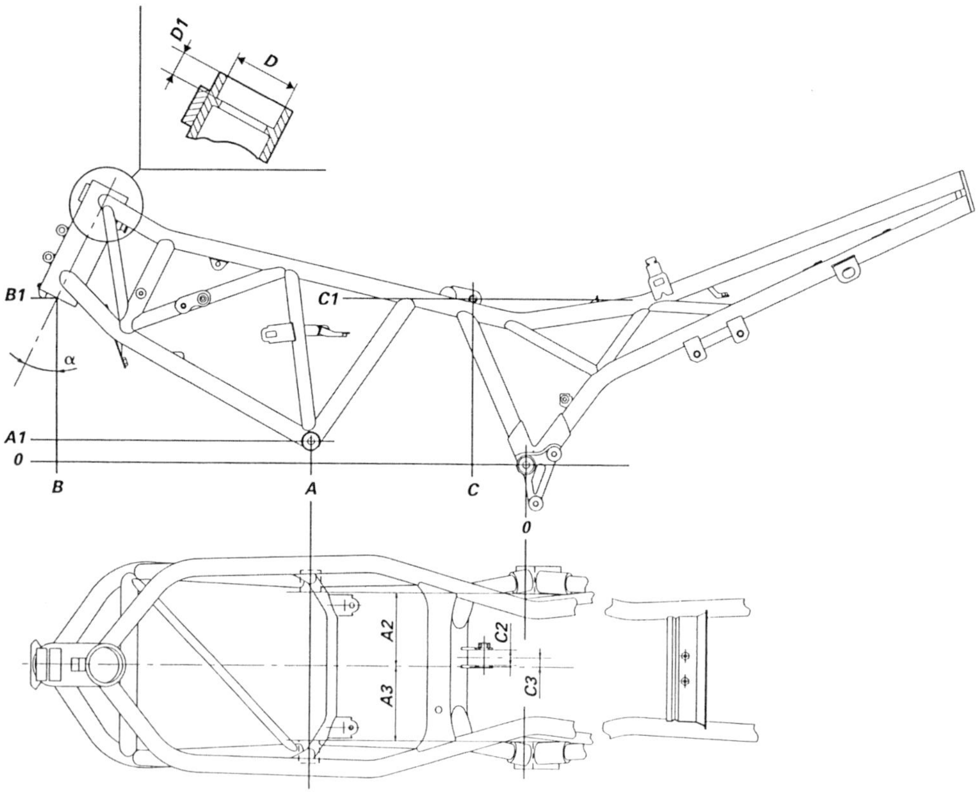

Although the frame of the 1998 Supersport was strongly derived from that of the earlier Supersport, the rear subframe was entirely new.

front wheel), the front end was considerably more taut and direct. Rear suspension action from the cantilever swingarm was also improved with more rear wheel travel. Contributing to the quicker handling was a wheelbase of 1,395mm (55 inches), the shortest of all current Ducati motorcycles. The Brembo brakes were also from the ST2. At the front were twin 320mm discs with P4 30-34 calipers. The caliper mounts were wider apart to improve rigidity and the calipers different internally with greater fluid capacity. Both the clutch and front brake PSC 16 master cylinders were also a new generation with revised lever ratios, these also having

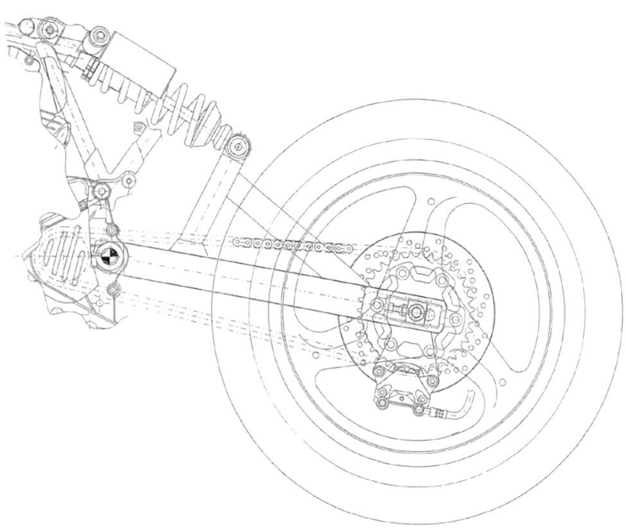

The aluminum cantilever swingarm and single Showa shock absorber were also similar to the earlier version. The longer shock absorber effectively steepened the steering head angle and provided quicker steering.

While Terblanche still favored the white-faced Veglias and these appeared on the prototype, the production Supersport had a 916-style instrument panel. The aluminum handlebars, while mounted on top of the fork yoke, provided an aggressive riding position. Other details were top-of-the-range, including remote-reservoir master cylinders and adjustable levers. This is a 750 with non-adjustable front forks.

Compared to the earlier Supersport the front end was significantly improved. The 43mm Showa forks were more rigid, with a larger (25mm) axle and the brake calipers featured wider mounts. The new Brembo wheels were also lighter and stronger than before.

remote reservoirs and adjustable levers. All the brake and clutch lines were braided steel. The rear brake was also shared with the ST2, with a 245mm disc, Brembo P 32 G caliper and PS 11 master cylinder. Compared with the earlier Supersport the brakes were a noticeable improvement.

Where the new Supersport really did differ in concept from the earlier version was in the riding position. The handlebars were still located above the top triple clamp, but were lower and pulled back 15mm to be closer to the rider. The footpeg position was similar and to maintain uniformity within the range. Footpegs and controls were from the 916. While the early prototypes used the long serving white-faced Veglia instruments, production models were fitted with 916 instruments with new graphics. The taillight and rear license plate bracket were from the ST2, and finally there were acceptable rearview mirrors. With a more sporting riding position than before, the Supersport also promised better back-road behavior and it didn't disappoint. The feel from the front end was vastly improved and even at slower speeds the new Supersport had a directness in the steering that the older Supersport lacked. If any criticism could be leveled at the Supersport it was the moderate power. The chassis could have undoubtedly handled more power.

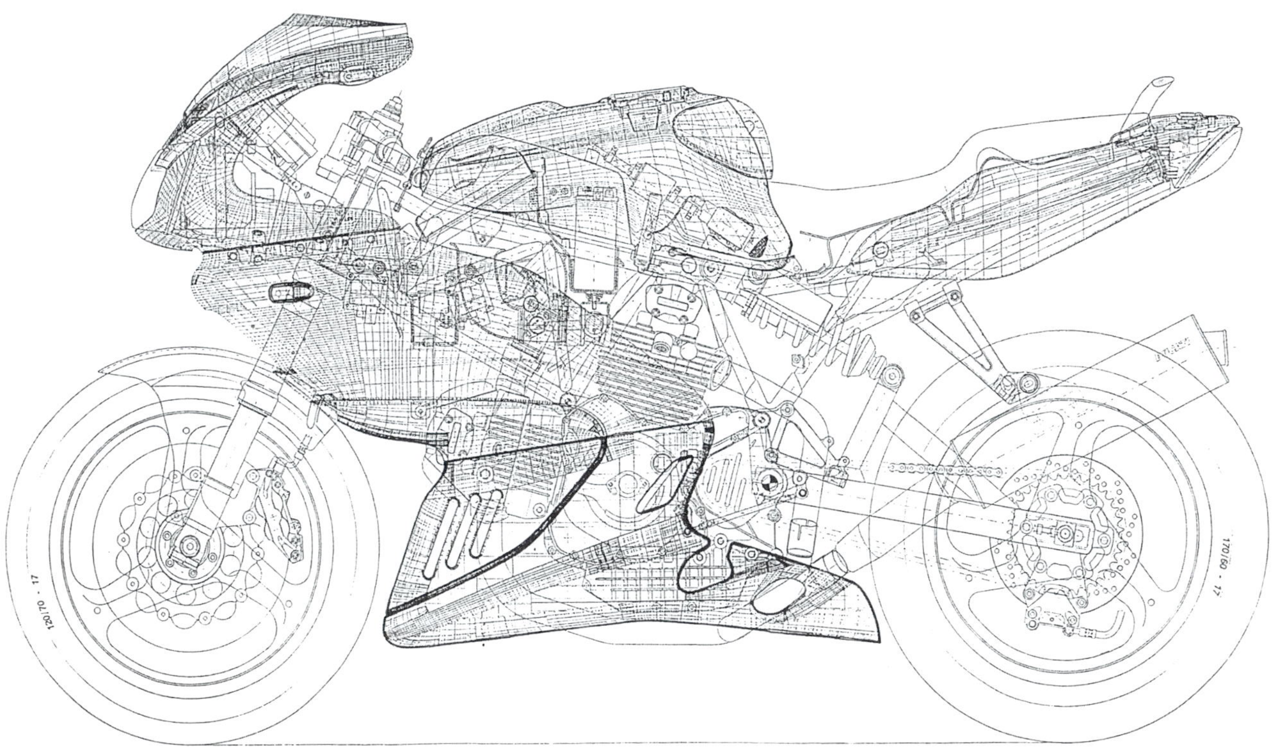

The 1998 900 Supersport was the first Ducati designed with the aid of a computer. This sped up the design process and enabled the new Supersport to go into production in record time.

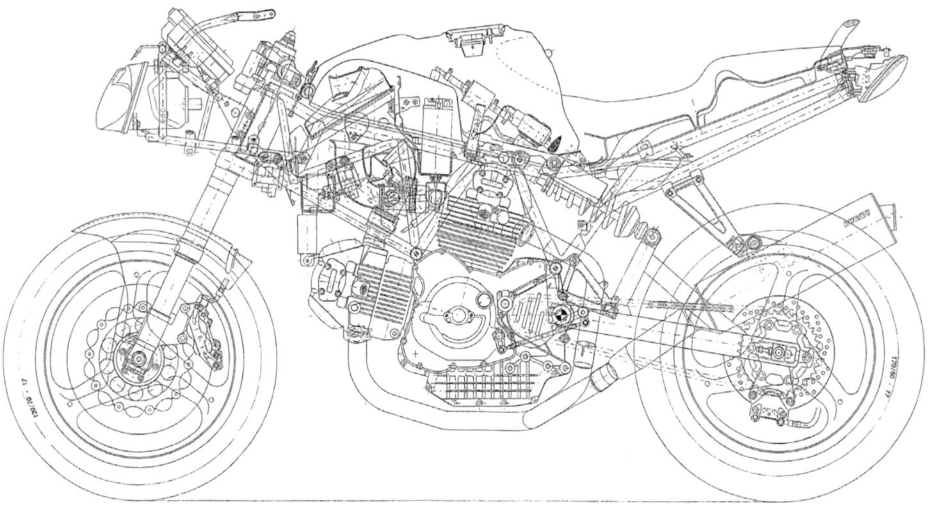

Underneath Terblanche's new bodywork was a compact motorcycle that used the air-cooled 90-degree V-twin to its best advantage. So good was the basic chassis that it really didn't require modification.

Pierre Terblanche's bodywork was strikingly different to the earlier Supersport, the full fairing incorporating improved ducting to cool the rear cylinder. The general style was inspired by the racing Supermono and incorporated a new parabolic headlight to replace the aging rectangular unit of before. While the 18-liter (4.76-gallon) fuel tank utilized the same underneath section as before, the shape was quite different. A striking feature was the incorporation of a neoprene tank pad as a stock item. Because of the stronger front forks and larger silencers the 900 Supersport was slightly heavier than before at 188kg (414 pounds), but 92kg (202 pounds) of that was on the front wheel. No dual seat cowling was fitted and the colors were red and yellow. In line with other faired 1998 models there were no tank decals, the DUCATI marking being confined to the fairing only. This continued through 1999. Initially offered only with a full fairing, production began in March 1998. It became available in Europe during May and in the United States in July, with production of 4,585 units during the year. Sales to the U.S. for the year ending March 1999 were 580. At the Munich Intermot of 1998 a half-faired (½ Carena) version was also shown, the specifications otherwise unchanged for 1999. Sales for the Supersport range compromised 18 percent of the total Ducati market.

900 Supersport 2000

There were few changes to the 900 Supersport for 2000, these confined mainly to decals, brakes and riding position. The engine was unchanged, now incorporating oil jets to spray the underside of the piston crowns. Unlike the 2000 model year 900 Monster the Supersport continued with the air-/oil-cooled cylinders and still produced 80 HP at 7,500 rpm. While the chassis also continued as before, the frame and wheels were now dark metallic-gray, with slightly revised decals on the red or yellow bodywork. 900 appeared on the fairing, there was a DUCATI logo underneath the headlight and a DUCATI SUPERSPORT logo on the top of the fuel tank. The Plexiglas windscreen was higher and the fairing received a transparent protective layer to prevent stone chips. In response to criticism of the rather sporting riding position and improve comfort, the handlebars were raised a further 12mm, and the neoprene tank protection made thinner. As with the 900 Monster, the clutch master cylinder was reduced to a PSC 12 for an improved hydraulic ratio. Along with other model year 2000 Ducatis the sidestand was without an automatic return, and now fitted with an anti engine-start sensor. In line with the rest of the 2000 range the brakes on the 900 Supersport were also upgraded. The front 320mm discs now had aluminum carriers, and there was a new PSC 16mm master cylinder using racing radial master cylinder technology. The braking system was identical to that of the 1999 748. For 2000 the tires were either high-performance Metzeler MEZ3 or Michelin TX. The sizes were unchanged.

900 Supersport 2001

There was some development to the 900 Supersport for 2001.The engine featured a number of minor updates, but the option between fully- and half-faired versions unchanged. Colors were red or yellow with

The 2000 900 Supersport was little changed from 1999.

a metallic gunmetal gray frame and wheels, metallic silver-gray engine, new rearview mirrors, and gray seat and fuel tank protection. Engine updates included totally air-cooled cylinders, split timing-belt rollers for enhanced set-up accuracy, new KTM oil cooler, new-design clutch slave cylinder, new Bosch timing sensor and a new starter motor ratio.

All 2001 Supersport twin-cylinder engines featured an improved lubrication system, with incremented flow rate thanks to an enlarged pump suction unit. In Ducati air-cooled twin-cylinder engines, oil circulation plays a key role in ensuring an even, progressive warm-up to operating temperature and controlling the temperature of vital parts exposed to extreme heat to avoid abnormal peaks even under the harshest riding conditions. This improved oil circulation in the key areas of the cylinder head helped maintain temperature uniformity, improving reliability and service life.

The 900 Supersport received a new Sachs shock absorber for 2001.

The 900cc engine also inherited the air-cooled cylinders from the 2000 750cc Monster. With their more efficient heat dispersion capability, the new cylinders provided greater thermal-mechanical stability compared to the previous combined air-/oil-cooling system. Special oil jets located at the base of the cylinders—introduced on the 2000 750 engine—assured effective cooling of the piston crown, wrist pin, con rod small-end and big-end bearing. A new high-efficiency KTM oil cooler improved cooling efficiency.

Another significant technical update was the introduction of split belt rollers for the toothed camshaft belts. These belt rollers disengaged the gear wheel from the shaft, enhancing cam timing accuracy. The maximum deviation from optimum theoretical timing was now ±2 degrees. This contributed to more consistent in performance, with the power and torque

Ducati Mike Hailwood 900 Evoluzione

Unveiled at the Munich Intermot of September 1998 was the Ducati Mike Hailwood 900 Evoluzione concept motorcycle. Pierre Terblanche went to AKA design in Hitchin, north of London. Over an 11-week period he worked with a three-dimensional model on the computer and constructed a full-size clay model. The idea behind the Evoluzione was to recreate the NCR racers of the late 1970s. While using an air-cooled two-valve fuel-injected 900 Supersport engine as a basis, the engine was tidied externally through the use of sump covers to hide the oil cooler and lines, with the ignition coils on the camshaft bearing supports on the cylinder heads. The engine had polished engine cases reminiscent of the earlier round-case Ducatis, but apart from the clutch was that of a standard 900 Supersport. The clutch was one of the more special components on the bike. Weighing a mere 800gm, it was a slipper design with three plates and a diaphragm spring by Poggipolini and Zornik.

Terblanche created this mock-up in England.

The tubular-steel frame was a special construction by the Dutch company Troll, placing the engine as far forward in the frame as possible while retaining the same offset as the normal 900 Supersport with a 23.5-degree steering head angle. Though a twin-shock swingarm in the style of the original Hailwood Replica was initially considered, this was discarded for a

Pierre Terblanche with his spectacular Mike Hailwood Evoluzione of 1998. With its emphasis on light weight and simplicity, this possibly represented the Supersport concept at its zenith.

Terblanche always fondly remembered the NCR racers of the late 1970s and his Mike Hailwood Evoluzione was homage to those machines. Dummy sump covers hiding all the wires and oil cooler lines emphasized the cleanliness of the engine design. This is the prototype.

tubular single-sided swingarm with Öhlins 125 Grand Prix shock absorber, and modern 916 fork. The wheelbase is still a very short 1420mm. Wheels were Marvic, the rear being 6.00 x 17-inches with a 200/50 x 17-inch

The production MH900e differed in a number of details from the prototype, including the normal turn signals.

tire. To minimize unsprung weight a single 305mm disc was used at the front. The disc was a product of Mislav Zornik and constructed of Selcom, a carbon silesium combination. Using only a single front disc enabled the other brake caliper mount to be machined off the fork and a single-sided stainless steel bracket installed to locate the front mudguard.

One of the more advanced features was the one-piece fairing and fuel tank. Designed to keep as much weight on the front wheel as possible, this unit was a nylon polymer, rotationally molded and heated while rotated. The rear indicators were in the exhausts, with gases exiting through a Super Trapp-style exit. The Valeo headlight was quite small, only 80mm in diameter. Other unique features were the voice-activated ignition system and television rearview camera. When the MH900e finally went into production in May 2000 and in 2001, many of the special features on the prototype were absent. The engine was similar to the 900 Supersport, producing slightly less power (75 HP at 8,000rpm). The production version didn't include voice-activated ignition and television rear view camera. The front fork was the non-adjustable type of the 750 SS and the front brakes the usual 900 Supersport semi-floating 320mm set-up with P30/34 calipers. The rear disc was 220mm with a Brembo twin-piston caliper. An adjustable gas-charged Paioli shock absorber controlled the tubular-steel swingarm. The tubular-steel frame featured a 60mm backbone tube,

A single Paioli shock was fitted to the production MH900e.

integrated with a series of smaller-diameter steel wishbones. Wheelbase was 1,415mm and the steering head angle a steep 23.5 degrees. The specific five-spoke Brembo wheels were shod with sporting Michelin Pilot tires, 120/65 x 17 and 170/60 x 17. A 130mm headlamp replaced the small prototype style, and the rear turn signals were no longer incorporated in the exhausts. The weight was 183kg. The MH900e was initially sold only on the Internet, with the first production machines becoming available in May 2000. The very first production example was delivered at the World Ducati Weekend at Misano in June 2000. The total production was 2,010, most sold to California and Japan as 2001 and 2002 model year versions.

The front braking was by twin discs on the production version. The headlight was also a larger diameter.

Also new was an Öhlins shock absorber and more rigid aluminum swingarm.

on all engines now close to maximum rated levels. Other updates included a new Bosch timing sensor and a new starter motor ratio. The neutral indicator was improved for more precision, and there were new oil cooler connectors. As on all 2001 models the troublesome clutch slave cylinder was also updated. The CPU received new mapping to smooth out the power delivery, particularly in the low- rpm range, although the peak power and torque were unchanged, the Supersport 900 producing 80 HP at 7500 rpm and 7.7 kg/m at 6500 rpm.

Chassis updates included larger, 12mm engine bolts, a lighter sealed for life battery, and simplified wiring. The 43mm fully adjustable Showa fork was unchanged, but a new Sachs rear shock absorber, with progressive damping proportional to travel and more comfortable static calibration, appeared this year. Setting the 900 apart from the 750 this year were five-spoke Brembo wheels in gunmetal gray, the design similar to the wheels on the 996. Detail improvements to the ergonomics this year included revised seat padding and new rearview mirrors.

900 Supersport, 900 Sport 2002

For its final year as a 900, the 900 Sport joined the 900 Supersport, both available in half- fairing and

A new color, metallic-gray with red wheels, was available for the 900 Supersport in its final year.

The budget 900 Sport was also added to the line-up for 2002.

full- fairing versions. The engine was unchanged from the previous year and the 900 SS retained the fully adjustable Showa front fork. Also new for the 900 SS was an Öhlins rear shock absorber. This was fully adjustable for preload, compression and rebound damping, and also ride height. Separating the 900 SS from the 900 Sport was a new aluminum swingarm, providing a 40 percent increase in rigidity over the previous version. This was a beautiful construction and a new rear fender and chain guard accompanied the new swingarm. The 900 Supersport was also available in metallic gray, with red five-spoke wheels, alongside red and yellow. The 900 Sport retained the earlier three-spoke wheels, and included a non-adjustable Marzocchi front fork and steel swingarm. This was available in matte black. With the new 1000DS Supersport about to be released, after five years the *nuovo* 900 Supersport was discontinued. Now, more than a decade on it remains one of the least appreciated sporting Ducati models.

750 Supersport 1999

For 1999 the 750 Supersport was resurrected in the guise of the new 900 Supersport and shown at the Munich Intermot in late 1998 in two versions, fully and half-faired (½ Carena). Also designed by Pierre Terblanche the half fairing represented a new approach to the concept and was significantly larger than earlier versions of the half fairing on Supersports. The 750 Supersport was intended as an entry-level Supersport, and apart from electronic fuel injection, the five-speed 750cc engine was the same as that for the 750 Monster. Thus it carried the same engine number sequence (ZDM 750 A2 C) and featured all the 1998 revisions to the crankcases, clutch, engine covers and timing belt covers. While the 900 Supersport received new camshafts the 750 still used the cams from the 750 Monster. The low, 9:1 compression was also retained, and the valve sizes were 41mm and 35mm. The primary drive was also unchanged with 33- and 61-tooth straight-cut

For 1999 a smaller 750 joined the 900 Supersport, both also being available with a half fairing and in either red or yellow. The 750 engine was similar to that of the 750 Monster and featured 900-style timing belt covers.

gears, although the final drive was 15/40, still with the 98-link D.I.D. 520 VL4 5/8 x 1/4-inch chain. Due to the fuel injection the power was increased to 64 HP at 8,500 rpm with maximum torque of 6.9 kg/m produced at 6,000 rpm. The CPU was the same Marelli 1.5 CPU as the 900 Supersport, this also transforming the running characteristics and smoothness of the engine. However, although the power and torque peaks were a wide, 2,500 rpm apart, the 750 needed to be revved quite hard to achieve reasonable performance.

The frame was identical to that of the 900 Supersport, but as with earlier 750 Supersports, featured a steel swingarm with a different chain adjustment system and rear axle. For some reason this was also longer than the aluminum version of the 900, increasing the wheelbase to 1,405mm (55.3 inches). The wheels were 1999-spec

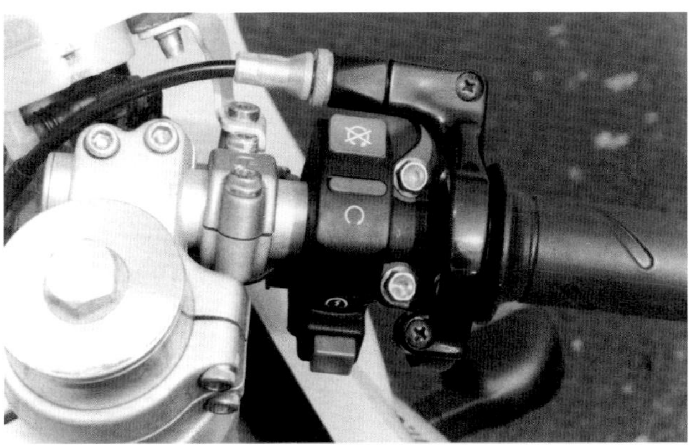

With the electronic fuel injection came a much neater throttle and starter switch setup.

The footpegs and levers on the post-1998 Supersport were 916-inspired and much more attractive than the earlier type that had originated back with the 750 Paso of 1986.

Updates for the 2000 750 Supersport mirrored those on the 900.

Brembo GA/Si7 of the 900 Supersport, although the rear was a narrower 4.50 x 17-inch. Suspension also followed the style of the earlier 750 Supersport, the 43mm Showa front forks non-adjustable, but providing the same fork travel as the 900. The rear suspension was by the Showa GD 132 of the 900 Supersport. The tires were excellent Bridgestone BT57, the front now a 120/70-ZR17 instead of the lower-profile 120/60 on earlier 750 Supersports. The rear was the usual 750 160/60, but now a ZR17. Many of the ancillary components on the 1999 750 Supersport were improved over its predecessor. The brake and clutch levers were adjustable, the master cylinders having remote reservoirs and the brake and clutch lines were braided steel. The braking system was shared with the 900, with the same revised calipers and master cylinder. With a dry weight of 183kg (403 pounds) the 1999 750 Supersport was heavier than its predecessor, but offered improved weight distribution with 90kg (198 pounds) on the front wheel.

750 Supersport 2000

For the 2000 model year the 750 Supersport shared all the small cosmetic and ergonomic revisions with the 900. Unlike the 900, the 750 retained the PSC 13 clutch master cylinder and gold-painted wheels and frame. The engine and chassis were unchanged except for a Sachs Boge shock absorber similar to that of the 2000 Monster. As before, both full- and half-faired versions were available in red or yellow. The tires for 2000 were either Bridgestone BT57 or Dunlop D207 in unchanged sizes.

750 Supersport, 750 Sport 2001

New for 2001 was the budget 750 Sport, with a single front disc brake, and while both 750s shared the 64 HP engine as before, a 34 HP version was also built to comply with new license restrictions in Europe. All engines shared the updates incorporated on the 900 (air-cooled cylinders, split timing-belt rollers, KTM oil cooler, new-design clutch slave cylinder, new

The budget 750 Sport was released for 2001. This had a single front disc brake.

Bosch timing sensor, and a new starter motor ratio). Other shared updates included the 12mm engine fasteners, lighter battery, simplified wiring, more precise neutral sensor, and new oil cooler connectors. The 750 Supersport now shared its adjustable Sachs shock absorber with the 900, the 750 Sport inheriting much of the specification of the previous 750 Supersport. Setting the Sport apart were steel clip-on handlebars, and a single 320mm Brembo front disc brake with a four-piston P30/34 caliper and PS13 brake master cylinder. The 43mm Showa front fork was non-adjustable and it was only available as matte black with a

Modifications to the post-1998 Supersport

While the style of Terblanche's Supersport was controversial, there was no doubt that functionally the new Supersport was a significant improvement over its predecessor. In terms of outright handling the Supersport was the equal or better than any other Ducati, the combination of light weight, excellent low and mid-range power, and quick and stable handling being unsurpassed. At the time of its release Ducati's chief tester Andrea Forni said that the Supersport was the finest handling motorcycle ever on the tortuous Apennine passes where the testing was carried out. Therefore, for general street use, the brakes and front suspension required little or no modification. The Supersport only really benefits from weight saving, increased horsepower and possibly replacement of the rear shock absorber. Even the 750, with its non-adjustable fork, represented a significant step forward over the earlier model in terms of handling.

The biggest problem for owners seeking to modify a post-1998 Supersport, including the exhaust, was replacing an EPROM couldn't reprogram the ECU. The only way to alter the mapping of the ECU was to use a flashload program that downloaded a new map into the ECU from an external computer. For the 2000 model year Ducati Performance offered an engine tuning kit that included twin carbon-fiber racing mufflers, a K&N air filter, and a replacement CPU. The claimed power increase from this kit is approximately 7 HP. Apart from replacing the heavy mufflers, further weight saving can be obtained through lighter wheels and body parts.

The 2002 model was the final 750 Supersport, still very similar to Terblanche's first edition.

metallic gray frame and wheels. Both the 750 Supersport and 750 Sport had gunmetal-gray frame and wheels, metallic silver-gray engine, new rearview mirrors, and gray seat and fuel tank protection. The colors for the 750 Supersport were still red or yellow, with a half or full fairing

750 Supersport, 750 Sport 2002

As with the 900, the 2002 model year was to be the last for the 750 before the 800 replaced it. Thus, the 750 engine, like the 900, was also unchanged from 2001. There were also no changes to the chassis specification, but as with the 900 SS the 750 SS was available this year in metallic gray with red wheels. For 2003 there was a new small-capacity Supersport, the 620, alongside the new 800 and 1000 DS. The 620 was discontinued for 2004, and the 800 for 2005. Effectively replaced by the Sportclassic range, the 1000 Supersport finally ended in 2006. It was an ignominious end to a great line of Supersports initiated in 1973.

INDEX

Appendices Download Information

Appendices are available for download at ducatindex.com. The download is a printable PDF. For those of you who don't wish to view the information on a computer or print it out at home, you can purchase simple printed versions of the index from the publisher at octanepress.com. Go to the *Ducati Belt-Drive Two-Valve Twins Restoration Guide* page to order your printed copy of the index. You can also call 512-334-9441 to order a copy.

The appendices are extensive and consist of more than 50 pages.

They include:

Detailed production figures, listed by year and model variation

Valve timing specifications

Clutch composition (number of plates, thickness, and part number, plus updates made to the specs)

Gear ratios

Stock gearing

Carburetor specifications (carburetor model number and brand with stock jet and needle sizes)

General specifications (bore, stroke, compression ratio, displacement, valve clearance, tire sizes, brake types, wheelbase, seat height, dimensions)

Fuel and other fluid capacities

Fork types